Luminos is the Open Access monograph publishing program from UC Press. Luminos provides a framework for preserving and reinvigorating monograph publishing for the future and increases the reach and visibility of important scholarly work. Titles published in the UC Press Luminos model are published with the same high standards for selection, peer review, production, and marketing as those in our traditional program. www.luminosoa.org

T0074567

Capitalizing a Cure

Capitalizing a Cure

*How Finance Controls the Price
and Value of Medicines*

———

Victor Roy

UNIVERSITY OF CALIFORNIA PRESS

University of California Press
Oakland, California

Suggested citation: Roy, V. *Capitalizing a Cure: How Finance Controls the Price and Value of Medicines*. Oakland: University of California Press, 2023. DOI: https://doi.org/10.1525/luminos.141

Cataloging-in-Publication Data is on file at the Library of Congress.

ISBN 978-0-520-38871-0 (pbk.)
ISBN 978-0-520-38872-7 (ebook)

28   27   26   25   24   23
10   9   8   7   6   5   4   3   2   1

CONTENTS

CHRONOLOGY OF KEY EVENTS

Late 1960s   Scientists at US federal health agencies begin a decades-long effort to elucidate the clinical and public health consequences of viral hepatitis.

1987   Gilead Sciences is founded in Silicon Valley.

1989   The Hepatitis C virus is identified by scientists at Chiron, the National Institutes of Health (NIH), and the Centers for Disease Control and Prevention.

1991   Chemist Ray Schinazi begins receiving public investments for nucleoside research.

Late 1990s   Without cell culture techniques to grow the virus in labs, drug companies struggle to test hepatitis C compounds.

1998   Pharmasset is founded out of Emory University by Ray Schinazi based on research funded by NIH and the Veterans Administration.

1999   Pharmasset receives the first of 16 NIH grants.

2001   A publicly funded lab and company led by virologist Charlie Rice begins distributing replicon technology, enabling drug companies to test compounds against hepatitis C.

2002   Roche makes $2 billion on interferon-based treatments for hepatitis C priced at $36,000 per treatment course.

2004   Pharmasset completes raising about $55 million in venture capital funding.

2005   Pharmasset's Michael Sofia begins developing PSI-7977 using a prodrug method; in 2008 it will become the company's lead candidate for a hepatitis C drug.

2007   Pharmasset raises $45 million with its initial public offering and is listed on NASDAQ.

2010   Gilead's share price plateaus due to limited growth prospects, though it has accrued $24 billion in HIV revenue since 2004.

2011   Vertex launches telaprevir, the first direct-acting regimen for hepatitis C, priced around $60,000 per treatment course.

Gilead acquires Pharmasset for $11.2 billion for its PSI-7977, later named sofosbuvir.

2014   Gilead receives FDA approval for the first combination sofosbuvir-based treatment and sets the list price at more than $90,000 in the United States.

Health systems in many high- and middle-income countries ration care for hepatitis C due to the high price of treatment.

Gilead voluntarily licenses access to hepatitis C intellectual property to 91 low-income countries. Civil society groups launch patent opposition cases in high- and middle-income countries.

2015   Egypt mobilizes a mass treatment campaign with sofosbuvir treatments under $1,000 per course.

The US Senate investigation releases a report describing Gilead's pricing strategy.

2016   Gilead makes $46 billion on hepatitis C drugs in the first three years of sofosbuvir use and spends over $32 billion on payouts to shareholders.

Wall Street begins to sour on Gilead due to the diminishing growth prospects of curative hepatitis C treatments.

From 2016 to 2020, Gilead raises its US HIV treatment list prices annually and bets over $40 billion on new acquisitions.

2017   AbbVie launches an eight-week combination treatment for hepatitis C priced at $26,400.

Gilead estimates that sofosbuvir-based medicines have treated 1.5 million people globally.

Seventeen US state Medicaid programs loosen their treatment restrictions.

2019   Gilead launches a generics subsidiary to offer sofosbuvir-based treatments at $24,000 for certain US health systems.

Pandemics, Wall Street, and the Value Playbook

In late June 2020, as COVID-19 exacted a devastating human toll across the world, we got our first glimpse into a critical question: how might drug companies price new treatments for a global pandemic? With significant investments from the US government, the pharmaceutical company Gilead Sciences attempted to show that a drug called remdesivir could help treat COVID-19. As an antiviral drug, remdesivir offered none of the immunity of a vaccine, but a clinical trial led by the National Institutes of Health suggested that it could lead to quicker resolution of symptoms and a reduction of hospitalization days (from 15 to 11). Whether it actually saved lives—or in clinical parlance, offered a mortality benefit—appeared doubtful at best.[1]

That same month, I was completing my internship year as a physician at Boston Medical Center, a safety-net hospital that had become an epicenter for COVID-19 care and treatment. With few treatment options at the time besides oxygen and watchful waiting, remdesivir offered a small glimmer of hope. But beyond its potential clinical significance, the treatment also carried important economic implications. Experts estimated the treatment cost $10 to manufacture, but Gilead's patents over remdesivir gave it monopoly power over the price.[2] As the first major drug to be approved to fight COVID-19, remdesivir's price was closely anticipated, both for its cost to health systems but also for the ways drug companies and governments might deal with paying for the future health technologies needed to effectively confront the pandemic.

After weeks of speculation, Gilead announced its pricing: $2,340 for a five-day course for developed-country governments, including the US Veterans Affairs and Indian Health Service systems, and $3,120 for Medicare and Medicaid as well as all US private insurers.[3] The prices immediately drew consternation for being too high—and too low. The consumer watchdog group Public Citizen called the price "offensive" for a drug "that should be in the public domain," citing US public investment of at least $70.5 million in the riskiest development stages for remdesivir, along with over $700 million in publicly financed coronavirus research since the SARS outbreak.[4] By this view, the US government was also implicated in this pricing outcome for failing to use its public power to safeguard the value it had helped create through its own investments. Given the large patient population that could require COVID-19 treatments, this pricing was expected to yield a huge financial windfall for Gilead while causing new budgetary challenges for health systems. In referring to Gilead, Peter Bach, a health policy expert at Memorial Sloan Kettering, remarked, "This is entirely predictable. . . . They take the highest number anybody has floated, they cut down a bit from there, and they say now they're the good guys."[5]

Indeed, in an open letter explaining the pricing, Gilead's CEO, Daniel O'Day, wrote, "We believe that pricing remdesivir well *below* value is the right and responsible thing to do" (italics added).[6] But how was O'Day conceiving of value? From his perspective, value was the savings the drug offered health systems by shortening hospitalizations. By Gilead's math, the potential average savings amounted to $12,000 per patient, making the drug's price good "value for money." Conveniently, the strategy also allowed Gilead to forecast nearly $3 billion in revenues just for remdesivir by the end of 2020—in the thick of a grim pandemic year.[7]

Yet some on Wall Street felt Gilead *undersold* the treatment's value. Geoffrey Porges, an analyst with the SVB investment bank, argued for $5,000. And even that, Porges said, would be underselling remdesivir, because it "ignores the enormous societal value that everybody else gets from making a patient less infectious, for getting a patient back into the community, for getting them back to work sooner. . . . All of those societal benefits aren't even considered in this price."[8] His view begged the question: could any price be too high for a drug or treatment amid a pandemic? Curiously, some policy thinkers seemed to think that any effort to curb prices would be dangerous. In a *Washington Post* editorial headlined "Beware of Underpriced Drugs for Covid-19 Treatments," economist Craig Garthwaite argued that failing to pay *higher* prices for treatments like remdesivir would mean calamity: "Said plainly, we must convince biotechnology firms that we will pay for the value they create. . . . Come in too low, and the long-term cost may be high, both in dollars and lives."[9] Higher prices, by this argument, were not only a reflection of the value of new and better treatments, but also the only route to their discovery and development.

I was finishing my first draft of this book just as the pandemic gained steam in the spring of 2020. Though my book was about a different infectious epidemic, hepatitis C, the arguments over "value" felt disconcertingly familiar. In the years prior to my residency training, I had researched and published on Gilead's new curative treatments for hepatitis C, which had triggered a political firestorm with launch prices north of $80,000 per course.[10] In investigating the politics and the financial model underlying their development, I heard similar claims regarding drug pricing and value from Gilead, its allies, and even many policy experts. Better health, they argued, would only be possible if we were willing to pay more for a better treatment. These claims were being made even as access to treatment was restricted and deferred for millions of patients with hepatitis C around the world, disproportionately harming marginalized patients—low-income people and racial minorities, people who inject drugs, and those currently or formerly incarcerated. Now, even amid a global pandemic, echoes of this playbook seemed to be unfolding—a dynamic that, as I describe in the concluding chapter, would grow even more stark with the failure to equitably deploy vaccines for COVID-19.

Though the scale and severity of the COVID-19 pandemic challenged any contemporary comparison, my research into hepatitis C had helped identify an underappreciated yet shared culprit for unprecedented prices and unequal access to medical technology: the growing reach of finance into how we value health and determine who heals and who suffers. This book takes us into the development of curative medicines for hepatitis C and the ensuing struggle over treatment access to illustrate what happens when medicines become financial assets controlled by shareholders in speculative markets. Drawing on scholarship in sociology and political economy, historical research into scientific and business developments, and rarely analyzed corporate documents and earnings-call transcripts, the book illustrates the pivotal decisions and financial actors that shaped the price of these medicines. Rather than taking high drug prices and inequities in access as a natural outcome, we will see how "financialized" drug development has been socially constituted, and also how this economic calculus faces resistance and contestation from people striving for innovation that better meets patient and public health needs.

In a June 2020 note to Wall Street amid Gilead's pricing moves, Geoffrey Porges harkened back to World War II, quoting then US secretary of war Henry Stimson: "If you are going to try to go to war, or prepare for war in a capitalist country, you have to let business make money out of the process or business won't work."[11] Yet this historical allusion falls flat precisely because it is ahistorical—failing to consider, for example, the major government-led mobilization behind the mass production of penicillin in World War II, the large-scale public investments in COVID-19 biomedical research, or the major changes in how contemporary pharmaceutical businesses make money. In contrast, this book's social and historical analysis reveals the distinctive *kind* of capitalism practiced today by pharmaceutical businesses and its profound and morally troubling consequences for patients and society—a set of realities that the leaders of the World War II era might have found deeply unfamiliar and concerning.

Introduction

The Politics of Drug Pricing and the Value of a Cure

How much should a miracle drug cost?
—BLOOMBERG BUSINESSWEEK COVER STORY, JUNE 2015

Price is the wrong discussion. . . . Value should be the subject.
—GREGG ALTON, FORMER GILEAD SCIENCES EXECUTIVE[1]

It is not prices that determine everything, but everything that determines prices.
—PIERRE BOURDIEU[2]

By the mid-2000s, hepatitis C had infected approximately four million people in the US and some 70 million across the world.[3] Spread through the blood, the virus elicits a reaction from the body's immune system that scars liver tissue over the course of years.[4] While many people with the virus do not feel any symptoms, a significant minority fall ill with the progression of liver disease, and some die from liver failure.[5] The treatments at that time involved interferon, a drug with limited effectiveness and noxious side effects, akin to cancer chemotherapy. Even when patients knew their diagnosis, most avoided the treatment. In this pre-COVID-19 world, hepatitis C would become the leading infectious killer in the United States, killing more people in 2014—about 20,000—than all other infectious diseases combined; it would also claim the lives of nearly 400,000 people globally in 2016.[6]

Yet a new drug, launched in December 2013, heralded relief from this suffering. The pharmaceutical company Gilead Sciences received approval from the US Food and Drug Administration (FDA) for sofosbuvir, which had produced sterling results in clinical trials. Recognizing sofosbuvir's promise back in 2011, Gilead had bought Pharmasset, the government- and venture-backed company that had developed the compound, for $11 billion—at that time the largest acquisition price in biotechnology history. After phase III trials, a combination treatment pairing sofosbuvir with one of Gilead's compounds showed cure rates north of 90% and would receive FDA approval in 2014, just ten months after sofosbuvir itself.

Yet the jubilation for science was quickly met with contention following Gilead's next move: the US launch price of the sofosbuvir-based treatment was near $90,000. From the company's view, the price was reasonable—only incrementally higher than previous hepatitis C treatments, which exceeded $70,000 but offered far lower cure rates from longer and more toxic regimens.[7] While the drug was estimated to cost only about $100 per treatment course to manufacture, Gilead also viewed its price as representing a reward for the billions the company had spent buying Pharmasset and bringing the treatment through the final stage of clinical trials.[8] For health systems with tens of thousands of hepatitis C patients who could benefit from this better treatment, however, the price was a serious problem.[9] The health of patients hung in the balance.

The US case highlights a struggle that played out across the world between health systems and Gilead, particularly in high- and middle-income countries. In response to Gilead's prices, US state-run Medicaid programs instituted "eligibility requirements" that limited the treatments to those in the most advanced stages of disease.[10] Patients faced delays and denials. Even until 2018, for example, the Medicaid program in Texas was denying most patients' treatment requests, though the state was estimated to have over 500,000 patients with hepatitis C. Through Medicare, the publicly financed insurer for people over the age of 65, thousands of older patients were receiving the treatment. But without the ability to negotiate drug prices with companies, Medicare officials worried that the treatment—and other highly priced breakthroughs in the future—would strain the federal budget.[11] The Finance Committee of the US Senate, one of the most powerful stewards of budgets and costs in the healthcare system, paid close attention to what was unfolding with hepatitis C treatment. In July 2014, the committee launched a bipartisan investigation into Gilead Sciences and its hepatitis C pricing strategy.[12] Citing the cost of the treatment to the overall US health system and concerns over treatment restrictions, Senators Wyden and Grassley sought answers from the company on the rationale it used to set its prices for hepatitis C treatments.

In the summer of 2015, during my field research into the debate that was raging over hepatitis C drug pricing, I found myself in a policy meeting in Washington, DC, observing physicians, representatives of federal health agencies, and patient advocacy groups as they deliberated over how to realize the potential of these curative therapies.[13] Though many were concerned by the high prices charged by Gilead, they also worried that all this focus on the price was shifting attention away from the value and efficacy of the drugs.

Since their launch, the medicines had been dubbed the "$1,000-a-day pill" in the popular press. CBS's *Evening News* ran multiple prime-time stories on hepatitis C that centered on the treatment's price.[14] Even *Bloomberg Businessweek* had featured the price of these treatments on their cover earlier in the summer, with the headline, "How much should a miracle drug cost?"[15] In the view of many physicians and public health experts who had long worked on hepatitis C, this media coverage, alongside the ongoing political consternation, was diverting attention from the extraordinary potential for these new treatments to cure disease. After the decades-long wait for better treatment options for patients with hepatitis C, the attention on price was wearing thin.

Rising to address the meeting, one public health official seemed to have a rejoinder to the question posed by Bloomberg's cover story. "These drugs are of high value," they said. Citing a recent study, this person insisted, "They could cost up to $1.4 million and they would still be cost-effective!" While this official did not think the prices *should* be in the millions, they believed high prices could be justified given their curative potential. It was up to health systems to pay. I would hear this refrain—that the "value" of these medicines justified their price—throughout my research into the development and pricing of hepatitis C treatments.

From this view, health systems would be wise to pay for treatments, even at prices they might deem high, because the medicines represented a significant advance from the previous standard of care and could save the health system billions in averted hospitalizations and transplants. This position echoed the views of a powerful player in the debate. In the 2015 story accompanying the *Bloomberg Businessweek* cover, Gilead's senior executive Gregg Alton said that "price is the wrong discussion." Instead, he urged, "value should be the subject."[16]

I take a different view. We *do* need to tackle price. Prices for new medicines are reaching unprecedented levels, and creating a crisis for health systems and patients. We must get to the bottom of why this is happening. Yet questions of value—what value is, who creates it, and how it flows in our economy—are also crucial. As I witnessed first-hand in the debates over hepatitis C, particular narratives of value were used to justify higher drug prices while obscuring the dynamic way value is created and extracted in contemporary drug development.

This book thus pursues the subjects of both price and value. But rather than take up the conventional wisdom urged by Alton—that prices simply represent the value of health improvements developed by industry—I took a different approach. I examined history, tracing the dynamics of drug pricing and the notions of value underpinning the development process behind sofosbuvir-based treatments. An illuminating but underappreciated explanation emerged: the reach of finance into drug development and public health. Even as contention over drug pricing has intensified, however, the role of financial logics and actors has been largely obscured from public view. Instead, the struggle over rising drug prices has been dominated by industry arguments about "risk" and "value." We turn to these prevailing arguments next.

RISK, VALUE, AND THE POLITICS OF JUSTIFICATION IN THE DRUG AFFORDABILITY CRISIS

In their first two years, sofosbuvir-based medicines brought Gilead Sciences nearly $46 billion in revenue, making it the most profitable drug launch in history.[17] By then, hepatitis C treatments had become part of a growing political battle over the rising prices of prescription drugs. Industry observers and health policy analysts warned that hepatitis C medicines were just our first glimpse of a wave of new drugs with unprecedented prices coming in the next decade or so.[18] In this future dystopia, drug prices ranging from $100,000 into many millions would be the new norm. Indeed, that future is already here, with many cancer therapies priced in the hundreds of thousands, and a treatment for infants with a rare muscular disease priced by Novartis at $2.6 million in 2019.

Such drug launches spawned an intensifying crisis in drug affordability and access for health systems and patients around the world. In low-income countries, many medications were inaccessible due to the intellectual property protections that allowed multinational drug companies to charge monopoly prices. Gleevec, a cancer medication, exemplified this crisis: its manufacturer, Novartis, had charged $2,200 for one month's treatment in India, before the country's Supreme Court struck down its patent claims.[19] Even high-income countries with publicly financed health systems struggled to cover new drugs for conditions like cancer, cystic fibrosis, and hepatitis C.

In the United States, with its private insurance system, high drug prices were being passed onto patients in the form of rising copayments and premiums, and a growing number of patients were having to choose between prescriptions and other expenses, like rent and food. One survey showed, for example, that three in ten patients had not taken their prescribed medications in the prior twelve months due to cost.[20] Such prices also disproportionately affect the health of racial and ethnic minorities, with Black and Latinx people more likely to ration medicine due to cost—and thereby suffer complications of chronic conditions.[21] These grim consequences led to growing calls for drug pricing reform in the US and around the world.[22]

Yet accompanying the political struggle over high drug prices has been another debate: the arguments used to justify them. This debate has formed around two central arguments used by the pharmaceutical industry. First, drug companies argue that high drug prices are a reward for the enormous costs of research and development (R&D) and the risks these investments entail; second, drug companies, *à la* Gregg Alton's exhortation, defend high drug prices by pointing to the economic value of future health produced through innovative treatments.

Let us start with the first rationale. For decades, the industry has argued that the price of new drugs needs to be put in the context of the soaring costs of R&D. Since the early 1990s, the pharmaceutical industry has supported a group of economists at the Tufts Center for Drug Development who generate data to buttress this view.[23] They find that the average cost of developing a drug has escalated over the past three decades, from $231 million in 1991, to $802 million in 2003, to $2.6 billion in 2014.[24] These estimates are based in part on assumptions about the long time horizons, high rates of failure, and opportunity costs involved with drug development.

This industry argument is strongly linked to their advocacy of intellectual property protections, since patents give drug companies the pricing power they can then use, by their view, to finance risk-laden R&D. In the popular rhetoric and even legal discourses used in these debates by many policymakers, business executives, and scholars, patents are often viewed as governing a "fair exchange."[25] In this transaction, customers access the inventor's product in exchange for the investor's recouping the cost of developing that product, plus some profits to reinvest in further research.

Yet critics have argued that the industry's figures are likely grossly inflated. In interpreting the 2004 Tufts study that reported $802 million per drug developed, for example, Light and Warburton used a different set of assumptions and independent data to give an estimate approximately 25 percent of the original: $180–231 million per approved compound.[26] Based on this and similar studies, critics claim that the high prices are not reflective of R&D investments and instead represent the industry's abuse of the monopoly power granted to companies via patents.

In recent years, as this argument has come under greater public scrutiny, the pharmaceutical sector has advanced a second rationale: that prices reflect the "value" they bring to health systems and society. This narrative relies on an alluring logic: "consumers" are willing to pay more for better health outcomes, and such payment will direct innovation toward producing more "high-value" therapies. More than a decade ago, health industry consultants described this shift toward a "value-based pricing strategy" as follows: "In essence, the fundamental pricing question has shifted from 'what price do we need to charge to cover our costs and make a good return?' to 'given market perceptions of value, which products can we profitability produce?'"[27] In the case of health, however, the "market" is not typically individual patients. With prices for patent-protected medicines many times the median wage of individuals, "value" is perceived through the eyes of the primary buyers: public health systems, and in the US, private insurers.

But "value" has multiple interpretations in the arena of pharmaceuticals, with significant differences between insurers and public health systems in the US and Europe. In Europe, national health systems assess value by making a comparative analysis between a new medication and the existing standard of care. Through "cost-effectiveness research," health systems weigh whether a new therapy adds enough benefit, in "quality-adjusted life years," for its incremental cost.[28] Manufacturers aim to price drugs within the ranges health systems are willing to pay for this additional benefit. This method of "health technology assessment" is used widely across Europe, most notably with the UK and its National Institute for Clinical Excellence (NICE). Value assessments have important merits that I discuss in chapter 4 and have been proposed by progressive reformers in the US as part of the solution to the drug pricing crisis. Yet even these European bodies have come under increasing pressure from the rising prices for new treatments, especially those that might benefit large patient populations.

In the more fragmented US system, however, with both public and private payers, pharmaceutical companies have typically been more resistant to any formal process of value determination.[29] The rising influence of the Boston-based Institute for Clinical and Economic Review and its value-assessment reports for new drugs—modeled in part on the British NICE—have many health policy experts calling for value assessment to be part of any prescription drug pricing reforms in the US.[30] But fearing that such a process will lead to pricing caps, the industry has used its lobbying power in Washington to thwart such efforts. Without institutional or legal mechanisms for assessing the benefits and prices of new medicines before approval, considerations about value center on the upper bounds of drug prices that a health system may be able to bear. These considerations of "value" are shaped by industry lobbying and marketing.

For example, one of the leading interpretations of value advocated by industry, which has migrated into mainstream policy debates, is that value is about both cost-effectiveness *and the savings* particular treatment outcomes can bring for health system payers by averting downstream disease. A fact sheet produced by Pharmaceutical Research and Manufacturers of America highlights this framing, claiming that "every additional dollar spent on medicines for adherent patients with congestive heart failure, high blood pressure, diabetes and high cholesterol generated $3 to $10 in savings on emergency room visits and in patient hospitalizations."[31] According to industry leaders and even many policy experts, paying higher prices now could create "public health value" for the future—such as averted liver transplants and hospitalizations in the case of hepatitis C. Media headlines like "These Drugs Cost $84,000—and That's a Good Deal," on the typically progressive policy-focused site *Vox*, capture the attractiveness of this position.[32]

Both explanations for these unprecedented drug prices—the expensive risks of R&D and the economic value of therapeutic advances—assume that prices correlate with some underlying objective sum. Yet both abstract questions of pricing and value away from the actual contexts in which drug development occurs. Neither approach, for example, could make sense of Gilead's $11 billion acquisition of Pharmasset. Was this a research cost? The public health value of a potential cure?

Or an artifact of financial market speculation? Even if both prevailing rationales correctly explained the reasons for rising drug prices, they have troubling normative implications. For example, if R&D costs are indeed increasing, is this a justification for ever-higher prices, or more a troubling sign of the extent of waste and inefficiency in the patent-driven system of drug development, as some have claimed?[33] The "value" argument is also vexing—it would mean that some of the most vital drugs for patients and public health should by definition cost the most for health systems and patients, regardless of consequences for access.

Rather than explanations of why drug prices have come to be what they are, I see these rationales as attempts to justify the industry's power over intellectual property and pricing. My investigation into drug pricing instead seeks to illuminate the social mechanisms that produce drug prices in the contemporary political economy. To pursue this understanding, I examined the existing critiques of the pharmaceutical industry for insights. I found important lessons, but also glaring blind spots.

DIAGNOSTIC BLIND SPOTS IN THE PRICE OF A CURE

I first learned of the heated debate over hepatitis C and drug prices soon after the launch of the initial sofosbuvir-based treatments in December 2013. At the time, I was in the early stages of a doctoral program at the University of Cambridge, where I was studying sociology and political economy. My doctoral studies took place in between medical training at Northwestern University in Chicago. The delays and denials of care I was learning about with hepatitis C went against the very purpose with which I was pursuing medicine.

As a medical student, I had taken the Physician's Pledge, a modern-day version of the Hippocratic Oath which begins by stating that "the health and well-being of my patient will be my first consideration."[34] For me, at least part of practicing this pledge meant using available life-preserving technologies, like new medicines, to treat illness and take care of the vulnerable. But those taking care of patients with hepatitis C often faced a quandary. Two clinicians in the US's Indian Health Service put it well in *JAMA*: "Earlier treatment can prevent advanced liver disease, but late-stage liver disease is needed to qualify for treatment. For a clinician, explaining this circular logic to a patient can be frustrating for both parties."[35] Thousands of encounters like this one—with physicians having to explain to patients why getting treated would not be possible at the time—occurred across the US and the world.

The pledge that we take as doctors sets out an ideal. Yet by itself, medical anthropologist Danya Glabau writes, this ideal "falls short in describing the real state of things in the world, or how to fix them."[36] Caught between the ideal to which I had pledged and the material realities that patients faced, I searched for explanations. And here I was struck by the plain inadequacy of the ongoing attempts to dissect high drug prices. When the Finance Committee completed its 18-month investigation into Gilead's hepatitis C pricing, the headline of the final report flashed across their website: "Wyden-Grassley Sovaldi Investigation Finds Revenue-Driven Pricing Strategy behind Hepatitis Drug."[37] The headline fell flat not because the charge made by the committee was not true, but because of how little it explained.

At a conference on hepatitis C a week after the release of the Senate report, I listened as one of the conference leaders, a physician and liver specialist, referred to the report with resignation: "This is just how capitalism works."[38] For some, like this physician, the contradiction between the ideal of care and the reality of drug prices needed simply to be accepted as a byproduct of the natural laws of our prevailing economic system. Yet this physician's acceptance exposed a stark blindness. "Capitalism" is an economic system created by people, organizations and institutions—not simply handed down from above. Furthermore, it is not a monolith but has various incarnations across time and space. What interested me were the specific institutional and political factors that shaped the particular incarnation of capitalism from which sofosbuvir and its price emerged.

Several incisive critiques of the pharmaceutical industry have advanced an important and by now accepted explanation for the drug pricing outcomes we see: the enormous political and economic influence of these companies. In her 2005 book, *The Truth about the Drug Companies: How They Deceive Us and What to Do about It*, Marcia Angell, a former editor of the *New England Journal of Medicine*, offered a trenchant analysis of the influence of the pharmaceutical industry in using patents to charge high prices—and spending more money on marketing than on R&D.[39] In *The $800 Million Pill*, Merrill Goozner debunked the industry's myths about R&D costs and described instead how many of our most significant medicines have come through public investment.[40] On the specific question of sofosbuvir-based treatments, the economist Jeff Sachs concluded in a piece titled "Gilead's Greed that Kills" that the US government needed to tame the company's "untrammeled corporate greed and the monopoly power."[41] These critiques bring into view a core dynamic that is fundamental to any discussion of drug prices: power.

Identifying the power of the pharmaceutical industry is important. But to understand how we have arrived at our current predicament of drug pricing requires a more complex dissection of power. This dissection involves situating the most obvious rationale for the actions of drug companies—profit maximization—in the wider social and political-economic context that shapes drug pricing outcomes. To be sure, part of this is the overt power companies can exercise through government-granted patents. Yet as I was observing in the arguments over the "value" of hepatitis C medicines, this power also functions through forming categories of thinking and frames for debate used by authorities across an array of elite fields like medicine and public policy. This evokes an array of questions. For example, what are the institutions of power that influence drug companies? And how does this power influence drug development and public health? Mapping the machinations of the industry is a critical empirical and political task for challenging the status quo, but by itself it does not give us the systemic analysis we need for envisioning and enacting new possibilities.

THE MISSING DIAGNOSIS: FINANCIALIZATION

To share an initial set of findings from my research into the systems that had shaped Gilead's sofosbuvir strategy, in July 2016 I coauthored a short article for the *British Medical Journal*.[42] Within forty-eight hours, Gilead's executive vice president, Gregg Alton, countered with a post on the *BMJ*'s website listing a set of counter-arguments.[43] Unsurprisingly, Alton noted the risk Gilead and the wider pharmaceutical industry had undertaken on hepatitis C research and the significant value sofosbuvir-based medicines offered to society. (We later responded, using some of the evidence laid out in this book.[44]) This public counter—a post in response to a journal article—was an unusual move. Maybe, in pulling back the curtain on drug development and pricing, I had struck a nerve.

In my emerging analysis, I was coming to understand that the etiology of these unprecedented drug prices had a name: *financialization*. As elucidated by economic historians and sociologists, financialization is the growing influence of the financial sector and its imperatives over our economy and, in turn, our society.[45] In this analysis, since the 1970s the financial sector, rather than being a productive engine for investment, as it was in the postwar era, has increasingly contorted our economy around share prices, quick returns, and speculative boom-and-bust cycles, as witnessed with the 2008 global financial crash.

This book argues that the logics and institutions of finance reign supreme far beyond the financial industry; they have come to dominate how pharmaceutical businesses operate and how we price and value new medicines. Understanding this phenomenon is key to explaining why Gilead paid billions to buy a promising compound, for example, or why a medicine priced at nearly $100,000 could be argued by the industry and by many health economists to be a "good value" for society. How did finance come to have this power, and how might this analysis apply to new medicines?

Finance is, of course, critical to innovation. Writing in the first half of the twentieth century, the Austrian economist Joseph Schumpeter recognized that the new industries and technologies had not materialized on their own.[46] Their creation required credit, which provided entrepreneurs with capital for the experimentation, failure, and learning needed for innovation. He understood the source of this credit to be banks, which he called the "headquarters of capitalism." Alongside banks, however, another major source of capital for innovation existed during the postwar economic boom: the retained capital of large industrial companies. Companies like Xerox, AT&T, and IBM reinvested their earnings in large innovation laboratories to pursue the development of new markets and products.[47] But then this dynamic changed. As the financial sector grew in the 1970s and 1980s, with budding actors such as new stock exchanges and hedge funds emerging alongside banks, the sector became less and less about long-term investing in innovation and manufacturing and more about financial products geared to short-term gains. Businesses, ranging from General Electric to Pfizer, followed suit.

At least three shifts have been implicated in the rising power of finance. First, as sociologist Gretta Krippner documented in her book *Capitalizing on Crisis*, a series of political decisions that began in the 1960s and continued into the 1980s transferred power from the government to financial markets.[48] After a significant postwar boom, US policymakers were confronted with how to allocate increasingly scarce resources in the face of slowing growth and rising inflation. Instead of making these decisions themselves, however, they increasingly decided to grant power to what they deemed "depoliticized" financial markets by deregulating interest rates and foreign capital flows to make capital less scarce. This expanded the role and ultimately the size of financial market actors in allocating capital across the economy, from homeowner loans to municipal infrastructure. The launch of the 401(k) system and Reagan-era rollbacks of financial-sector rules accelerated the power and place of financial markets in our economy.

Second, the growing power of financial markets led to an explosion in financial speculation, with "institutional investors" like pension and mutual funds exercising newfound muscle in financial markets. In the deregulated market, financial actors like banks also turned from the traditional role of taking deposits and making loans to the widespread use of "securitization," which meant turning loans into financial products which could then be packaged and traded in financial markets.[49] The prices of these "securities" were subject to the speculative whims of financial markets, in which forecasts of future earnings drove value and provided the basis on which traders could gain returns.[50] Yet this casino-like betting game could also result in boom-and-bust cycles of speculative markets, as epitomized by the global financial crisis in 2008.

Third, as stock markets turned into a paramount force in the economy, "maximizing shareholder value" became the reigning ideology of corporate governance and business strategy.[51] As Gerald Davis described in his book *Managed by Markets: How Finance Reshaped America*, this ideology focused corporations on strategies aimed at meeting financial market expectations instead of making investments in goods and services.[52] Companies increasingly pursued financial maneuvers, like leveraging acquisitions and borrowing money, to generate short-term growth. To hit Wall Street's double-digit growth expectations, for example, General Electric expanded its consumer lending and financial services businesses at a pace that outstripped its investments in making innovative electrical products. A GE executive later remarked, "We had to decide whether we wanted to be a tech company that solves the world's big problems or a finance company that makes a few things."[53]

I contend in this book that the development of medicines is far from immune to such forces and has also become deeply entwined with the rising influence of finance. Though largely overlooked in controversies over access to medicines, emerging political economy scholarship has begun to illustrate how finance has structured the pharmaceutical industry, making it more short-term and extractive. In his 2006 book *Science Business*, for example, business scholar Gary Pisano documented how the emerging biotechnology sector of the 1980s and onward focused on monetizing intellectual property in financial markets to draw in capital, rather than using firms' own retained capital for research. But only a few businesses (like Biogen, Amgen, and Genentech) have been successful in this model; Pisano argues that the short-term makeup of much of the speculative capital behind new ventures is ill-suited for the long-term, uncertain work of converting complex science into usable treatments.[54]

William Lazonick and colleagues have focused on the effect of stock-market-driven imperatives on pharmaceutical research and development. In one paper, for example, they showed that drug companies increasingly downsize early-stage research deemed too risky, and instead distribute large sums of capital to shareholders to "maximize shareholder value."[55] Lazonick and others have also explored how biotechnology companies come to be valued in the tens and hundreds of millions—even billions—without ever having developed a therapeutic product. Such "productless IPOs" are traded on stock markets based on their speculative potential, rather than any products or revenues.[56] This structure of speculation lets financial actors trade on share price and derive financial gains.

While this scholarship provides a helpful orientation to how financial-sector imperatives can shape business strategy, it has largely "black-boxed" questions of drug pricing and value by focusing on macro sector-level data rather than the political economy of particular businesses and medicines. We need further research that interrogates the relationship between financialization and specific drug pricing outcomes and orientations of value. *Capitalizing a Cure* helps close this gap by tracing how organizational strategies and practices linked to financialization unfolded in the case of sofosbuvir-based medicines. Pursuing this account, in turn, demanded dusting off a set of analytical tools long pioneered in political economy, economic sociology, and science and technology studies, but little used in the world of public policy.

OPENING THE BLACK BOX OF PRICE AND VALUE: CAPITAL, ASSETS, AND POWER

A 2015 profile in *Fast Company*, "How Drug Company Gilead Sciences Outpaces Its Competitors—and Common Diseases," honored Gilead as one of the most innovative companies in the world.[57] "It can take up to 15 years to bring a drug to market," the piece said—"Gilead did it in two." Ignoring the fifteen-plus-year drug development process, which involved crucial public investments, the article gave *Fast Company*'s readers a portrait of a lone, risk-taking company. The prices it can charge are cast as a commensurate reward. In the economic thinking that underlies such portraits, the power of contemporary business is the product of a "knowledge-based economy," in which novel technologies (information, digital, genomic) help solo entrepreneurs and pioneering businesses create newfound productivity and innovation. Yet an alternative view has also endured in economic thinking: that production is not an atomized activity but a social process.

In the early twentieth century, the economist Thorstein Veblen was also witnessing rapid economic change, with the emergence of industrial giants in railways, steel, and soon oil and automobiles. To many of Veblen's colleagues in economics, the power of these new corporations could be explained by new forms of technological productivity—as in many analyses of the contemporary knowledge economy.[58] In Veblen's view, however, economic power was not intrinsic to any technology or corporation. Instead, the power of new businesses rested in the means by which these businesses could control industrial knowledge within a community in an effort to accumulate capital. Veblen was concerned with *capitalization*, or the conversion of knowledge into something with future financial value. For Veblen and a line of subsequent scholars, control over industrial knowledge is not a given feature of an economy. Rather, this control is *made* by dominant economic actors through a set of social strategies and practices.

Alongside this work to dissect capital in a Veblenian tradition, contemporary scholars of biomedicine and innovation offer a lens into these control strategies in the specific realm of drug development—from the ways in which collectively developed science is turned into financial assets, to the way health itself comes to be valued in financial terms. Taking a lead from Veblen, I draw on this scholarship to glean three critical insights that help lift the cover off the black box of drug pricing and value.[59]

Innovation, Entrepreneurial States, and Capital as Control over Assets

First, Veblen conceived of economic production as a social process *derived from an array of assets in a community*. Assets can be tangible, such as material technologies, or intangible, such as knowledge. Capital, in this view, derives from the ownership and control over groupings of tangible *and intangible* assets by powerful economic actors within a given community.[60] In the context of pharmaceutical development, for example, intangible assets are things like intellectual property in the form of drug patents. In turn, the logics of pricing and value in drug development are intimately tied to the way this knowledge is produced and made financially valuable.

Akin to Veblen's concept of economic production arising in a "community," contemporary heterodox economists Lazonick and Mazzucato have described the innovation processes that generate and make use of knowledge as "collective, cumulative, and uncertain."[61] Let us take uncertainty first. Taking risks for the possibility of financial reward is central to value creation in the economy. But while businesses typically take risks by making bets with a knowledge of probabilities, as in a lottery, innovation requires confrontation with "Knightean uncertainty." Named after the economist Frank Knight, this kind of uncertainty involves situations where the odds of any rewards are *unknowable* beforehand.[62] Building the complex technical base behind biotechnology and genomics, for example, required long-term public investments in science before profitable products could ever be developed.[63] Confronting this uncertainty is not the work of solo actors.

The *collective* nature of innovative labor is a second defining feature of innovation processes. This labor depends on multiple public and private organizational actors—from universities to financial institutions, workers to government agencies.[64] In this collective activity of innovation, public-sector organizations are critical.[65] As shown by economist Mariana Mazzucato in her book *The Entrepreneurial State*, the patient, long-term capital of the public sector—particularly in the US, but across many countries—has been pivotal in managing the uncertainty involved in developing products, from mobile phones to pharmaceuticals to renewable energy. In Mazzucato's view, this investment does not crowd out private-sector actors; rather, the state's significant technology investments "dynamize in" private capital. These public investments, in turn, allow governments to take on "technological frontiers," where overcoming radical uncertainty and technical hurdles can translate to entirely new discoveries and unforeseen business opportunities.[66] For example, this risk-taking capital has produced new general-purpose technologies (e.g., semiconductors, the Internet, gene-editing technology) from which whole new sectors of the economy (such as biotechnology) have been born.

The collective nature of innovation is also critical to the third defining feature of innovation processes: they are *cumulative*. What organizations and fields learned yesterday becomes the starting point for what can be learned today, and tomorrow. The stages of biomedical innovation, for example—which are typically expressed as basic science, preclinical research, and then Phase I through Phase III trials— illustrate this cumulative quality. This reality creates a need for committed finance across an innovation process, so that knowledge can ultimately be translated into products and markets.

This *uncertain, collective,* and *cumulative* process, then, creates a community of knowledge that can be turned into assets. In Veblen's view, economic value—in the form of capital—materializes when certain actors are able to control intangible assets (like knowledge) and tangible assets (like drugs or factories) and turn them to their advantage.[67] While assets are not a new economic phenomenon, as illustrated by Veblen's work in the early twentieth century, what is important to understand is how contemporary pharmaceutical businesses gain and maintain control over assets. In investigating this process, science and technology scholar Kean Birch has observed that knowledge has become a pivotal "intangible asset" through various forms of political-legal rules regarding intellectual property.[68] These rules enable socially produced and often publicly funded knowledge, for example, to become "enclosed" by a single private actor. Beyond such initial acts of enclosure, private actors engage in an array of legal and financial strategies to protect and expand their control over assets. Maintaining the boundaries of asset ownership can be a fraught endeavor, however, as illustrated by the tens of millions of dollars pharmaceutical companies spend on litigation against each other in intellectual property disputes with billions at stake.[69] Assets, in other words, are constructs of the law, and the underlying politics of intellectual property.

Furthermore, Birch argues that rather than studying commodification (a preoccupation he charges fellow social scientists with) we should examine *assetization*: the transformation of something (e.g., knowledge) into a revenue-generating and tradable resource.[70] While commodities are objects that gain their value through *exchange*, Birch argues, assets gain their value through *ownership* and entail a different array of social strategies of valuation. For example, while rising demand tends to push *down* commodity prices over time as more producers are incentivized to enter a market, assets become *more expensive* as demand rises as they are more difficult to replicate, inherently or legally (via politically constituted ownership protections). Thus, the stakes over intellectual property are so high in drug development because assets have a crucial and distinctive economic meaning: knowledge is transformed into property that may yield a future income stream.[71] Control over assets, in other words, also depends on control over the future—a future with uncertain financial promise. To appreciate these financial implications, we lean on a second crucial insight.

Capitalization as Quantified and Future-Oriented Control

Veblen defined capital as a *quantified, future-oriented* form of control over assets: the value of assets is based on the expected future stream of earnings that can be derived from owning them.[72] To value these streams of earnings, business and financial actors use *capitalization* exercises in which future earnings are translated into a present value to guide decisions over capital allocation.[73] Furthermore, businesses not only anticipate capital in terms of future streams of earnings, but also in terms of whether assets will generate an *advantage* over their competitors.[74] In other words, capitalists do not pursue accumulation by some absolute register of "maximizing profits" but in *comparison* to competing businesses, sectors, and the stock market.

This dynamic of quantified and future-oriented control has been further shaped by the emergence of "maximizing shareholder value" as an ideology governing corporate strategy. From the 1970s onward, shareholders, not managers of businesses, were deemed to be more efficient allocators of capital in the economy. Scholars in law, economics, and finance advanced the notion that shareholders could use a singular metric—share price—to direct capital toward higher-growth companies and sectors. Pharmaceutical companies came to be assessed not on their current profitability but on their potential to deliver *growth* in profits to shareholders. Echoing Veblen's observation of differential accumulation, this shareholder-oriented growth is expected to be faster than what investors and traders could make in the stock market.

"Maximizing shareholder value," in turn, has influenced business strategy across the drug development process. I particularly draw on anthropologist Kaushik Sunder Rajan's 2017 book, *Pharmocracy*, in which he elucidates the structural vulnerabilities that such speculative, future-oriented growth logics create for pharmaceutical businesses.[75] The structural force of financialized capital has configured drug companies, Sunder Rajan argues, to pursue short-term strategies to acquire growth by buying promising drug assets—a phenomenon I investigate in chapter 2 in the context of Gilead Sciences.

Such acquisitions are one of the many examples within contemporary drug development in which economic actors perform capitalization exercises—exercises that in turn serve as important windows for social analysis. Traders on Wall Street, for example, weigh what the latest clinical trial results might mean for their day's bets. A small biotechnology company, with no products or sales, considers what a promising compound might be worth to another company. These predictions call to attention the sociologist Jens Beckert's insight that actors' perceptions of the future need to take center stage in our understanding of economic action— "not only 'history matters,' but also the 'future matters.'"[76] Beckert reminds us that forecasts of the future are always contingent on what might happen in a web of social relations, which is why "capitalist competition is essentially a battle to establish and alter expectations." This battle leads to the third key insight.

Capitalization as Power and Hegemony

The two prior insights—that capital can be understood as the ownership and control over assets within a community *and* as a quantified, future-oriented form of control—converge on a third observation: *capitalization exercises reveal relations of power in society.* As several contemporary scholars have argued, methods of capitalization are far from simple pricing operations in a "natural" market.[77] Instead, as Nitzan and Bichler have detailed, capitalization exercises translate the roiling and complex interactions between capitalists and other social arenas into contingent forecasts of the future.[78] In the arena of drug development, for example, pharmaceutical companies' forecasts depend on the prices they anticipate being able to charge health systems and payers. This anticipation, in turn, relies on the relations of power between these companies and the various actors that shape drug pricing policy. As I describe at several points in the book, one way this power is readily visible is in their lobbying of government officials. But analyzing the sofosbuvir case also requires understanding a different kind of power. One of the particularly salient and puzzling features of the case is how the prices of sofosbuvir-based medicines were justified not only by the industry but also by many policy experts, who deemed them "value-based." The concept of "value" became the dominant lens through which most other discussions of the treatments were filtered.

In unpacking the influence of this logic in the debate over drug pricing, I call on Sunder Rajan's application of the concept of *hegemony* (drawing on social scientist Antonio Gramsci) to the modern pharmaceutical industry. Hegemony, in Sunder Rajan's reading, describes not a straightforward relationship of coercive dominance but the power to establish a new "common sense" within a society at a given time. The new common sense, in this case, centered on the notion that a high price for a cure represented its value to society.[79]

In pursuing a hegemony over value, part of Gilead's strategy involved mobilizing certain epistemic practices that are used by health policy experts and public officials to "value" new treatments and most effectively allocate public budgets. Sociologist Joseph Dumit's book *Drugs for Life*, in which he uncovers a critical set of such epistemic practices, is a useful starting point for this analysis. In his tracing of postwar American biomedicine, Dumit describes a series of innovations in clinical medicine that have changed the locus of financial value in modern biomedicine. Instead of only treating "felt illness," using medicines to make sick people feel better, we now also treat "statistical illness," using medicines to reduce the risk of downstream morbidity and mortality. This potential to reduce future disease risk, in turn, has been converted into a tractable source of revenues for drug companies through the production of long-term treatments for conditions like diabetes and hypertension.

Building on Dumit's analysis, I investigate the emergence of pharmacoeconomic methods of valuing the future benefits of such medicines in financial and population-level terms. Health systems and manufacturers use cost-effectiveness studies to determine whether a medicine is good "value for money." Public health modelers calculate the "prevention value" of new medicines. Health, in this framing, is an asset whose economic value can be measured through statistical methods. Public health officials and health policy experts, in turn, increasingly use these valuation practices to "rationally" allocate budgets to the treatments with the most economic value. While many of these methods have important uses, what is crucial to unpack is how a financialized drug development process can motivate drug companies like Gilead to appropriate the ostensible rationality of these practices to justify their prices.

Gilead's position that high prices reflected the value of a cure, in turn, engendered a deeply contested politics of drug pricing. Some health systems responded by restricting access to a life-saving cure; others challenged the company's intellectual property and bargained for lower prices. Sunder Rajan's reading of hegemony as a dynamic, fluid form—one that is open to challenge—is thus also important to consider. Such a reading brings to the fore John Kenneth Galbraith's concept of *countervailing power*. In a 1952 book on the topic, Galbraith argued that the economy was not an even playing field, as imagined by neoclassical economists.[80] Rather, some actors, such as big corporations, are able to gain and expand power, with attendant negative social and economic consequences. The only way to restore balance or change the dominant position is for other organizations to exercise countervailing power. This could be another company, but it could also be government, unions, or social movements. In the arena of drug pricing, the role of governments is pivotal as they are the main rule-makers (over intellectual property, regulatory approval, pricing regulation) and the main buyers of medicines. Civil society organizations also play an important role by challenging drug companies in different arenas of struggle, whether through pressuring governments to act or directly challenging intellectual property claims in courts. A crucial subject of investigation, then, is the extent to which the countervailing powers are activated and mobilized and how this shapes outcomes like drug prices and access to treatment.

Summing Up: Three Analytics for Capital and Finance in Biomedicine

Taking these literatures together, what can we learn for an investigation of drug pricing? Three key analytics can guide our study of drug pricing and debates over value.

The first analytic involves knowledge labor. Knowledge production in biomedicine is an uncertain, cumulative, and collective process entailing significant investments by governments, which also play a critical role in setting the political-legal rules (e.g., patents) that govern how knowledge can be translated into capital via relationships of ownership and control.

The second analytic involves financial value. Capital is a quantified and future-oriented form of control used to pursue advantage, with assets valued based on the expected stream of future earnings—a process shaped by shareholder-oriented corporate governance.

The third analytic involves power. The capitalization exercises at the heart of business strategy reveal the broader relations of power at stake in a community—including hegemonic positions but also potential countervailing powers that are engaged in social struggle.

As we examine the ways finance influenced the pricing and valuation of sofosbuvir-based medicines, I link these three analytics of capital to my particular orientation to studying drug prices, value, and financialization in this case.

A SOCIOLOGICAL ACCOUNT: THE CASE OF SOFOSBUVIR-BASED TREATMENTS

The sofosbuvir-based treatments for hepatitis C are well suited for an investigation of price and value. These treatments were launched as breakthrough therapies for an infectious disease affecting large numbers of patients, but they were also highly priced products that challenged health systems and led to a significant political struggle. This combination makes these treatments a paradigmatic example in health policy discussions related to drug pricing and biomedical innovation. In the primary public drug pricing forum organized by the Obama administration, for example, sofosbuvir was cited repeatedly.[81] As the most profitable drug launch in history (at the time) and also a major advance for public health, these treatments were held up as a study in how innovation should work—and also how our current systems of innovation are broken. This consternation played out in full public view, ranging from the significant news coverage detailed earlier in this chapter to the launch of a Senate investigation.

This outsize influence in the public debate makes sofosbuvir a particularly salient case. My interest draws inspiration from the anthropologist Marcell Mauss, who wrote that certain cases have "an excessiveness which allows us to better perceive the facts than in those places where, although no less essential, they still remain small scaled and involuted."[82] The political conflict that accompanied sofosbuvir's pricing generated a large array of publicly available evidence—including fifteen-hundred-plus pages of internal corporate documents reproduced in the Senate report. With the broad array of evidence in this case, lessons abound about how we as a society might consider making, pricing, and valuing future breakthrough therapies.

Research Questions and Concepts of Financialization, Price, and Value

To unearth these lessons, I pursued two central questions. First, what is the influence of financialization on pricing and value in the process of biomedical innovation? This assessment of pricing and value, in turn, motivates my second question: how does financialization shape outcomes for public health and future innovation? I pursued the answers to these questions with specific concepts of financialization, pricing, and value in mind.

First, financialization here refers to a political-economic system in which the structural power of the financial sector and its logics influence biomedical innovation. Rather than offer an *a priori* definition of financialization in the realm of biomedical innovation, I traced the relationships between the financial sector and the organizational strategy of pharmaceutical businesses. I then synthesized my findings to offer a more composite description of how this political-economic system operates (chapter 4).

Second, I viewed drug prices as products of specific social trajectories that are in turn results of prior business strategies and social struggles. For example, I situated sofosbuvir-based prices in the context of the prices of previous hepatitis C medicines. I also analyzed the ways in which financial actors anticipated future prices for hepatitis C assets (and ultimately sofosbuvir) throughout the drug development process. This allows me to best account for the precise launch prices charged by Gilead in the US as well as other major markets. My research also carries onward from the launch by looking at how health systems responded to Gilead and the subsequent prices and deals that emerged.

Third, throughout the study I considered value in two ways: in terms of the valuation practices economic actors use in a particular moment, and also in terms of the "flow" of value that materializes across an innovation process. Drawing on Veblen and work on capitalization, I delve into how sofosbuvir-based medicines are valued by financial markets throughout the innovation process in terms of their potential for future accumulation. I also trace how this future- and growth-oriented view of value colonizes representations of value in public health policy, as Gilead drew on a set of moral-economic discourses as well as valuation practices to buttress their view that high prices are a reflection of the value of future health. But in making these claims about value, Gilead and the pharmaceutical indus-try—as well as the many policy experts that aligned with this view—made crucial omissions that required a deeper analysis.

Here I juxtapose the narrow representation of value adopted by dominant eco-nomic actors with the systemic and dynamic view offered by Mariana Mazzucato in her 2018 book *The Value of Everything*. In her conception, the key questions in defining economic value are how "outputs are produced, how they are shared across an economy (distribution), and what is done with the earnings that are created from their production (reinvestment)."[83] Value, in other words, is not just the price that a buyer is willing (or often forced, in the case of medicines) to pay—it is dynamic. Innovation thus involves processes of what Mazzucato calls *value creation* (i.e., how new, higher-quality products are created) and *value extraction* (i.e., how the rewards from this creation are distributed in the economy and soci-ety). Fundamental to our understanding of value is thus also the role of public investment in drug development, as well as what Gilead did with the money it collected from sofosbuvir-based medicines. For many observers, the production of a curative therapy was in itself a signal achievement, indicating the effectiveness of existing innovation models. Rather than stopping with the launch of the treat-ments, however, I trace the innovation process forward to study treatment access for patients, as well as Gilead's decisions in financial markets after the launch of sofosbuvir-based medicines. These data complicate simple stories of valorization and allow us to consider the tensions that plague financialized drug development.

Building a Sociological Account

To answer the two central research questions, I developed a sociological account of the pricing and valuation of sofosbuvir-based treatments. Much like a clinician combining patient history with quantitative lab data to make a clinical diagnosis, I take "account" as a double entendre *à la* Stark: a set of *numbers* (such as R&D investments, revenues, shareholder payouts, and patients treated), as well as a *narrative* of the innovation process.[84] Each gave the other context. This account was sociological because I took a processual view of the developments that underpinned the creation and deployment of these treatments. This involved tracing the social process from the key scientific steps that made sofosbuvir-based treatments possible all the way to the treatment-access struggles that ensued from their launch. Studying this process, in turn, involved interrogating the relationships of power between multiple public, business, and financial actors—not just the work of one drug company.

I generated this sociological account in a provisional and iterative manner, toggling between the theoretical frames described in this chapter and the data I collected. A primary methodological tactic I employed in collecting and interpreting these data was to rely on documentary evidence as my primary type of source (see the appendix for an overview of my data sources). While I interviewed business leaders and financial analysts along with scientists and public health officials, no interviews are cited in the account. In relying on documentary evidence such as earnings-call transcripts, media accounts, and corporate documents, my research illustrates that much of what I critique about financialized drug development is already said openly, in public and in reports, by capitalists themselves. This book thus follows in the tradition laid out by Joseph Dumit, who wrote that "exposé alone is not critique; one must show how the system reinforces the worst tendencies despite being conscious of them."[85] In building an account of sofosbuvir medicines, my aim is to show how these worst tendencies (such as ongoing double-digit revenue growth and the scale of shareholder value extraction) have become naturalized and assimilated into the current system—and why we should find this less tolerable and more in need of change than many will argue.

To be sure, employing such a method to studying a single drug meant that I had to draw certain boundaries around the account. First, in focusing on sofosbuvir, I could not cover the dozens of compounds that drug companies pursued but that failed in clinical development—for hepatitis C and otherwise. Some analysts, and certainly industry allies, may fret that this underplays the role of private drug development. To provide greater context to private-sector efforts, I included available quantitative data on Pharmasset and Gilead's R&D costs beyond sofosbuvir during the times in which they made their biggest bets on hepatitis C. But the larger point I make in the book is that the exercise of summing up development costs in a financialized model of drug development reveals how drug prices bear no relationship to the division and costs of innovative labor and instead become tethered to speculative stock market expectations.

A second boundary: because I focus on US-based companies in Pharmasset and Gilead, my analysis centers largely on the American case of financialized biomedicine. While the financialization of pharmaceutical corporations may have important geographic variation based on the location of headquarters—an empirical question and potential direction of further research—I link this US-focused analysis to global consequences for treatment access. Given the enormous role that US-based public investments and private pharmaceutical corporations play in the global landscape of R&D and access to health technologies, this lens provides useful policy insights and can also generate questions regarding pharmaceutical companies in different geographic settings.

A third decision I made relates to my analysis of actors within the financial system. Instead of dissecting each individual actor, I examined groups of them—such as venture capitalists, institutional shareholders, and corporate executives—and their function within the drug development process. To be sure, each of these groups of actors has some internal variation: for example, two venture capital funds may take different approaches to risk tolerance or duration of investment. While a different book or research agenda may look at each of these groups and their influence on drug development, my emphasis was to trace the innovation process and the ways multiple groups of financial actors intersect with the process to shape individual corporations like Pharmasset and Gilead. In describing each group of financial actors (in chapter 2), I pointed to the range of possibilities typically available to them and how their strategies played out in this specific case. Mindful of these choices in my investigation, the sociological account that emerges faithfully answers the two research questions I set out to answer.

CHAPTER OUTLINES

The next three chapters follow the role of financialization in the innovation process that led to curative sofosbuvir-based therapies for hepatitis C. This sociological account starts in chapter 1, "Capitalizing Science," which chronicles the creation and of publicly funded research and its conversion into financial assets. At the center of this tale is the launch and evolution of Pharmasset, a company that emerged from publicly funded research at Emory University to develop the key curative compound for hepatitis C, sofosbuvir. Drawing on political-economic scholarship on assets and speculation, I show how the presence of financial markets as well as forecasts of growing drug prices and market valuations created opportunities for investors and traders to make significant returns in periods far shorter than the time it takes to develop a new medicine. This chapter ends in 2011 with Pharmasset's executives, now with a promising compound for hepatitis C in hand, searching for a suitor.

Chapter 2, "Capitalizing Drugs," investigates the extractive strategies that drive larger pharmaceutical companies as they hunt for growth to feed their shareholders. By documenting the history of Gilead—the eventual manufacturer of sofosbuvir-based treatments—this chapter unpacks how "maximizing shareholder value" has shifted the focus of drug companies away from life sciences research and toward the acquisition of promising and lucrative compounds. The focal point of this chapter is Gilead's $11 billion acquisition of Pharmasset in 2011. The chapter than traces how Gilead used the lion's share of its hepatitis C profits to distribute capital to shareholders and stockpile it for future acquisitions. This financially extractive model, however, would depend on the deeply contentious question of the prices drug companies charge health systems for medicines.

The closing act in the story is chapter 3, "Capitalizing Health," which begins with Gilead setting its prices and follows the role of financialization in shaping struggles for access to treatment in the US and around the world. The chapter documents Gilead's "value pricing" strategy, whereby in high- and middle- income countries the company based its pricing of sofosbuvir-based treatments on its expectation that health systems would be compelled to pay more for a better treatment. To execute this strategy, Gilead sought to establish a *hegemony of value*, in which paying more for the value of future health could be held up as a commonsensical idea accepted by policymakers, academics, and public officials. Even as this strategy generated significant political contestation in the face of mammoth financial accumulation, the chapter ends with Gilead turning to yet another cycle of financial maneuvers involving drug price hikes and acquisitions because of a staggering dynamic in financialized capitalism: Wall Street soured on sofosbuvir-based medicines because, as curative drugs, they *eliminated the very market for growth* on which their value as assets rested.

Chapter 4, "From Financialization to Public Purpose for Health," synthesizes the influence of financialization on the pricing and value of new medicines for hepatitis C and builds momentum for alternative directions. Equipped with the evidence from sofosbuvir-based treatments presented over the previous three chapters and drawing on wider industry data, I detail how drug prices have become fastened to the expectations of extractive financial markets. This financialized system of drug development produces a triple crisis: for access, for future curative breakthroughs, and for democratic governance. To craft a pathway toward equitable and affordable access, I lay out a "public-purpose" system for biomedical innovation. Such a system would involve enacting a public option for drug development and adopting a set of principles that would steer the wider system toward intentionally prioritizing access and investment in medicines that address the unmet health needs of patients and populations. A concluding chapter foregrounds financialized biomedical research amid COVID-19 and considers the possibilities and hurdles for a transition to a world in which science can be put more fully and equitably in the service of human health.

Capitalizing Science

Public Knowledge into Pharmaceutical Assets

I cannot imagine that, had there not been an NIH funding research, that there would have been a biotechnology industry.

—PAUL BERG, 1980 NOBEL PRIZE WINNER IN CHEMISTRY[1]

Financial capitalism is dependent on the constant searching out, or the construction of, new asset streams. . . . What we can see now is an impulse to identify almost anything that might provide a stable source of income, on which more speculation might be built, being brought into play.

—LEYSHON AND THRIFT, *THE CAPITALIZATION OF ALMOST EVERYTHING*[2]

In the mid-1970s, physicians and scientists at the National Institutes of Health (NIH) were stumped. Patients receiving blood transfusions were developing liver inflammation, but the cause was unknown. Scientists suspected a virus, but found that neither hepatitis A nor B, viruses which had been identified in the prior decade, was the culprit.[3] Though this mystery virus did its damage slowly and often unbeknown to the patient, clinical studies that tracked these patients showed that it could cause liver failure, and ultimately death, over time.[4]

The virus eluded scientists for another fifteen years, making it difficult to develop diagnostics and know the level of threat it might present to patients and public health. Harvey Alter, a physician and research scientist at NIH involved in the hunt for this pathogen, recalls a poem he wrote back then: "Oh GREAT LIVER in the sky / Show us where and tell us why / Send us thoughts that will inspire us / Let us see this elusive virus / If we don't publish soon / They're going to fire us!"[5] The long wait would end in the late 1980s, when a company called Chiron, in its search for new markets for diagnostic tests, worked with scientists at public agencies to uncover the molecular structure of the virus. In 1989 this group of scientists, including Alter, published a landmark paper describing the virus and its genome.[6] They called it hepatitis C.

Even after its identification, however, the virus remained furtive in other ways, just beyond the grasp of chemists and the few companies targeting the pathogen. Ten years after the identification of hepatitis C, the hunt for drugs against it had borne little fruit. Epidemiological studies suggested that three to four million people in the US were infected—primarily as a result of injecting drug use, as well as blood transfusions received before the early 1990s.[7] As many as three-quarters of infected patients remained undiagnosed. Yet at the turn of the millennium, physicians had few options to offer even their diagnosed patients. The existing interferon-based treatments, a toxic regimen requiring a year of weekly injections that offered cure rates of only 30–40%, was often a last resort, used only for the sickest patients.

This chapter traces what transpired next: the capitalization of publicly financed and cumulative knowledge into private assets for financial markets. This process—central to financialized drug development—would shape the trajectory and price of a potential breakthrough for hepatitis C.

In the late 1990s, scientists with public funding would overcome a key obstacle to hepatitis C drug development by discovering a method to test potential compounds in the laboratory. These public investments led drug companies to join the fray of hepatitis C treatment, and within a decade several were in pursuit. One upstart company would emerge in 1999 from a publicly funded lab. The company would go on to raise over $50 million from venture capital and get traded on the stock market—even as it accumulated $330 million in deficits, had no sales, and would never bring an approved drug to patients. Yet a compound developed by this company would ultimately become the backbone of a curative treatment for hepatitis C.

With science capitalized into assets, particular future and growth-oriented logics of price and value dominated the speculative markets where these assets were owned, traded, and sold. For investors and traders, these speculative markets offered a high-stakes opportunity to make sizable gains from bets on hepatitis C compounds, in periods far shorter than the time needed to develop those compounds into usable treatments. This opportunity for speculation, in turn, depended on an uncertain and fraught promise: unprecedented drug prices and market valuations.

OVERCOMING A TECHNOLOGICAL HURDLE:
THE REPLICON TOOL AND AN ENTREPRENEURIAL STATE

Throughout the 1990s, the deadly hepatitis C virus confounded scientists and chemists in their pursuit of treatments. Viruses are *intracellular parasites*, meaning they work inside human cells and hijack their machinery to reproduce. But unlike most viruses, hepatitis C did not grow in cell cultures generated in laboratories.[8] The reasons were unknown at the time. A handful of private labs had identified the structure and function of parts of the virus that are critical for its replication—most importantly the protein "subunits" called NS3 and NS4a proteases, as well as the NS5b polymerase.[9] But without any ability to grow the virus in cells, scientists could not test whether their compounds actually inhibited viral activity. Scientists remained vexed by this puzzle through much of the 1990s. Trials of different culturing approaches yielded little success.[10] One scientist lamented the "painfully slow process" and the "struggle to establish research tools and cell culture systems for HCV" (that is, hepatitis C virus) as critical factors holding back progress in the field.[11] Without a way to test drug compounds against it, drug development for hepatitis C was stalled.

Growing a Stubborn Virus and the Development of the Replicon

In the mid-1990s, government-funded German scientists, led by Ralf Bartenschlager at Heidelberg University, began to tackle this puzzle.[12] After their initial attempts to reproduce the hepatitis C virus failed, they tried another route: instead of growing the entire hepatitis C genome, what if they could reproduce just a part of it—the part that contained the main viral proteins involved in replication? They constructed a line of genetic code with only the internal proteins thought to be critical for hepatitis C replication.

They then inserted this line of code (or "genome") into cancerous liver cells, which by their very identity replicated very rapidly. This would allow them to see whether copies of the virus could be produced. Bartenschlager's team found what they had long sought: hepatitis C genetic material (RNA strands) of the anticipated size and correct protein units teeming inside the cancerous liver cells.[13] In other words, drug companies could finally test whether their compounds worked against the parts of the virus that enabled its replication, such as the NS3/4 proteases and the NS5b polymerase. If that worked, it could mean stopping the virus, and the disease, in its tracks. This research tool, in which strands of genetic material are replicated within cells, is known as a *replicon* (Figure 1).

For veteran science journalist and writer Jon Cohen, who attended an NIH meeting on hepatitis C in June 1999, reports of the replicon were the "show stopper."[14] The implications for drug discovery appeared to be significant. Discussing Bartenschlager's work, leading hepatologist Stanley Lemon said, "If these results hold up, they'll be enormously useful for drug screens."[15] The group described the replicon in a November 1999 paper in *Science*, completing nearly five years of work.[16]

Yet the replicon had limitations. Charlie Rice, a leading hepatitis C scientist in the United States, noted: "Bartenschlager's replicon was a landmark discovery in its own right, but the frequency with which you could initiate viral RNA replication was low."[17] That is, the hepatitis C genome in Bartenschlager's replicon only replicated itself in approximately one out of every million host cells, which added a cumbersome step of selecting the right cells for testing.[18]

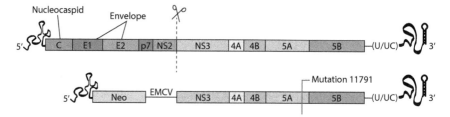

FIGURE 1. The replicon for hepatitis C. While the full hepatitis C genome (*top*) could not be replicated in the lab, the replicon version (*bottom*)—trimmed to include the main proteins needed for viral replication—could. This development set the stage for scaling up the testing of potential antiviral compounds. Source: Marshall (2000).

A virologist at Rockefeller University in New York, Rice had spent nearly a decade studying the virus and the parts and steps required for its replication.[19] As he examined Bartenschlager's replicon, Rice knew that considerably boosting viral RNA reproduction would be critical to realizing the replicon's potential for drug development.

To pursue a better replicon, Rice would rely on sources of public support that existed because of a major expansion of investments in scientific research by the US government in the latter half of the twentieth century. Before World War II, US government support for scientific research was modest. But successes in publicly financed wartime mobilization across an array of technologies, including penicillin, drew the interest of leaders like president Franklin Roosevelt, who saw such investments as a potential route to postwar prosperity. In his famed report *Science, The Endless Frontier*, FDR's chief scientific advisor, Vannevar Bush, mapped out a vision in which "the Government should accept new responsibilities for promoting the flow of new scientific knowledge. . . . These responsibilities are the proper concern of the Government, for they vitally affect our health, our jobs, and our national security."[20]

The Public Health Service Act of 1944 inaugurated a more intentional public investment strategy for health, with prior iterations of government laboratories transformed into the National Institutes of Health (NIH). NIH grew rapidly in the postwar years, from a total budget of $8 million in 1947 to $1 billion in 1966.[21] These investments aimed to improve public health, and also to give the US an economic and national-security edge in the Cold War.[22] NIH expanded from a handful of centers in 1949 to fifteen institutes by 1970, and twenty-seven by 1998. Scientists at these institutes found their physical home at NIH's Bethesda, Maryland, campus and formed what is known as the organization's "intramural" (or internal) research program.

As in many areas of clinical advances, NIH's Bethesda campus had played a pivotal role in viral hepatitis research. Physician-scientists like Harvey Alter had performed long-term clinical studies to identify the virus's deleterious health effects. Their work led to the identification of the other viral hepatitis pathogens, such as A and B, that would sharpen the focus on pursuing hepatitis C. NIH scientists also led the initial tests in the 1980s, even before the virus had been identified, to show that the mystery pathogen could be eliminated from the bloodstream with the use of a treatment known as interferon.[23] Though the early studies demonstrated interferon to be effective in only a small percentage of patients, the finding was still noteworthy: the pathogen's elimination in these patients proved that the virus had some vulnerabilities that scientists could exploit. With the identification of the virus in 1989, much of NIH's focus shifted toward a better understanding of the biology of hepatitis C in hopes of developing treatments that could significantly outperform interferon.

Investments in hepatitis C research stretched far beyond Bethesda, extending to university laboratories across the US that received grants through NIH's Extramural Research Program. This decentralized network represented approximately 80% of NIH's budget, which doubled from $8.9 billion in 1990 to $15.6 billion in 1998.[24] A primary mechanism for financing extramural research has been the R-01 grant, which provides funding to senior scientists at universities across the US. These renewable grants, historically the longest and most widely used avenue for NIH funding, provide three to five years of funding disbursed annually over the period of the award.[25] With R-01 grants as a key vehicle, NIH supported hepatitis C research across the US that elucidated viral replication and pathophysiology, at places like the Scripps Research Institute, Emory University, and the University of Georgia, as well as Charlie Rice's work at Washington University in St. Louis and later the Rockefeller Institute.[26] Combined with private philanthropy (most notably from the Greenberg Family Foundation), these NIH grants would enable Charlie Rice and his lab build on the work of the Bartenschlager lab to make crucial improvements in the replicon tool.[27]

Rice's team aimed to make the replicon reproduce at far higher rates.[28] Their strategy: to hunt for genetic mutations that would make the replicon more productive. Led by a scientist in Rice's lab, Keril Blight, they rebuilt the replicon system using Bartenschlager's data. Support for the research came from NIH grants that amounted to $3.4 million between 1999 and 2003 (when much of the replicon work was carried out). This was part of an overall NIH investment of $10.8 million between 1993 to 2005 in Rice's hepatitis C–specific research.

With this financing, Rice's lab identified mutations that produced a more infectious strain of the virus than the one used by Bartenschlager's team.[29] The new replicon produced abundant viral proteins in one of out of ten host cells, rather than one in a million. "That really makes a big difference," Rice said at the time. "It is going to allow us to do genetic studies on a much shorter time scale".[30] This replicon technology was further refined in the coming years by both Bartenschlager's and Rice's labs, with drug developers eagerly awaiting the technology to use in their hunt for anti–hepatitis C compounds.[31]

To share this new technology with drug companies, Charlie Rice turned to a small biotechnology company he had previously founded, named Apath.[32] Rice had envisioned Apath as a vehicle to get the fruits of his discoveries into the hands of other firms and scientists working on therapeutic advances.[33] To make good on this vision for Apath and the replicon technology, state investments would again come into play.

Sharing the Replicon Widely with the Small Business Innovation Research Program

Apath would look to a little-known government funding stream, the Small Business Innovation Research program (SBIR). Begun with a legislative act by the US Congress in 1982, SBIR requires government agencies with a research and development (R&D) aim (such as NIH) to invest part of their budget in domestic small businesses that show a strong potential for technology commercialization.[34]

SBIR grew out of an emerging policy debate in the 1970s and 1980s about the role of government in incentivizing innovation and private entrepreneurship.[35] As part of his broader agenda to promote small business during a period of economic stagnation in the 1970s, Massachusetts senator Ted Kennedy wanted to make it easier for entrepreneurs to commercialize promising technologies and start new businesses.[36] After a successful pilot within the National Science Foundation, the SBIR program was replicated across the federal government through the bipartisan passage of the 1982 Small Business Innovation Development Act.[37] In 1992, to further bridge the perceived gap between basic sciences and commercialization, Congress funded the Small Business Technology Transfer (STTR) program, in which small businesses must formally collaborate with a research institute (typically at a university or nonprofit) to receive a grant.[38]

SBIR and STTR are primarily intended to fund precommercial technology development. All agencies (such as NIH or the Department of Energy) with extramural research budgets of over $100 million are required to set aside a small percentage of their research budgets for these programs. In the decade between 2007 and 2016, NIH's SBIR and STTR programs together provided $3.53 billion in grants to small businesses advancing products for biomedicine. Across federal agencies, SBIR alone has reported the creation of 700 publicly traded companies due to its program between 1982 and 2016, with those companies attracting approximately $41 billion in venture capital investments.[39]

Two decades after its launch, SBIR would help Apath's efforts in hepatitis C. In its first five years of SBIR support, between 1999 and 2004, Apath received $4.26 million, including a $750,000 grant in 2002 to further develop the replicon.[40] The funding gave Apath the capacity to build a business organization capable of manufacturing and distributing the replicon across academic and industrial laboratories.

In a 2000 *Science* article reporting on the discovery, Rice shared Apath's plans for commercializing the replicon.[41] He made his strategic interests clear. Not wanting to do anything that would "impede academic research," Rice assured the interviewer, "I think that sharing material for academic research should be done with as few strings as possible".[42] Within two years, private and public labs began to acquire the replicon, which was dubbed Blazing Blight 7 (for its co-inventor Keril Blight, one of the scientists in Rice's lab). Apath offered nonexclusive licenses to use the technology.

In the field of hepatitis C, the replicon served as a kind of "general-purpose technology" on which almost all subsequent drug development was based. Examples of other general-purpose technologies are the Internet, semiconductors, and nanotechnology. Though the replicon is not a general-purpose technology on the kind of scale that crosses industries, it had an effect on all subsequent hepatitis C drug development. Marc Collett, then the head of discovery research for a small biotechnology company, ViroPharma, commented, "That's definitely a breakthrough that every group has used."[43] One of the many companies to use Apath's replicon around this time would be a small startup in Atlanta called Pharmasset that would be pivotal in making a cure for hepatitis C.[44]

An Entrepreneurial State, Curative Directions,
and Value Co-creation in Hepatitis C

Public investments played a pivotal role in the development of the replicon, which in turn shaped the trajectory of all subsequent hepatitis C drug development. As this chapter later presents, government financing was one element of public investment in the science that made sofosbuvir-based medicines possible (Table 1). While I do not provide a total figure for these contributions, a study by Harvard's Program on Regulation, Therapeutics, and Law that examined the underlying patents and linked them to public funding sources found at least $60.9 million in direct and indirect US public investments in the science that ultimately produced sofosbuvir.[45] The authors note that this is a striking figure because it approximates the amount of private funding Pharmasset would later report in their development of sofosbuvir. But numbers alone do not tell the story.

Situating this financing and the development of the replicon in the technology-development process disrupts the conventional narrative of government's role in innovation. While public investments in science are often labelled "basic research" as opposed to the more "applied" work carried out by the private sector, the story of the replicon shows us that these categories are often blurry. Programs like SBIR, for example, explicitly finance businesses to develop technologies—as they did for Apath in the creation of the replicon. Of course, the COVID-19 pandemic brings the state's role in the later stages of innovation into sharp relief, with major direct public investment in clinical trials and even the manufacturing of vaccines.

TABLE 1 Important public contributions behind sofosbuvir drug development

Phase of contribution	Description and significance	Public actors
Replicon development (1995–2002)	German and US scientists created a research tool called the replicon that enabled hepatitis C drug development to accelerate.	German government (German Research Society, Ministry for Education and Research); US government (NIH R01 and R37 grants)
Replicon commercialization (2000–2003)	The replicon was manufactured and distributed by Apath, a company supported through multiple major NIH grants, to enable hepatitis C drug development across company labs.	NIH Small Business and Innovation Research Program
Nucleoside science (1991–2007)	Antiviral development by Emory University and University of Georgia researchers formed the basis for Pharmasset's viral hepatitis research.	NIH R01 and R37 grants, Veterans Affairs (VA) Office of R&D
Pharmasset launch (1998–2004)	Sixteen early-stage grants provided important financial support— and market signals to venture capitalists.	Small Business and Innovation Research Program, VA, Emory
Sofosbuvir development (2005–2008)	The prodrug method developed by McGuigan (UK) in the 1990s was used by Pharmasset to develop sofosbuvir.	British Medical Research Council, European Research Council, Belgian government (for McGuigan); NIH grants in 2005 and 2006

SOURCES: NIH RePORTER database; Barenie et al. (2020). See the text for citations of key papers.

In thinking about the replicon and other public investments in hepatitis C technology development detailed later in this chapter, Marianna Mazzucato's conception of the *entrepreneurial state* provides a useful map. Far from crowding out private funding, as often claimed by critics of government, the risk-taking investments by public agencies "dynamize[d] in" private capital, as Mazzucato puts it.[46] Until the replicon, private capital had largely languished on the sidelines, as the problem of efficiently testing candidate compounds had dissuaded all but a handful of pharmaceutical companies from taking on hepatitis C. Yet with a new tool that dramatically expanded innovation possibilities, the industry began to direct capital toward hepatitis C.

This is an example of what Mazzucato calls the state's role in "co-creating" value in innovation, as public investments in technologies like the replicon enabled a much larger market for hepatitis C drug development.[47] Yet this process also demonstrates the opportunity for contradictions *within* the state—on the one hand, financing research for the purpose of improving human health, but on the other spurring private commercialization in ways that can later come to undermine treatment access. This conflict is not a given. Rather, it is shaped by the conditions of financialization, which will come into full view in chapters 2 and 3.

The public investment in overcoming technological uncertainty both accelerated the rate at which drug developers could test compounds, and, as Mazzucato points out, shifted the *direction* of the innovation process—in this case, toward therapies that could result in increasing rates of cure for all patients with hepatitis C. Instead of treating only the sickest patients (with toxic interferon-based regimens), the replicon enabled drug developers to find targets that directly halted the replication of the virus. Such "direct-acting" antiviral compounds promised a short, simple, and safe course of treatment for hepatitis C. Further improvements in the replicon also allowed testing of compounds on the multiple genetic variations of the virus.[48]

The significance of this achievement would gain recognition. In 2016, when the prominent Lasker Prize committee chose hepatitis C as a major medical advance to spotlight, they awarded Rice and Bartenschlager's early-stage scientific and technological work on the replicon, along with Michael Sofia's later work to eventually develop the curative compound.[49] The crowning recognition would come in 2020, when Charlie Rice would win the Nobel Prize in Medicine for his team's replicon research (along with Harvey Alter and Michael Houghton, who discovered the virus).[50] The replicon would not be the last advance made possible by public investments in the search for hepatitis C treatment.

THE TRIPLE HELIX: PUBLIC AND PRIVATE SCIENCE IN THE LAUNCH OF PHARMASSET

In the spring of 1998, an Emory University scientist, Ray Schinazi, launched a company called Pharmasset. From the very beginning, his intentions were clear. "I coined that name," Schinazi would tell a reporter later. "It's actually 'pharmaceutical assets' and the idea was to create assets that would be sold to companies. That was the initial business plan."[51] Rather than build a durable enterprise, Schinazi's ambitions exemplified what was at the time a relatively new form of pharmaceutical venture: one founded to land the lucrative rewards of being bought by another company. One of the company's main assets would turn out to be sofosbuvir, the curative backbone of hepatitis C treatments. Pharmasset's assets, however, did not appear out of thin air. Rather, the company emerged through long-term public investments in science and technology development and also the particular approach of the US government to patents and intellectual property. This approach enabled the conversion of publicly funded science into private financial assets and would shape the pricing and value logics governing the trajectory of sofosbuvir.

*The Development of Nucleoside Chemistry and the Public Science
behind Pharmasset*

Before starting his venture, Schinazi benefited from decades of public support for drug development focused on nucleoside chemistry. Nucleosides are chemical precursors to nucleotides, which are the building blocks for DNA and RNA. Schinazi's research focused on synthesizing "analogues" to these nucleosides, which then get modified by the body and are taken up by viruses. When viruses take up these analogues into their growing DNA or RNA chains, the analogues gum up the chain and block further viral replication.[52] Nucleosides, then, carried the potential to abort viruses. In the 1980s into the 1990s, many large pharmaceutical companies avoided these compounds, as nucleosides were deemed to have a high risk of toxicity because they also interfered with the production of genetic material by human cells.[53] Two institutions would give Schinazi the long-term funding necessary to figure out how to make safe and effective nucleosides: the Department of Veterans Affairs (VA) and NIH.

Schinazi came to Atlanta in the early 1980s, running a laboratory at the Atlanta VA hospital while also joining the faculty of Emory University.[54] Since the early postwar years, the VA—a publicly funded national health system for military veterans—had expanded a nascent set of research projects into a fully fledged research program whose breakthroughs included the first cardiac pacemaker (1958), concepts that led to the development of the CT scan (1960), and liver transplantation (1968).[55]

Schinazi has credited the VA as important for the successes of his Laboratory of Biochemical Pharmacology. He enjoyed space for a staff of nearly 40, equipped with the latest technologies, as well as a state-of-the-art animal research facility, critical for preclinical testing of potential drugs.[56] In a nationally broadcast interview, Schinazi shared that in the 1990s and 2000s seven-eighths of his salary came from the VA system. He would translate these resources into research into new nucleoside therapies, most notably for HIV/AIDS and hepatitis C, both of which affect veterans in large numbers. For this work he would later receive the VA's William S. Middleton Award, its highest honor for biomedical research.[57]

NIH was another primary source of financial support for Schinazi. Like Charlie Rice, Schinazi was the beneficiary of NIH's extramural funding; his support included R-01 grants as well as the special R-37 National Merit Award.[58] The latter goes beyond the R-01 grant by giving exceptional scientists the opportunity to pursue projects that are "more adventurous," that carry "greater risks," and that take time to develop: these awards are given typically for *no less* than five years and can be renewed for a total ten-year window of research. According to a separate analysis performed by the access-to-medicines group Knowledge Ecology International, Schinazi was a principal investigator under 64 NIH grants between 1991 to 2012, involving $10.5 million in public funding. He filed a total of 49 patents that disclosed federal funding, with NIH and the VA listed as two of the principal federal agencies.[59]

By the late 1990s, Schinazi had developed multiple compounds that could serve as leading candidates for development. He and his team had iterated on a prior discovery by a Canadian team to produce a nucleoside compound, emtricitabine, that showed particular promise for HIV.[60] This work expanded their knowledge of nucleoside activity against viruses, a direction that Schinazi and his team hoped to carry forward into antiviral compounds for hepatitis C. In a preview of the approach he would take toward hepatitis C, in 1996 Schinazi launched a small biotechnology company, Triangle Pharmaceuticals, to further develop emtricitabine in clinical trials. In 2004 the compound would be acquired for $464 million by a company that would also later be central to the hepatitis C tale: Gilead Sciences.[61]

Though Triangle would ultimately sell for a lucrative return, in late 1990s the company became embroiled in legal challenges related to its nucleoside compounds.[62] Seeking a fresh start, Schinazi sought to launch Pharmasset as a vehicle through which a larger array of nucleoside compounds could be developed into valuable "assets" for established pharmaceutical companies to buy. Building on his years of HIV research, Schinazi sought financing for this new venture. One stream (documented in further detail in the next section) would be over $50 million in venture capital gained through several rounds of financing between 1999 and 2004. But another key stream remained the US state and its SBIR program, the same source that had funded Apath and the development of the replicon.

Between its initial founding in 1999 and the discovery and development of the more efficient replicon by Apath in 2002, Pharmasset's focus remained on other nucleosides for HIV and hepatitis B virus.[63] However, after the development of the replicon accelerated interest in discovering drugs for hepatitis C, NIH granted Pharmasset funding to develop compounds against the virus. Over the course of the company's first seven years, NIH would support Pharmasset with $2.46 million in public financing through sixteen SBIR grants. Of these, six grants between 2002 and 2006 specifically supported hepatitis C drug development, an investment of $1.61 million.[64]

Though Pharmasset's venture capital funding would far exceed its initial NIH funding, these SBIR grants were important to Pharmasset's early formation. As Keller and Block describe, the importance of an SBIR grant is not limited to the amount of money. SBIR grants provide a kind of "signaling and certification" to venture capital of the promise of a given technology. Keller and Block traced the relationship between venture capital and SBIR grants in five different years between 1995 and 2009. In the life sciences in particular, roughly 20% of venture capital investment went to firms that had previously received one or more SBIR awards.[65] Pharmasset was one of these. The company featured each of its sixteen SBIR grants prominently on its website, showcasing them to potential investors as badges of public support.[66]

Alongside his long-standing support from NIH and the VA, Schinazi positioned the company as a nodal point in a network of research universities benefiting from public funding in the Atlanta area. An *Atlanta Business Chronicle* article described the configuration of the cofounders: "Schinazi has a team of 30 researchers at Emory continuing to discover new drugs. [Dennis] Liotta has about 15 researchers and another founder, Chung Chu at the University of Georgia, has about 20. The fourth founder is scientist Jean Pierre Sommadossi of the University of Alabama at Birmingham."[67] A journalist covering Pharmasset's origins highlighted these early-stage employees: "Most of them are top scientists from around the world who bring more than 100 patents and the beginnings of 8 potential drug formulas to the company."[68] Indeed, a study by Harvard's PORTAL research group found that during the mid-to-late 1990s Emory University and the University of Georgia received at least seventeen public grants from NIH that were directly or indirectly related to the later development of sofosbuvir. This configuration—taxpayer-funded university research being used to start a biotechnology company like Pharmasset—was possible in part because of a shift in political and legal arrangements that had begun nearly two decades earlier.

Patents, the Bayh-Dole Act, and the Conversion of Public Science into Private Assets

The early 1980s witnessed a significant shift in the political-legal rules governing science and technology in the US that made it easier for publicly funded knowledge to be turned into financially valuable assets. The dominant narrative behind this shift was that a bipartisan group of policymakers saw a need to respond to the economic slowdown of the 1970s and believed that promoting business through the commercialization of new advances in science and technology—including those developed with public funding—could help. The purported national goals of the shift were to promote American jobs through high-tech industries, and to gain an edge in an increasingly competitive global market. A raft of changes followed in the 1980s, making it easier for the nascent biotechnology sector and the pharmaceutical sector, for example, to commercialize knowledge generated with public funds for new technologies and markets.[69]

One specific change came with the 1980 Bayh-Dole Act, which permitted inventions developed with public funds to be patented by a university or a professor rather than be owned by the government.[70] This fostered a new environment of commercialization for universities and researchers. As an administrator at Emory University explained, "The theory was that a lot of innovation was coming out of federally funded research, but it was all owned by the government and 'sitting on the shelf.'"[71] That administrator, Todd Sherer, was the head of Emory's Technology Transfer Office, a new kind of organization that multiplied across American universities in the 1980s and 1990s. They helped university professors apply for patent protection for their discoveries and supported the commercialization process.[72]

This new legal setup shifted the stakes of research: for university administrators, any research by faculty might generate valuable intellectual property from which the university could gain royalties; and for university professors like Ray Schinazi, discoveries could be converted to private, licensable products attracting capital rather than staying in the public domain.[73]

In the mid-1990s Schinazi and Emory took advantage of this change with their compound for HIV/AIDS, emtricitabine.[74] Emory patented the compound, which Schinazi had developed based on the prior work of Canadian scientists and with public funding. The university then later licensed it to Triangle Pharmaceuticals, Schinazi's spin-off business.[75] When Gilead subsequently bought Triangle for $464 million and then began selling emtricitabine as part of a combination HIV therapy in 2004, Emory University made $540 million in royalties—the largest royalty payment to a university up to that time.[76] A sizable slice, some $200 million, was split between Schinazi and his two co-developers at Triangle.[77]

The Bayh-Dole Act, along with the broader regulatory shifts of the early 1980s, signified a break from previous pathways for innovation. Science and technology scholar Sheila Jasanoff writes that Bayh-Dole "changed the long-standing presumption that publicly funded work could not be privately owned and exploited".[78] In his work on the emergence of the biotechnology sector, business scholar Gary Pisano detailed the shift in incentives for publicly funded scientists: knowledge assets were now to be monetized by academics with a direct economic interest in research efforts.[79] This configuration of university labs, public funding, and small enterprises has been dubbed a "triple helix," with many innovations tracing their genesis to this triad.[80]

The Bayh-Dole Act produced a new political-legal contract that sanctioned the conversion of public science into private financial assets. But it presented a risk: the government would be granting control over knowledge to new owners, who might use it in ways that went against the public interest. To guard against this risk, the act contained a "march in" provision, which enabled the US government to license any intellectual property that emerged from federally funded research in the case of public health need.[81] Though this step has been contemplated on multiple occasions, it has never been taken.

Beyond the Bayh-Dole Act, a broader system of intellectual property protections granted by the US government for pharmaceutical development also applied to the emergence of companies like Pharmasset. The patents granted by the US Patent and Trademark Office give companies twenty years of protection for new drug compounds.[82] Some of this period is used by companies to further develop and test drug compounds and to seek regulatory approval, so the "effective patent life" can be shorter. Companies typically use multiple maneuvers—such as pursuing patents for minor changes or manufacturing processes—to extend their control, often for much longer than twenty years.[83] Alongside this temporal dimension is a geographic one: patent laws have become increasingly globalized, driven by countries in the "global North" and multinational pharmaceutical companies. For reasons I describe in later chapters, these changes give pharmaceutical companies with patents easier access to global markets in which to sell drugs.

This intellectual property landscape had two important implications for Pharmasset. First, the shifts produced by Bayh-Dole gave Schinazi and his cofounders the organizational and political-legal environment in which to commercialize public science into private financial assets. While sofosbuvir would be developed later in the company's evolution and development efforts, this environment enabled Schinazi to use his publicly funded nucleoside research at Emory University and the VA as a foundation for the company's startup phase. Emory University retained stock in the company.[84] Universities like Emory thus became big financial winners in this legal setup, receiving public investments as well as royalties and capital gains from owning intellectual property made possible by these investments. Notably, no US public-sector organization—such as NIH or the VA—was a shareholder in the company their investments had made possible.

Second, owning patents for compounds with *possible* therapeutic value—even if they were years away from human clinical trials or FDA approval—formed the basis of the company's value. In other words, Pharmasset's value in financial markets would come not from the sales or profitability of any medicine but from the forecasts of *potential* global earnings from its ownership of certain assets. This strategy, which Pisano calls "monetizing intellectual property," would take on heightened importance in an era of financialized drug development.[85] For the larger companies that would later buy companies like Pharmasset, owning patents—and the potential value of earnings that might come with them—would be a way to meet the growth expectations of financial markets. For small companies like Pharmasset, monetizing patents would be their *raison d'être*—the primary mode and rationale for their existence. Rather than using its own capital from prior sales and earnings—of which it had none—Pharmasset would use patents to attract speculative capital for its continued R&D efforts.

Sofosbuvir as a Hybrid Advance: Public Science Meets Private Asset

While Pharmasset relied on the mobilization of this speculative capital, the company's later breakthrough would be made possible by the application of publicly funded science. This breakthrough, the development of sofosbuvir, would reveal the critical role of public investment and knowledge production across the stages of technology development. But it would also illustrate a pivotal dynamic underpinning financialized drug development: the enclosure of collectively produced knowledge into privately owned assets.

As Pharmasset pursued its initial set of compounds for hepatitis C in the early 2000s, the company saw promise in PSI-6130, a nucleoside synthesized by one of its chemists, Jeremy Clark, that showed activity against one of the main parts of the virus. By 2004, the company had filed patents on the compound and launched a partnership with Roche to further test its effectiveness. But Pharmasset's scientists knew the compound had an important limitation: when it entered the blood circulation, it morphed into multiple chemical versions, reducing its overall potency in the liver.[86] This chemical unraveling limited its effectiveness in eliminating the virus from the liver. While Roche continued its clinical trials for the drug, Pharmasset's own scientists pursued research into other potential hepatitis C compounds.

One of these scientists, Michael Sofia, had come from one of the "Big Pharma" companies, Bristol Myers Squibb, and he was eager to make a mark in a smaller biotechnology business like Pharmasset. He examined the PSI-6130 effort and began searching for an alternative direction based on several crucial questions.[87] Was it possible to reduce the pill count, lower the dosage, and increase the potency of the compound even further than PSI-6130 could? A more potent compound might eliminate the need for the toxic interferon altogether, which would dramatically increase the number of patients who might benefit from treatment.[88]

To develop a compound that transcended PSI-6130's limitations, Sofia and his team at Pharmasset built on methods pioneered in antiviral and cancer therapeutics. The reason for PSI-6130's limitations was known: once in the bloodstream, the compound was blocked from completing a pivotal step that would optimize its potency in the liver.[89] Sofia surmised that bypassing this blockage was the key to successfully attacking the part of the virus the compound targeted, the NS5b polymerase.[90] He needed a "Trojan horse," something that would help him stealthily deliver the compound to the liver in its most potent form. To solve this problem, he drew on the work of scientists who had confronted similar challenges, particularly with the HIV pathogen. One of these scientists was Christopher McGuigan, a British chemist at Cardiff University who had worked with colleagues to develop a particular "prodrug" method. A prodrug is an inactive substance that the body's enzymes can convert into an active drug.

In a prodrug method, an additional chemical structure called a phosphoramidate is added to the base compound and serves as a "mask" until the compound reaches the liver.[91] The idea would leverage existing physiology: because the liver is often the first place a drug is absorbed and modified, Sofia hypothesized that the mask would fall off in the liver, revealing a chemical structure ready to undergo the necessary modification steps to bind to and inhibit the virus's NS5b polymerase.[92] This way the compound would have its greatest effect in precisely the organ where hepatitis C was wreaking its damage. Sofia figured he had found his Trojan horse.

McGuigan had pioneered this method in collaboration with Belgium scientist Jan Balzarini over the prior fifteen years.[93] Based at Cardiff University in the UK, McGuigan's team led the effort to develop this phosphoramidate structure and method, first in the context of HIV and then for other viruses (like hepatitis C) and cancers.[94] The initial breakthrough came in 1992 when McGuigan was working to improve AZT, a treatment for HIV.[95] In a seminal 1996 paper describing the approach, McGuigan, Balzarini, and their collaborators cited four public sources of funding: the British Medical Research Council, two programs of the European Commission, and the Belgian government.[96] Between 1993 and 2013, the McGuigan team published 85 research papers on their method, creating a large network of citations and possible applications for their prodrug approach. When the UK government later sought to profile impactful public investments in research, McGuigan's work was highlighted as a critical contribution to broader antiviral drug development for hepatitis C, including Pharmasset's eventual compound.[97]

Sofia applied this publicly available knowledge about phosphoramidate prodrugs to Pharmasset's hepatitis C research.[98] Trying multiple versions of a phosphoramidate "mask" fixed to a base PSI-6130 structure, Sofia ultimately found one that resulted in a profound decline in the virus. The new structure would be named PSI-7977, and later receive the name sofosbuvir (after its lead scientist). In 2008, after three years of preclinical testing by Sofia and his team, PSI-7977 became Pharmasset's lead candidate for a hepatitis C treatment. Documenting this process in chemistry and medical journals after the development of sofosbuvir, Sofia cited McGuigan's prodrug method (and McGuigan's papers) as the pivotal and defining step in arriving at the curative compound.[99]

Thus the sofosbuvir structure and its curative function constituted a hybrid public–private outcome (Figure 2), recombining publicly funded and available knowledge in the context of a private business traded in financial markets. The cumulative and collective nature of the process also reveals one of the hazards of financialized business models that rely on turning socially produced science into private assets: fierce battles over patents.

Such battles not only unfold only between drug companies and the civil society groups that challenge intellectual property claims in courts of law in a bid to expand access to treatment (which I describe briefly in chapter 3)—they also occur between drug companies themselves. For example, Pharmasset's patents generated significant controversy and became the subject of multiple lawsuits eventually levied at Gilead.[100] As Bourgeron and Geiger illuminate in their work on hepatitis C patents, Gilead's claims over sofosbuvir patents were haunted by its "molecular predecessors."[101] Roche, for example, claimed in March 2013 that Gilead infringed on Roche's license because *sofosbuvir* was connected to PSI-6130, the compound at the heart of the earlier Pharmasset–Roche business partnership. Merck also challenged Gilead in this period, seeking royalty payments and suing the company for patent infringement. By this time, Merck had bought Idenix, a company founded by one of Ray Schinazi's colleagues, Jean-Pierre Sommadossi, at about the same time as Pharmasset. A legal question central to Idenix's and subsequently Merck's case against Gilead was whether Pharmasset's chemist Jeremy Clark had first synthesized the PSI-6130 compound that would go onto be a precursor to the lucrative sofosbuvir—or if scientists at Idenix had already made a similar development.[102] Idenix would also later closely collaborate with McGuigan's lab.[103] Merck challenged Gilead for patent infringement and in 2016 won a $2.54 billion award, but it was overturned on an appeal that was later upheld by the Supreme Court.[104]

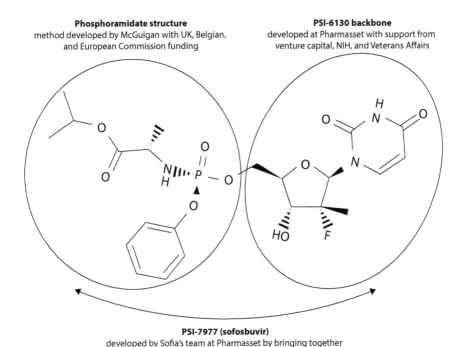

Phosphoramidate structure
method developed by McGuigan with UK, Belgian, and European Commission funding

PSI-6130 backbone
developed at Pharmasset with support from venture capital, NIH, and Veterans Affairs

PSI-7977 (sofosbuvir)
developed by Sofia's team at Pharmasset by bringing together phosphoramidate and the PSI-6130 backbone

FIGURE 2. Organizational and financial sources of sofosbuvir structure.

As Zeller has noted in his work on intellectual property monopolies, the "socialization" of innovative labor "makes it difficult to assign the elements of an intellectual achievement to specific actors or firms."[105] In the face of this fraught reality, the US intellectual property system relies on expensive litigation and legal machinations to resolve the specific contours of such claims. Drug companies, in turn, must become specialists in intellectual property battle strategies as they seek to maintain control over socially produced assets.

To lay claim to the sofosbuvir compound as its intellectual property, Pharmasset moved quickly to file applications with the PTO in 2007 and received a patent in 2008. The company then began to prepare for early-stage human trials in 2009 and 2010.[106] Over the course of these two years, Sofia's application of the prodrug method would be validated in several Pharmasset-led early-stage clinical trials, with each trial showing promising results. Though the numbers of patients were relatively small, the compound showed results heretofore not witnessed in hepatitis C. In the Phase II trials for example, sofosbuvir cured hepatitis C at rates higher than 90% in multiple cohorts among 564 patients.[107] A remarkable advance for patients appeared within reach. Pharmasset used the capital from shareholders to run these trials, at a total cost of $62.4 million. But the company's executives also wrestled over what to do next with their prized asset. The answer to this question would be shaped by the financialized trajectory along which the company had already travelled.

SOFOSBUVIR AS AN ASSET AND A RELAY RACE
OF FINANCIALIZED CAPITAL

The early 2000s brought an expanding search for hepatitis C therapies, with the advent of the replicon drawing in a growing field of emerging companies and private finance capital. Yet this entry of speculative capital would illustrate key features of financialized drug development.[108] With no internal sources of finance and no products or revenue, Pharmasset would be structurally oriented to meeting the demands of an array of external and speculative forms of capital, from venture capital to stock markets. These finance capitalists were drawn by the economic promise of its hepatitis C assets. At play in these valuations, in turn, would be the future prices investors and traders anticipated for hepatitis C drugs. Defined by specific growth-oriented logics of price and value, these financial markets would let these actors bet on drugs over periods far shorter than it would take to develop any compound into a usable treatment.

Financial Markets and Pharmasset:
Venture Capital, Corporate Capital, and an IPO

As Pharmasset embarked on developing its pharmaceutical assets in the early 2000s, it searched for sources of financing to carry forward its research efforts. Neither direct public funding beyond NIH's SBIR program, nor bank financing, would work. Though the state had been a critical source of patient capital in an earlier stage, SBIR grants (highlighted earlier) would not be sufficient for phase I and II trials. According to a US government study using data from that period (2004–2012), the average phase I anti-infective clinical trial cost about $4.2 million, and a phase II trial, $14.2 million.

Furthermore, while hepatitis C was a growing public health concern in the late 1990s and 2000s, NIH had not developed a plan to scale up financing of hepatitis C drug development, particularly public funding of clinical trials.[109] This lack of mobilization contrasts with the case of HIV/AIDS, in which political movements had ultimately instigated broad-based public-sector investments in drug development.[110] Similar political support had yet to be engendered for hepatitis C at the national level or in the US or abroad. Among the reasons offered by physicians and public health analysts for this relative silence: the chronic and often invisible nature of hepatitis C and the marginalized status of many patients with the virus.[111]

Bank loans were also not an option for Pharmasset. The project's high uncertainty and the lack of collateral of a small biotechnology company without any approved products made it unsuited for bank financing.[112]

Instead, Pharmasset would turn to a source that had become more common for biotechnology enterprises since the 1980s: venture capital. Quite unlike the government, venture capital funds typically provide capital to early-stage businesses in exchange for an ownership share.[113] This capital comes in phases, with companies attracting "rounds" of funding based on the extent of their financial promise. Venture capitalists usually aim to "exit" their ownership after several years and "cash out" their investment when an investee company is acquired by a larger firm or becomes publicly traded on the stock market. Reflecting the typical scale of venture capital investments in biotechnology companies at that time, by 2004 Pharmasset had raised $55.3 million to finance its nucleoside development work.[114]

This venture capital financing mechanism did not emerge from spontaneous market activity. It was fostered by two regulatory shifts undertaken by the US government in the 1970s and 1980s and influenced in part by new business interests. First, the Bayh-Dole Act, as described earlier, allowed venture-backed startups to emerge from university research by monetizing publicly funded knowledge.[115] Second, in 1979 the government promulgated a regulatory change that let pension funds invest much more of their assets in venture capital, which until then had been deemed to carry too much risk.[116]

With a new class of university startups in which to invest, as well as new sources of pension-fund financing, venture capital skyrocketed. In 1978, venture capital amounted to only a sliver of economic activity, with a total of $216 million in commitments.[117] And pension funds made up only 15% of that. Ten years later, in 1988, pension funds accounted for nearly half of a total of $3 *billion* committed to venture capital funds.[118] At the height of the dot-com bubble, in 2000, venture capital reached $120 billion in investment, though this fell to $23 billion in 2004, the year of Pharmasset's final major round of venture financing.[119] In the 1980s and 1990s, the biotechnology sector emerged as one of the leading destinations for venture capital, with approximately 20% of a total of $108 billion directed to drug and device development companies.[120]

Yet the scale of these investments in individual research projects would be modest, as it was spread across hundreds of firms. In biotechnology, for example, the median total investment by venture capital funds in the early 2000s was approximately $50 million.[121] This could not sustain the long and expensive effort typically required to develop initial compounds into approved drugs. The modest and short-term investments of venture capitalists meant that Pharmasset needed more capital. The company turned to two other potential sources: a larger pharmaceutical company, and the stock market.

By the spring of 2004, Pharmasset had what it viewed as a promising pharmaceutical asset in PSI-6130.[122] Because the compound had shown profound inhibition of the virus via binding to the NS5b polymerase protein both in the replicon and then in rats, Pharmasset decided to pursue early human trials.[123] But many questions typical of early-stage drug development remained, including how much of the compound would be needed for the desired effect, and whether it would be safe in humans. With no experience in hepatitis C clinical trials, Pharmasset looked to an approach that had grown in the past two decades in the biotechnology and pharmaceutical sector: the "strategic partnership" between small enterprises and established companies.

These have been pursued in the industry as a way of joining up the supposed comparative advantages of small companies (with few or no approved products) and larger ones (with established revenues). Small biotechnology companies can supply established businesses with compounds from early-stage research often deemed too risky for larger firms, and larger businesses can provide clinical trial expertise to small companies with little background in the development process.[124] In the past three decades, such alliances have become more common, especially as large companies have outsourced early-stage research.

Several months after closing their final round of venture capital and patenting PSI-6130, Pharmasset struck a partnership deal with Roche, a large Swiss-based pharmaceutical company.[125] As the manufacturer of the leading hepatitis C treatments at the time (the interferon-based Pegasys and Copegus), Roche saw potential in using PSI-6130 to expand its antiviral strategy. The interferon treatments were toxic, akin to cancer chemotherapy, and many patients avoided taking them until their disease was in its later stages.[126] The public list price for the regimen was about $40,000, and the market for hepatitis C, which also included interferon products from Roche's competitor, Schering Plough, had grown to over $2 billion in sales by 2004.[127] Roche hoped that by pairing interferon with a compound like PSI-6130, they could make their treatments less toxic and more usable by patients at an earlier stage of the disease.

Leveraging its recent experience in hepatitis C clinical trials (for their interferon regimens), Roche aimed to conduct further investigations of the efficacy and safety of Pharmasset's compound in humans. Roche agreed to provide an upfront payment, further milestone payments of up to $105 million, and royalties on Pharmasset, in exchange for global rights to any compound and its associated revenue (minus royalty payments);[128] Roche also gained shares in Pharmasset.[129]

Over the next six years, during which the two companies partnered on clinical trials for PSI-6130 and its modified versions, Roche directed $44.5 million to Pharmasset.[130] But this relatively small sum—in the face of the tens of millions necessary for later-stage clinical trials—would be only one part of the relay race of financial actors from which Pharmasset would seek capital. The company would then turn to another source to sustain their R&D efforts: the stock market.

By 2006, Pharmasset was preparing for an initial public offering (IPO): converting itself from a privately held company to one that would be traded on the NASDAQ stock exchange.[131] Two factors shaped this move. An IPO would enable Pharmasset's venture capital investors to exit and "cash out"; it could generate a new round of capital to finance clinical trials. Pharmasset's IPO on NASDAQ, on April 26, 2007, raised $45 million, with the stock trading at $9 per share.[132] Four institutional shareholders—pension funds like Fidelity, and hedge funds like BlackRock—each held more than 5% of these shares. Pharmasset's $45 million "valuation" was based on its three clinical-trial-stage nucleoside compounds: the PSI-6130 compound being developed with Roche, as well as one for hepatitis B (clevudine) and one for HIV (racivir).[133] For each compound, Pharmasset saw the potential for major revenue, as anticipated improvements in the treatments had the potential to lead to higher prices and more patients being treated. With 15 million people chronically infected with hepatitis C in the major markets of the US, Europe, and Japan, Pharmasset's senior leadership believed its development efforts could produce compounds that would bring it a substantial share of the market for hepatitis treatments.

Financial markets bet on this promise as well. The potential of its drug assets enabled the company to raise further capital in the stock market by issuing new shares, with five separate rounds of follow-on financing bringing $345.9 million in capital.[134] Pharmasset spent some of this on clinical trials, in 2010 and 2011, for the compound that would ultimately be sofosbuvir.[135] These follow-on rounds also allowed new shareholders to trade on Pharmasset's rising stock price, which rose in 2010 and 2011 and reached $85 per share in October 2011 on the news of clinical trials showing a major breakthrough in hepatitis C treatment.[136]

Such trading on pharmaceutical assets, many of which may never receive regulatory approval or generate earnings, has been facilitated by the specific configuration of NASDAQ. Unlike its older sibling, the New York Stock Exchange, NASDAQ allows companies with no record of profits (like Pharmasset) to execute an IPO.[137] Like the venture capital system, NASDAQ was a product in part of the US state: the exchange was created in 1971 as the world's first electronic stock market, with the encouragement and guidance of the US Securities and Exchange Commission. NASDAQ would begin to take off in the 1990s with the rise of venture-backed technology companies. The presence of NASDAQ enabled a highly liquid financial market through which venture capitalists could exit their initial investments and subsequent traders could enter and exit based on fluctuations in share price. In Pharmasset's case, these price changes were shaped by development milestones and clinical trial results, which influenced shareholders' perceptions of the company's future value.[138]

By 2011, Pharmasset would be valued at nearly $5 billion, though it had no approved products, sales, or profitability. This disjuncture was a common feature of small biotechnology companies and was true of Pharmasset from day one. When Pharmasset raised $40 million from a series D round of venture financing in 2004, the company had run an operating loss in each year since its founding, for a total of $15.8 million in deficits, and was not expected to be profitable for years into the future.[139] When Pharmasset raised $45 million in its IPO and then follow-on financing in equity markets nearing $350 million, it had an accumulated deficit of $330 million and no compounds in phase III trials (Table 2). These forms of speculative capital would be fueled, in turn, by specific logics of risk, value, and price that would be entirely tethered to financial markets. We turn to these logics next.

TABLE 2 Pharmasset's sources of financing, 1999–2011 (millions of US dollars)

Period	Financing source	Amount
1999–2004	Venture capital	53.81
2000–2005	Small Business Innovation Research program	2.46
2004–2010	Roche partnership	44.50
2007	Initial public offering	45.00
2008–2011	Follow-on equity financing	345.87
	Total financing, 2000–2011	491.66
	Total operating loss, 2000–2011	(313.9)

SOURCES: Pharmasset SEC filings; S&P Capital IQ database.

Paying Out on Assets:
Speculative Capital and the Logics of Price and Value

Why did this chain of speculative financial actors get behind an unproven business like Pharmasset? The most obvious reason is that each actor, from venture capitalists to shareholders, aimed to make money. But the *way* they aimed to make this money is crucial for our understanding of the financialization of biomedicine and its consequences for drug pricing and value in drug development. These speculative actors make their money on the basis of two political-economic features of financial markets.

First, to mitigate risks and garner rewards, financial markets offered capitalists the opportunity to "exit" Pharmasset in periods far shorter than the time it takes to develop a drug. Lazonick's analysis of stock markets—less vehicles to provide capital for innovation, and more mechanisms for business transactions and trading on share prices—sheds light on this process. Second, financial markets enabled actors to make these gains by speculating on rising valuations for Pharmasset's drug assets on the basis that health systems would one day be compelled to pay more for better treatments. Beckert's description of "imagined futures" in capitalists' expectations reveals how forecasts of future earnings streams can fuel speculative transactions.[140] Taken together with the analysis of shareholder power in chapter 2, we begin to see how financial-market-driven drug development is intertwined with unprecedented drug prices.

This first dynamic relates to the temporal dimension of speculative capital. These financial actors did not get involved as part of a long and risky "development marathon" seeking to bring a drug all the way from the bench to the bedside. Rather, they were part of a "relay race" in which they aimed to accrue earnings in periods far shorter than it would take to make a new medicine. In other words, from venture capitalists to traders on Wall Street, they enter, as Powell et al. put it, with "the terminal point in mind."[141] Yet the speculative bets enabled by financial markets varied among the actors, with contrasting time horizons and at stages of the drug development process containing differing levels of risk. A venture capitalist might make a three-year bet on a business in its fledgling, startup phase; a trader on Wall Street might make a two-day bet on the results of a late-stage clinical trial.

Venture capitalists in biotechnology typically seek a 40–75% rate of return on their investments.[142] These returns are said to be warranted because unlike day traders on Wall Street, venture capitalists provide capital at unproven, early stages of a business and must wait for a payout. Venture capitalists also view themselves as "active investors" who use their technical and business expertise and networks to transform nascent businesses into potentially "high-value" enterprises. Partners at venture capital funds with a biotechnology focus typically have a background in biomedical research or medicine, which they use to evaluate potential technologies for investment. They also serve on the boards of the businesses in which they invest, using their technical and financial expertise to shape management decisions over talent, technology, and strategy in the critical early stages.[143]

While venture capitalists take greater risks than other speculative capitalists, they mitigate these risks in several ways. One way is to come in *after* the public sector has financed the most uncertain stages of technology discovery. As one of Pharmasset's venture capital backers for their series B round, MPM Capital's Luke Evnin, noted in a 2014 blog post: "Due to NIH funding now also going towards programs that demonstrate commercial potential, our 'start ups' are much further along by the time we invest—even though they may still be straight out of academia."[144] Another way to mitigate risk: venture capitalists use multiple financial-market strategies to "exit" their investments typically after three to five years. Either through the acquisition of their investee firm by a larger business or via an IPO, venture capitalists seek to transfer their ownership to other shareholders while generating a gain based on the valuation of the acquisition or IPO.[145] Evnin shared his venture capital fund's preference for exiting via acquisitions: "When we approach an investment, we really think about who's the buyer and what will we have to show that buyer? Is this a team and a product portfolio that will get us there?"[146] Finally, venture capitalists spread their capital across many assets, betting that a few big wins will cover losses in other investments. Yet because venture capital does not provide the scale and duration of capital required to fully develop and approve a drug, companies like Pharmasset continue to depend on other forms of external capital to sustain their research efforts.

At the IPO stage, institutional shareholders (such as mutual funds, hedge funds, and insurance companies) and stock markets enter the picture. Through his historical work, Lazonick shows us that while stock markets *can* provide capital to businesses, as is commonly held in popular discourse, this is not their primary function.[147] To be sure, the IPO is an example where the stock market functions to provide capital to young businesses. Yet the IPO mechanism also creates a market for speculative trading in which ownership is transferred from venture capitalists to other shareholders.[148] This transfer produces a "market price" based on the value that new shareholders forecast for the company at the time of its launch on the stock market. This price—represented in the company's stock price—then enables financial market exchange in which traders pursue financial accumulation—sometimes over mere hours, as in the case of day traders. Across the life cycle of a business listed on a stock exchange, Lazonick demonstrates that the stock market serves more as a mechanism for trading, via which shareholders can use their wealth to pursue capital gains, rather than as a vehicle to finance businesses in a durable way.

Indeed, the liquidity of financial markets (the relative ease with which traders can enter and exit) enables large financial rewards. Across biotechnology, stock markets have largely been kind to both venture capitalists and Wall Street traders. An analysis of annualized returns between 2000 and 2010 of 1,400 venture capital funds shows that life sciences venture capitalists made 20% returns (higher than in information technology).[149] Another analysis found that a trader who bought shares in all 340 biotech IPOs from 1979 through 2000 and held on to those shares until January 2001 or until a company was acquired would have realized an average annual return of 15%, almost twice the average gain on the S&P 500 during that time.[150]

This leads into the second dynamic of financial markets: how do these actors collect this scale of rewards? The economic sociologist Jens Beckert's observation that "expectations should be seen as central to the explanation of economic outcomes" provides insight into the motivations of speculative capitalists.[151] Financial actors did not seek to make money from Pharmasset's profits—the company had none—but by speculating on Pharmasset's future earnings and the company's resulting "market valuation." Trading on these valuations, in turn, gave speculative actors the chance to "buy low" and "sell high." Underlying these valuations, however, are specific expectations regarding drug pricing and pharmaceutical value.

As Beckert explains, the social bases of such expectations are to be found "within the power structures in which market actors find themselves." Based on its patents and the political power of the pharmaceutical industry, for example, Pharmasset's leaders and capitalists in financial markets plausibly expected that health systems could be compelled to pay higher prices for a better treatment. Interferon-based treatments for hepatitis C already cost well over $30,000 per treatment regimen in 2004, yet they produced severe side effects with a curative response in less than half of the patients that took them.[152] Wall Street analysts and Pharmasset's leaders anticipated that higher prices and market valuations over time would be contingent on therapeutic improvements.

This amounted to a kind of "pricing escalator," in which the price of current treatments set the pricing floor for future treatments, with each new generation priced incrementally higher based on the "value" it could offer health systems (Figure 3). Indeed, a retrospective study of launch prices for hepatitis C drugs in the US found that a 1% increase in cure rates was associated with a $1,000 increase in price.[153] This ability to turn pricing predictions into realized outcomes was due to the political influence that the pharmaceutical industry pursued through lobbying and other strategies I describe in the next two chapters.

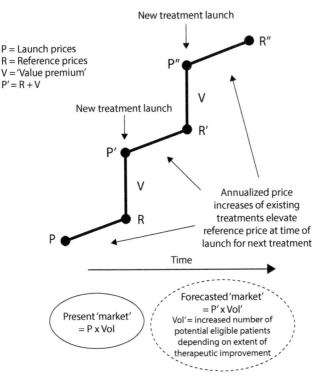

New treatment launch

P = Launch prices
R = Reference prices
V = 'Value premium'
P' = R + V

R"

P"

New treatment launch

V

R'

P'

V

R

P

Annualized price
increases of existing
treatments elevate
reference price at time of
launch for next treatment

Time

Present 'market'
= P x Vol

Forecasted 'market'
= P' x Vol'
Vol' = increased number of
potential eligible patients
depending on extent of
therapeutic improvement

FIGURE 3. The pricing escalator and expansion of market valuation. In this schematic view, the price of the existing standard of care serves as a reference (R), with a next-generation treatment garnering an additional price (D) based on its purported differential value. Higher prices (R + D), combined with the larger numbers of patients who stand to benefit from a better medicine, produce forecasts of expanding market valuations. These valuations attract bets from speculative capitalists. See chapter 3 for more on how this pricing comes to be represented as "value pricing" in policy debates.

These higher prices, in turn, would be combined with forecasts of large patient populations that could benefit from a better treatment. While the toxic interferon treatments could only be used on later-stage patients, the industry and Wall Street predicted that improvements could mean that everyone could be treated—even asymptomatic patients. Pharmasset captured these predictions in the SEC filing for its IPO.[154] In documenting a modest improvement in interferon treatments (from 47% to 54% cure rate in clinical trials), for example, Pharmasset's leadership noted that sales of hepatitis C drugs increased from $1.3 billion in 2000 to more than $2 billion in 2002. With further improvements commanding higher prices for more eligible patients, the company predicted that the hepatitis C drug market would grow from $2.2 billion in 2005 to $4 billion by 2010 and $8 billion in 2015.

Even if it was years away, this anticipated earnings stream from financial assets—in this case promising compounds granted patents by the US government—attracted bets from speculative capitalists. Pharmasset would close out the decade with assets valued at nearly $5 billion. Yet with no revenues, products, or profits, it remained cash hungry. This financialized trajectory, in turn, would shape the options its executives had for the company's next steps. We end the chapter by considering these options.

Potential Pathways for Pharmasset: Durability or Disposability?

As Pharmasset entered 2011 with PSI-7977 looking to be a potent financial asset, the company's senior leadership had a decision to make, one typical of small biotechnology companies with compounds preparing for later-stage trials. Should they aim to grow as a durable, free-standing business, or become what has been called a "disposable" business, with the organization dissolved on the sale of its assets to an established pharmaceutical company?[155] Pharmasset's strategic planning and board meetings, captured by the US Senate investigation, reveal that two major considerations shaped the company's decision: the timing and results of further clinical data on PSI-7977 and competing compounds; and its possibility of growing into a diversified, global enterprise.

If Pharmasset were to find a partner or get acquired, they wanted it to be with the right company for the right price. Early indications from the phase II trials were that PSI-7977 would work most effectively if paired with a second compound, as in the combination therapies for HIV. Using PSI-7977 alone (a "mono-therapy") could lead to high rates of resistance and lower cure rates.[156] Pharmasset and several larger companies, such as Bristol Myers Squibb, Gilead Sciences, and Merck, had developed compounds that might work in tandem with PSI-7977, but the data on those compounds still presented a murky picture, as few had made it into later-stage clinical trials.[157] Pharmasset's executives knew they could gain leverage by waiting.[158] With complete phase II trials for PSI-7977 to be released in late 2011, Pharmasset's compound would likely be in high demand.[159]

In the meantime, they also considered whether they could build a free-standing business. But here they saw major barriers. They would have to build marketing, regulatory, and distribution networks, which would require expertise and financial resources they did not have.[160] The larger companies had a major incumbent advantage, with the infrastructural and political power to shepherd drugs through the final stages of regulatory and global distribution. The executives also worried that after the launch of PSI-7977 Pharmasset would need to quickly diversify to other areas of therapeutic development, because a curative therapy for hepatitis C would not support the type of continuous growth their shareholders would want. The company's viability as a single-product business remained a looming question, and the leadership remained wary of the risks in developing other products. "Given the substantial time frame from research program initiation to product launch," they observed in a 2011 board meeting update, "it is highly unlikely that any *de novo* research program will provide the necessary revenue in the required timeframe" to deliver growth beyond hepatitis C.[161] Sticking to their original vision of the company—making assets to be sold to Big Pharma—appeared to be the most viable strategy.

PHARM(ASSET)

This chapter reveals the dynamics of pricing and value intertwined with sofosbuvir's financialized trajectory. By tracing how science came to be capitalized, with publicly financed and cumulative knowledge converted into valuable assets controlled by financial markets, three key features of this trajectory come to light.

First, value creation in the drug development process would be contingent on the state. The very possibility of sofosbuvir depended on public investments. All through the development of the replicon, nucleoside science, Pharmasset's launch, and the prodrug approach, public investments—primarily in the US but also in Europe—co-created value by "crowding in" private capital and setting the direction of the innovation process toward finding curative medicines. This private capital would be mobilized by the state not only through public investments but also through the state-sanctioned political-legal setup that allowed the patenting of collectively developed knowledge. Universities like Emory were big financial winners in the process, receiving public funds and royalties from intellectual property. This process turned knowledge into a financially valuable asset—the kind of asset that Schinazi, as the founder of Pharmasset, one day hoped he could sell to large companies.

Second, as a small biotechnology business with no products or revenue, Pharmasset was structurally tethered to an array of external financial actors. This chain of speculative financial actors—from venture capitalists to traders on Wall Street—bet on the future of Pharmasset's compounds, over time horizons far shorter than the time it would take to develop sofosbuvir. Of these financial actors, venture capitalists took on the biggest risks by making early investments in unproven compounds, thereby creating value in the evolution of Pharmasset. But the presence of financial markets—whether through acquisition and IPOs or liquid stock markets—provided each of these actors the opportunity to mitigate risks by being able to "exit" long before the fate of sofosbuvir would be determined in clinical trials or FDA regulatory review.

By the end of 2010, Pharmasset would be valued north of $5 billion, largely on the promise of PSI-7977, the compound that would become sofosbuvir. Yet Pharmasset's investments in the drug had amounted to only $62.4 million, and the R&D investments over the life of the firm totaled $271 million—about 5% of its market valuation.

This disjuncture between Pharmasset's financial market value and its R&D spending reveals the third feature: "value" in this speculative process was not commensurate with R&D investments or profitability. Instead, it reflected predictions—specifically, predictions of *growth* in Pharmasset's earnings potential. In valuing Pharmasset, speculative capitalists anticipated that health systems would one day pay more for a better hepatitis C treatment that could benefit a larger patient population. The high prices of existing treatments—over $30,000 at the time—made this a potentially wildly lucrative market.

Which path would sofosbuvir take in the hands of Pharmasset? Being acquired gave Pharmasset's shareholders a chance at a major reward, without trying to compete with incumbents that had significant global advantages. Lacking any approved products or the investments to develop the organizational capabilities for a durable business, Pharmasset thus viewed large companies like Gilead as potential suitors rather than as future competitors. To understand the pricing and value logics constituting sofosbuvir's next steps, then, we turn to Gilead—Pharmasset's most interested suitor—and the forces shaping its pursuit of growth.

2

Capitalizing Drugs

Shareholder Power and the Cannibalizing Company

The main urgency that the biotech model assuages are the strategic needs of big Pharma to outsource most of its R&D process.

—PHILIP MIROWSKI[1]

They have come back to the well every time. . . . Some people are joking and say "they should just hire you."

—RAY SCHINAZI, FOUNDER OF TWO BIOTECH COMPANIES,
PHARMASSET AND TRIANGLE PHARMACEUTICALS,
LATER ACQUIRED BY GILEAD SCIENCES[2]

While Pharmasset wrestled with what do with its promising hepatitis C asset, an array of established pharmaceutical companies viewed hepatitis C with hope and concern. Companies like Merck and Vertex were close to receiving approval for new treatments with higher cure rates than interferon-only treatments.[3] These new medicines, however, would still require patients to get weekly injections of the toxic interferon therapy. Many patients would likely continue to wait for better options. Given the large patient population and the prices (upwards of $50,000 per patient) that Merck and Vertex were expecting to charge, providing such an option seemed like it would be highly lucrative.

As a Vertex Pharmaceuticals executive put it, hepatitis C was "one of the largest pharmaceutical opportunities this decade."[4] Industry researchers and investment analysts expected the market to exceed $15 billion by 2015. As many as two dozen large and small companies were racing for this revenue, with the potential for drug compounds crystallizing. Graham Foster, a liver specialist and clinical advisor to several of these companies, put it bluntly: "There are half a dozen possible targets on the hepatitis C virus, so you don't have many things to test. There are hundreds of millions of people infected; the current cure rate is 60 per cent; and the drugs are virtually intolerable. . . . You'd want to play, wouldn't you?"[5] Yet as of 2011, none of the large companies that had decided to play appeared to be in a position to develop what physicians and patients desired: a treatment that would cure the disease at higher rates, and without toxic side effects.

This chapter follows Gilead Sciences' hepatitis C gamble to show how capitalizing pharmaceutical assets—using accumulated capital to acquire growth—served as a central strategy for Gilead and its competitors. Far from a spontaneous emergence of market activity as might be implied by standard economic analysis, this strategy was a product of a series of political-economic changes since the 1980s that gave shareholders in financial markets greater influence over corporate governance. At stake would be the very purpose of large "life sciences" companies like Gilead: were they developers of novel science, or specialists in acquiring financial growth? The answer would reveal the relations of power between financial actors, business, and government that shaped the trajectory of sofosbuvir's price as well as the economic value that materialized with it.

LIFE SCIENCE AMID SHAREHOLDER POWER

In the summer of 2011, Gilead Sciences was in a predicament: internal R&D efforts had borne little fruit in the previous few years. A publicly traded company with established flows of revenue from treatments for HIV/AIDS, Gilead's scope for further growth seemed limited, with many Wall Street analysts pigeonholing it as a single-disease business.[6] Though improved treatments for hepatitis C signaled a new revenue opportunity, Gilead's development efforts appeared stuck. When Pharmasset surveyed Gilead's history in a 2011 strategy document, it noted: "Today Gilead is left wondering what to do in HCV" (hepatitis C virus), due to a "lack of successes."[7] Seeking growth without the internal pipeline to realize it, the company would turn to a set of strategies that had worked before.

Gilead's Ascent through Recombining Innovation for HIV/AIDS

Launched in 1987 by a medical and business school graduate, Michael Riordan, Gilead Sciences initially focused on a new biotechnology called *antisense* that could be used to shut down proteins responsible for viral replication.[8] Naming the company after an ancient region said to be the source of a healing balm, Riordan wanted science to be at the core of its business and emphasized it by adding the word to the company's name. The list of principles used in orientation of new employees started with "Gilead's business is science."[9] But he fully recognized the turbulent influence of the environment in which the new biotechnology business was operating. The next principle on the list: "Finance has its ups and downs."

Unlike Pharmasset, Gilead did not emerge directly from a university; it was founded in Silicon Valley in the early years of biotechnology. As a result of the changes described in chapter 1, a growing abundance of speculative capital was financing new ventures.[10] Gilead began with $6 million in venture capital.[11] With no products or profits, Gilead went public in 1992, and its NASDAQ IPO raised

$86.25 million.[12] This investment was based on the promise of a new approach: the company had shifted away from its antisense strategy and had acquired the rights to compounds that held financial value in the eyes of Wall Street.

Under the leadership of John Martin, a medical chemist recruited from Bristol Myers Squibb with experience in antiviral research, Gilead focused on nucleoside science. Martin envisioned a two-pronged business model: "in-licensing" compounds from other companies and institutions while also attempting to build up its internal research capabilities. In-licensing in this context means gaining rights to a particular scientific asset in exchange for royalties to the previous owner, who may not have the technical capability or the financial desire to further develop it. Pursuing this in-licensing strategy, Gilead acquired rights to compounds from two institutes in Europe with whom Martin had worked while at BMS. In 2001 one of these compounds, tenofovir disoproxil fumarate (TDF),would be approved in treatment for HIV, becoming the only once-daily pill for the disease at that time.[13]

Gilead sought to go further than in-licensing, turning to outright acquisition of firms with promising compounds by making financial bets in exchange for ownership of those assets. After a minor acquisition in 1999, Gilead's second purchase in 2003, Triangle Pharmaceuticals, positioned the company for dominance in HIV/AIDS. For $464 million, Gilead gained ownership of a compound known as emtricitabine, which had already received FDA approval.[14] As described in chapter 1, Ray Schinazi, also the founder of Pharmasset, had founded Triangle in 1996.[15] Both TDF and emtricitabine, the backbone compounds in their HIV regimens, came from university laboratories; Gilead brought them together in single pills for simplified treatment regimens.

Within three years of its acquisition of Triangle, Gilead offered two main treatments for HIV/AIDS: Truvada, launched in 2004, and Atripla, launched in 2006. Truvada was a combination of emtricitabine and TDF, while Atripla added a third compound licensed from Merck.[16] Before this, patients with HIV/AIDS typically needed to take many medications multiple times a day, making it difficult to adhere to treatment and increasing the likelihood of side effects. Gilead's combination of several medicines into once-daily treatments like Truvada and Atripla made it the leading manufacturer of HIV medicines. By 2008, 80 percent of HIV patients in the United States received one of Gilead's medicines.[17] From its launch in 2004 to the end of 2011, Truvada generated $13.5 billion in total revenue.[18] Atripla amassed $11.2 billion by 2011, surpassing Truvada in yearly sales in 2010. Gilead's HIV strategy had paid off, allowing the company to expand during the 2000s from a small publicly traded company with no products and sales to a growing biopharmaceutical company with $8 billion in annual revenue in 2011.

Yet even with its successes in HIV, the company faced a structural predicament. Its share price had risen between 2006 and 2008, mirroring its growth in HIV drug sales. "The cash continues to pile up," noted a *Forbes* article. By the close of 2009, the company had nearly $4 billion in accumulated capital. But when this growth began to plateau, in 2009 and 2010, the share price slumped back to its pre-HIV range

FIGURE 4. Gilead's share price between August 2006 and October 2010. After rising from $16 to nearly $30 on the strength of HIV sales in 2006 thru 2008, in 2010 it fell and stagnated between $16 and $20. Sales growth from HIV continued but slowed, and the company did not have another product in the pipeline anticipated to generate new growth. Source: Google Finance, GILD.

(Figure 4). The same *Forbes* piece summed up the sentiment on Wall Street: "As its earlier galloping growth begins to slow, investors are starting to wonder what Gilead plans to do for a second act."[19] Gilead's position in the innovation process—and its decision as to what to do for its "second act"—would in turn be shaped by the latest iteration of a long-running debate over corporate governance in the twentieth century.

The Rise of Shareholder Power and the Crisis of Growth

Wall Street's dissatisfaction with Gilead's performance, even as the company amassed billions in cash from a viable earnings stream, illustrated a structural crisis confronting large contemporary pharmaceutical businesses. This structural crisis centered on growth: with "maximizing shareholder value" deemed by Wall Street to be the core function of a business, pharmaceutical companies were supposed to pursue short-term and ongoing growth and distribute that growth to shareholders. Yet this went against the long-term, risk-laden, and investment-oriented financial commitment required for drug development. This "financialization" of American corporations, begun in the 1970s, would have significant ramifications for pharmaceutical companies like Gilead.

Maximizing shareholder value has not always been taken to be the core task of US corporations. For much of the twentieth century, large corporations employing thousands or even hundreds of thousands of employees dominated the US economy. These companies relied on what economists Lazonick and O'Sullivan call the "retain and reinvest" approach.[20] By reinvesting the capital they had earned from sales of their existing goods and services, corporations—from pharmaceutical companies like Merck to General Electric, General Motors, IBM, AT&T, and Xerox—secured long-term growth.

For these companies, the primary role of shareholders was *not* to fund business. Contrary to today's prevailing mythology, most large businesses—from the birth of stock markets in the early twentieth century to today—have not needed money from their shareholders. Rather, as I described in chapter 1, aside from episodes where businesses undergo IPOs or issue new shares, the primary role of stock markets was to provide a vehicle for business transactions (acquisitions, for example) and trading in companies' stock.

The established businesses of much of the twentieth century preferred to use the retained capital from sales of goods and services to reinvest in employees, R&D, and other capabilities.[21] This strategy enabled a rising professional cadre of managers—rather than corporate shareholders—to have a greater degree of control over business strategy.

As Lazonick has chronicled, this cadre developed, through the maturing US system of higher education, to lead corporations by strategically investing retained capital in ways that could generate long-run economic growth. This dominant paradigm, in which corporations and their managers had control over their own resources and capital, allowed a "stakeholder" view of capitalism to predominate. By this view, corporate success depended on serving multiple interests, from customers to employees to local communities. In a famous 1932 debate in the *Harvard Law Review* over the purpose of corporations, professor Merrick Dodd argued that businesses were "an economic institution which has a social service as well as a profit-making function."[22] This stakeholder view of corporate governance would prevail well into the postwar era in the United States.

Yet this manager-led consensus broke down in the 1970s, amid headwinds from business slowdown, a challenging macroeconomic environment, and new scholastic fashions emerging from the worlds of law, finance, and economics.[23] After two decades of expansion in the 1960s and 1970s, the typical US corporation had become, many business analysts and economists argued, too large and diversified. Operating as conglomerates in unrelated industries, and with leadership too removed from actual processes to make informed investment decisions, US corporations performed poorly.[24] The macroeconomic environment exacerbated this slowdown. The rising powers in Japan and Germany, having recovered from World War II with skilled workforces and deep technical bases in multiple sectors, presented major new competition for the US. The "stagflation" of the 1970s—which brought together inflation from rising oil prices and higher rates of unemployment—added to corporate struggles. A growing perspective in academia and finance was that placing control in the hands of shareholders—away from corporate managers—would be critical to renewing prospects for economic growth. This shift toward shareholders would be underpinned by two core arguments.

First, on the "efficient-market hypothesis" promoted by economist Eugene Fama and his colleagues in finance, the main mandate of managers should be to distribute capital to shareholders, who could then allocate it to sectors and firms with better growth prospects.[25] This in turn would spur growth across the economy. Share price—as a measure of a firm's *potential* growth and corporate performance, rather than their existing profits—would serve as a market signal for this allocation of capital. This would reduce the ability of managers to pursue what financial markets might deem "inefficient" strategies.[26]

Second, as part of what has been dubbed the "law and economics" movement, legal scholars argued that any "residual" earnings of a corporation belonged to its shareholders, because shareholders had no contractual guarantee of reward—unlike salaries and payments to employees, vendors, suppliers. To discipline corporate managers to pursue this strategy, which came to be known as "maximizing shareholder value," these scholars argued for a "market for corporate control," in which companies with poor returns on their stocks could be the subject of takeover.[27] This idea came to fruition by the 1980s.

Financial deregulation, beginning in the 1970s and accelerating in the 1980s, gave rise to new powers for institutional investors—such as mutual funds, pension funds, and life insurance companies—which could now invest directly in corporate stocks. Aided by the lax enforcement of antitrust laws under the Reagan administration, these new financial actors bought up companies, fired their managers, and sold off divisions for quick profits.[28] Within a decade, nearly one-third of *Fortune* 500 firms had been acquired or merged. The sole measure of corporate performance became the higher share price and market capitalization of the company after the takeover.[29]

By the early 2000s, maximizing shareholder value—by generating growth and then directing capital to shareholders—became the reigning ideology of corporate strategy. And to bring executives further into the fold in pursuing this approach, corporate boards shifted their approach to compensation. Executives became major shareholders themselves, with compensation packages in the form of stock options alongside annual salaries.[30] This gave corporate managers a direct incentive to "maximize shareholder value."

Yet this ideology rested on a logic of growth at odds with the long-term risk-taking required for drug development. A typical drug takes ten to fifteen years to develop. But shareholders expect capital gains at a magnitude and on a timetable that can be incompatible with such risk-taking. For example, investment analysts on Wall Street typically expect growth in the pharmaceutical sector in the double-digit range—that is, about 10%, *annually*.[31] This expectation comes from comparing pharmaceutical companies against competing vehicles for growth or the overall "market rate of return"—what a trader or investor can garner from allocating their capital elsewhere in the stock market. These "returns" are assessed by Wall Street every few months on quarterly earnings calls, a practice linked to what some have dubbed "quarterly capitalism."[32]

This configuration of extractive growth—directed to shareholders on short time horizons and at significant scale—produces what Sunder Rajan has described as recurring episodes of structural "crisis" for pharmaceutical companies, like Gilead, that are in the ostensibly risk-laden and long-term business of drug development.[33] As Gilead entered into 2011, staving off this crisis and transcending the projections of Wall Street would be central to its strategy.

Overcoming Recurrent Crisis: From Research and Development to Search and Development

By the metrics of profitability, Gilead Sciences performed exceedingly well in the years leading up to 2011. Between 2009 and 2011, for example, Gilead's rates of profitability ranged from 33% to 38%.[34] In 2011, the average rate of return for the companies in the S&P 500 stood at about 8%. Gilead's profitability was largely due to its patent-protected revenues in a single therapeutic area: medicines for HIV. Between 2008 and 2011, Gilead's revenues climbed by about $1 billion each year, from $5 to $8 billion, with its HIV medicines making up 85% of that revenue.[35] But as the growth from HIV sales slowed, so did the company's share price. The fear that Gilead would remain a single-disease business, with limited prospects for higher rates of growth, was pushing the share price down. How could the company overcome this dim prognosis?

As Sunder Rajan described in his study of the pharmaceutical industry, Gilead faced two conundrums—looming patent cliffs and limited pipelines.[36] First, Gilead's existing products had a finite life based on the length of their intellectual property protections. Though the threat was not immediate, these "patent cliffs" still loomed over Gilead's prospects. The patent on their key HIV compound, TDF, would expire in 2017 in several key markets, including Europe, which threatened to expose their most lucrative HIV treatment regimens to generic competition in a little over five years.[37] Like other big pharmaceutical companies, Gilead would try to extend the length of its patents and their dominance in their current "market" via a number of dubious strategies (described in chapter 3).

Though Gilead's HIV treatment regimens had delivered steady revenue growth for the company, as the HIV epidemic plateaued they could not produce the magnitude of growth shareholders demanded.[38] But that growth was also threatened by another dynamic: limited internal potential for new drugs, or what are known in the industry as "drug pipelines." The very shareholder imperative to produce short-term growth undercuts a company's appetite for the long-term risks needed to develop new treatments. Instead, maximizing shareholder value has meant directing as much capital as possible to shareholders. Though Gilead's revenue totaled $33 billion between 2007 and 2011, the company invested $3.3 billion, or

10%, in R&D.[39] Meanwhile, it directed $9.9 billion (three times its R&D budget) to shareholders by buying up its own shares ("share buybacks")—a practice I detail later in this chapter.

Gilead's R&D investments included clinical trials for hepatitis C. Like many of its competitors among the large drug companies, Gilead faced a wider industry conundrum. A study by Boston Consulting Group found that of the 712 unique drugs for hepatitis C in company pipelines between 1995 to 2014, only twelve were ultimately approved in a major market. On the other hand, the same study found that of the drugs that made it to phase III trials, more than half made it across the finish line and were approved for clinical use. This dynamic of high failure rate from preclinical through phase II trials can help explain why Gilead—facing pressure to grow—looked to Pharmasset.

Gilead had brought two compounds to phase II trials, but both appeared to lack the effectiveness of competing compounds like PSI-7977. Monitoring Gilead's pipeline, Pharmasset's executives noted that "their protease inhibitor is not very potent and has a resistance problem," and observed that their other compound showed the potential for adverse heart-related events at the necessary dosages.[40] Evaluating Gilead's pipeline and looming patent expirations, an analyst with Bloomberg business said, "We continue to be pessimistic about Gilead's long-term growth." Yet this analyst upgraded the stock from a sell to a buy because of "a large share buy-back plan announced earlier this month."[41] This short-term focus epitomizes the contradictions of financialized drug development: decrying the company's lack of growth possibilities, while applauding it for distributing capital to shareholders that could have otherwise been reinvested to develop stronger pipelines.

To generate this near-term growth in the context of patent cliffs and limited pipelines, Gilead would turn to their preferred approach: acquisitions of promising drugs using their stockpiled capital. Reflecting on its position on an earnings call with Wall Street analysts, then-CEO John Martin said, "We typically like things where we can have impact on Phase III [of clinical trials] and where we can accelerate those products either into the approval process or into greater indications after the approval process."[42] Gilead's senior leadership saw their company as a late-stage *acquisition specialist*, buying compounds in their final steps of development and thereby taking control of potential future earnings streams just as the compounds neared and then crossed the regulatory finish line. Such an approach had worked for HIV; to produce the next wave of growth, Gilead would need it to work again for hepatitis C.

Gilead's approach had by then become common across the industry. A 2010 report by investment bank Morgan Stanley, "Pharmaceuticals: Exit Research and Create Value," synthesized a view that had come into vogue.[43] The report encouraged large pharmaceutical companies to "exit" risky, early-stage research in small molecules and instead focus on acquiring patents on promising compounds. In other words: "research and development" should become "*search* and development." This approach, Morgan Stanley argued, could lead to a three-fold increase in profitability. Internal research could be used to support external "search" strategies aimed at buying the right treatments. The industry has largely heeded this advice. A Deloitte report in 2015 reviewing the performance of 12 leading large and midsize pharmaceutical companies found that over 80% of the financial value of their drug pipelines came from "external innovation": assets they had acquired, or developed in partnership with a smaller company.[44]

As 2011 wore on, Gilead knew that losing out on the hepatitis C market could have dire consequences for the business. Its dependence on HIV treatments left the business in a vulnerable position, especially if one of its competitors, like Merck or Bristol Myers Squibb, were to "win" the hepatitis C gamble by coming to the market first or with a better treatment regimen.[45] Conceivably, a larger company could launch a takeover attempt to gain control of Gilead's HIV revenue stream.[46]

In August 2010 Gilead hired John McHutchison to lead their "search" for the right hepatitis C asset. An Australian doctor who had led many clinical trials in hepatitis C for multiple biotechnology companies, including early-stage trials for Pharmasset's PSI-7977, McHutchison was viewed as a leading expert on the potential of hepatitis C treatments then under development.[47] Pharmasset's senior leadership noted the hire, observing "the very clear signals from Gilead and John are that they will be making some strategic moves in HCV."[48] These strategic moves would require a major financial bet, as Gilead sought to beat its competitors in the rush to acquire growth.

CHASING THE GOLDEN SNITCH, AND A HEPATITIS C GOLD RUSH

By the summer of 2011, both Pharmasset and Gilead faced a strategic decision over hepatitis C: should they pursue a business "combination," and if so, what would be the right price? Pharmasset's primary concern was whether a suitor would pony up for its valuable hepatitis C asset, PSI-7977. For its part, Gilead could take a financial gamble, or one of its competitors might swoop in to buy Pharmasset instead. With PSI-7977 showing promising data in late-stage trials, Gilead began deliberations on how to approach a potential acquisition.

To assess Pharmasset's value to the company, Gilead hired Barclays Capital to run a financial modeling exercise called Project Harry. Drawing inspiration from Harry Potter, Gilead was Gryffindor; Pharmasset was Harry. The compound ultimately called sofosbuvir, PSI-7977, was akin to the golden snitch in a game of quidditch: acquiring it could mean winning the game of hepatitis C drug development.[49] Project Harry showed that Pharmasset would indeed be worth a big bet. A speculative race unfolded to acquire Pharmasset and its potential competing hepatitis C assets, as large companies gambled against each other on drugs in their late stages of development in hopes of acquiring future revenue growth.

TABLE 3   Key figures used in Gilead's and Pharmasset's capitalization exercises

	Gilead's Project Harry model (with Barclays Capital)	Pharmasset's Project Knight model (with Morgan Stanley)
Expected price for PSI-7977	$80,000	$36,000*
Cost of capital	10%	8%
Years of sales (from approval year to patent expiry)	2012–2030	2014–2030
Net present value (NPV)	$25.5 billion	$11 billion
NPV translated to Pharmasset share price	$250 per share	$136 per share
Market price of Pharmasset as of July 2011	$70 per share, or $4.8 billion	
Mean target price for Pharmasset forecasted by 16 Wall Street analysts	$100 per share, or ~$8 billion	
Final acquisition value	$137 per share, or $11.2 billion	

NOTE: Each of these figures was tested in modeling exercises with different assumptions to develop sensitivity ranges, but for simplicity I give the median figures here.

* In its modeling, Pharmasset assumed a price of $36,000, or about half of what they thought a final regimen would be priced at ($72,000). This is because Pharmasset anticipated that it would need to be paired with another compound to be the kind of simple, once-daily treatment with high cure rates that could gain a dominant market position (US Senate Committee on Finance 2015: 886).

This process of capitalizing drugs, in turn, would rest on power relationships central to financialized drug development—the industry's power to price drugs and accumulate capital to buy assets, as well as the role of stock markets in driving speculative financial gains for shareholders.

Accounting for the Future and the Powers to Capitalize PSI-7977

To determine the value of a possible acquisition, Gilead performed an accounting exercise that is common in business: capitalization. Put simply, in this scenario, capitalizing something, such as a pharmaceutical asset, means valuing it for its expected monetary returns. In one sense, capitalization exercises are a technical operation that guides how a business can allocate capital. Such exercises involve forecasting multiple variables, ranging from the length of PSI-7977's patent life, the likelihood of regulatory approval, the extent of potential competition, and critically, its potential future price (see the main figures relevant to my analysis in Table 3). Based on Project Harry's results, Gilead's models showed that the compound could be worth over $25 billion to the company, even after accounting for an estimated $10 billion acquisition cost. The figures were tested across ranges of different assumptions, but all the models reinforced the "value" that Pharmasset could offer Gilead.

Pharmasset's executives also assessed the value of their own company, and their capitalization exercises showed that PSI-7977 would be worth approximately $11 billion were it to remain in their own hands as a solo company. The difference between the two figures—$25 billion versus $11 billion—stemmed in large part from Gilead's anticipation that it could use PSI-7977 in combination with its own compounds to develop a single, daily oral tablet that would gain a large global share of the hepatitis C market. Given its regulatory, distribution, and marketing expertise, Gilead believed it could use this simplified treatment regimen to become the dominant manufacturer of hepatitis C medicines.

Valuing these streams of possible earnings from PSI-7977 required the application of *discounting*, an idea central to capitalization exercises. The idea is that money today is worth more to an investor or business than that same amount in the future. To determine the value of a future stream of earnings, businesses "discount" future cash flows, to get what is known as *net present value.*[50] As Muniesa has put it, the discounting process "signals how much a capitalist would be prepared to pay to receive a future flow of money."[51] The discount rate used by corporations like Gilead and Pharmasset is equivalent to the minimum rate of return expected by shareholders from their existing mix of investments; this is also known as the *cost of capital*. Only projects showing a return greater than the cost of capital would make an investment worth pursuing.[52] For example, Gilead used 10% as its cost of capital, based on the rate of return expected by financial market actors on the company's existing mix of shares and loans. And even discounting the future of PSI-7977's earning streams by 10%, Gilead's models showed that acquiring Pharmasset had a high probability of returns in excess of $25 billion—making it a potentially wildly successful bet.

Yet capitalization exercises are more than technical pricing operations carried out by businesses. They also reveal the dynamics of power that are at play in business strategy.[53] In his reading of Veblen, the political economist Gagnon observes that "not only are productive assets capitalized in the process, but also any institutional reality is capitalized as well, be it social, legal, political, cultural, psychological, religious, technical or anything else that can grant an earning capacity." On a basic level, a 10% cost of capital indicates the powerful imprints of the financial sector, which reward businesses for pursuing projects that have double-digit growth rates—rates of return significantly better than what might be made in the stock market otherwise. As Gilead's leadership sought to exceed the returns expected in financial markets, Project Harry would also reveal two other power relationships critical to financialized drug development: the pharmaceutical industry's power over drug pricing in the US and globally; and its power to spend accumulated capital to buy assets like Pharmasset.

One of Gilead's steps in valuing Pharmasset was determining the price it could charge for PSI-7977 on its approval. These predictions were not abstract calculations but represented confidence in the company's power to translate predicted prices into realized outcomes. For example, Gilead anticipated that health systems could be compelled to pay at least as much, but probably more, for a superior clinical outcome. In the Project Harry model, for example, Gilead assumed a price of $65,000 per patient in the US, while also testing a sensitivity range of prices $10,000 below and above that point.[54] They chose $65,000 for sofosbuvir's future price in the US based on the price of the existing standards of care for hepatitis C. Both Merck and Vertex's treatments, just recently approved, would be launched with total treatment costs exceeding $65,000 for many patients (depending on the amount of interferon required) and with lower cure rates.[55] Per Gilead's formulation, sofosbuvir-based treatments could one day offer a lower "price per cure" and thus be promoted as a good "value" for health systems. In interviews with US Senate investigative staff, Gilead said that this was a conservative estimate in the run-up to the acquisition; its focus was on the chance to sell in this rough price range to a large number of patients with hepatitis C.[56]

To execute this strategy successfully in the US—which large pharmaceutical companies typically consider their most lucrative market—Gilead could count on the political influence of the pharmaceutical lobby. With one of the most influential lobbies in Washington, DC, the pharmaceutical industry had spent $240 million just in 2011 and nearly $1 billion in the previous five years.[57] In European countries and Japan—the next-largest markets in which Gilead anticipated making significant revenues—national health systems typically have more negotiating power than in the US and are able to command lower prices. But the US launch price still mattered in this global context. In its Project Harry modeling, for example, Gilead forecast European and Japanese prices as a discount from the US price, at 75% and 57%, respectively.[58] Even with these discounts, high-income countries would offer enormous revenue potential.

Perhaps most critically, this accumulation strategy would rest on Gilead's anticipated control over PSI-7977's patents, with threats coming from two directions. With respect to corporate competitors, Gilead would later make significant investments in a legal armamentarium aimed at fending off patent litigation from companies like Roche and Merck. With respect to governments, Gilead could rely on national and global policy favoring patent monopolies. In the territories Gilead forecast as most lucrative, the US and Europe, governments have the power to license such intellectual property to generic manufacturers, but in recent decades they have rarely done so, even amid public health emergencies or with patents derived from significant public investments. Gilead also saw significant financial potential in middle-income countries, where millions were infected with hepatitis C. This potential would be shaped by the World Trade Organization's TRIPS Agreement, through which low- and middle-income countries have been forced to "harmonize" their patenting systems to grant protections to global pharmaceutical companies in their specific territories. (TRIPS stands for Trade-Related aspects of Intellectual Property Rights.) The pharmaceutical industry's lobbying efforts via the World Trade Organization and other supposed "free-trade" agreements aim to enact ownership claims over knowledge across as much of the world as possible.

The other power revealed by Project Harry's capitalization exercises was the ability of large pharmaceutical companies like Gilead to accumulate the capital needed to even fathom betting billions on Pharmasset. In each of its models, Gilead estimated a price tag in the range of $10 billion for Pharmasset and projected how it would mobilize the capital for this purchase. At the time of the acquisition, Gilead was already sitting on $10 *billion in cash*, primarily from its sales of Atripla and Truvada.[59] These sales were in part driven by price increases: Atripla, for example, rose from $13,800 per year in 2006 to $25,874 per year in 2011.[60] Payment for these treatment regimens came from public-sector programs across high-income countries. Even in the US, with its large private insurance markets, the public sector finances treatment for over half of all individuals diagnosed with HIV, through a special government program begun amid the AIDS epidemic in the mid-1990s, and 80% of HIV patients in the US were on a Gilead treatment regimen at the time.[61]

Gilead's position echoes Zeller's description of pharmaceutical companies as "accumulation centers" within global capitalism, with earnings stockpiled from their ownership claims over assets like HIV medications. By using its considerable patent protections and attendant market power to set and raise prices and then accumulate capital, Gilead could both redirect this capital to shareholders and leverage it to acquire further assets. As the company planned for a potential acquisition, it anticipated using this accumulated capital to pay for Pharmasset. With its stockpiled capital and a clear projection of the future financial value of PSI-7977, Gilead readied itself for the big bet.

The Stock Market and a Speculative Race to Buy Growth

In the summer and fall of 2011, the acquisition process unfolding between the two companies would reveal the key logics of the stock market in financialized drug development, less as a source of capital for innovation and more as a vehicle to drive speculative accumulation for shareholders. This speculative accumulation would be driven by two dynamics: pricing in asset-based markets, as highlighted by Birch; and the positioning of shareholders as major winners in stock markets, as described by Lazonick.

First, because drugs are configured via patents as financial assets, the acquisition process shows how increased demand can significantly raise the price and value of these assets in stock markets. As Birch has described, assets like patents for drug compounds gain their value via ownership of future earnings. When the demand rises for such assets, asset prices rise as well.[62] This asset-based dynamic contrasts with prices for commodities, which typically *fall* with increased demand as more producers are incentivized to enter the market. For example, between Gilead's first bet on Pharmasset in September 2011 and the acquisition in November, Gilead raised its bid by over $3 billion. Gilead initially bid $8 billion, or $100 per share. This bid rested on Gilead's use of forecasts by Wall Street analysts. While Pharmasset at the time was trading at about $70 per share, for a value of $4.8 billion, the analysts expected that forthcoming PSI-7977 trial data would boost Pharmasset's share price to near $100. Yet Pharmasset rebuffed Gilead's initial offer at this price, because its executives knew that their phase II trial was even more promising than many had anticipated. As described earlier, Pharmasset's own internal capitalization exercise led its executives to believe that their hepatitis C assets were worth about $11 billion, or somewhere between $135 and $140 per share.

Leveraging their private clinical trial data, Pharmasset drew Gilead into an auction process, inviting multiple companies to confidentially review the new evidence and make bids. Given the possibility of competition—even though none eventually surfaced—and new knowledge about PSI-7977, Gilead raised its bid to $125 per share. Pharmasset's executives again rejected the offer. Pharmasset's leadership were betting on a better negotiating position in November, when they planned to publicly release PSI-7977's clinical trial data at a major medical conference, the annual meeting of the American Association for the Study of Liver Diseases.[63] And this bet was correct: Gilead would raise its bid a total of three times.[64]

On November 20, 2011, Pharmasset agreed to be bought for $137 per share, or $11.2 billion.[65] This was the largest-ever price for the acquisition of a small biotechnology company at the time, but it fell right into the range of values that Pharmasset's senior leadership had expected to get for PSI-7977 as a stand-alone company.[66] With this bid from Gilead, Pharmasset could guarantee its shareholders a payout *now*, and avoid the multiple downstream barriers associated with bringing a drug to global markets.

This dynamic of an escalating price for Pharmasset's hepatitis C asset did not fit the conventional understanding of "market competition." Rather, it was connected to the distinctive economic dynamics of assets that Birch has described. Unlike with commodities, competition for assets like PSI-7977 helps to escalate prices, as potential owners look to gain control over a potentially lucrative revenue source.

These logics are reflected in the very discourse of those who have described this pursuit of hepatitis C assets. Illustrating this speculative, bubble-like dynamic, one close observer of antiviral clinical trials called the pursuit a "hepatitis C gold rush."[67] Gilead's acquisition only raised the stakes for competitors like Merck and Bristol Myers Squibb, which had long coveted hepatitis C drugs as a potential growth opportunity. Pointing to the competition over increasingly scarce assets, Andrew Berens, an analyst with Bloomberg, said, "We are going to see a land grab."[68] Within a month of Gilead's acquisition, Bristol Myers Squibb announced that it had bought Inhibitex for its INX-89 asset, at a price of $2.5 billion, or $26 per share.[69] On the prior day of trading, Inhibitex had been valued at $9 per share, with the price hovering even lower at the time of Pharmasset's acquisition.[70] Two years later, in June 2014, Merck made a similar move, buying Idenix for its

IDX-21437 asset at a price of $3.85 billion, or $24.50 per share. On its previous day of trading, Idenix had been valued at $7 per share.[71] The potentially lucrative market in hepatitis C, underscored by Gilead's bet on sofosbuvir, drove up the valuations of these smaller companies. Like Gilead, the large pharmaceutical companies all faced similar imperatives in financial markets: to acquire growth.

Alongside the asset-based dynamic that can push up prices in stock markets is a second dynamic: shareholders are positioned to be major financial winners. Pharmasset's shareholders emerged with significant gains from the acquisition, with the purchase price of $137 per share representing an 89% premium over the last trading day before the announcement, when it traded at $72 per share. At the time of the acquisition, five institutional shareholders, all pension or hedge funds, each held more than 5% of Pharmasset's shares, amounting to an aggregate 39% stake.[72] Ray Schinazi, the original founder of Pharmasset, received $440 million for his 4% stake in the company.[73]

Whether Gilead's shareholders would "win" now depended on whether the predictions for PSI-7977 would be realized. In the days of news coverage that followed, business analysts expressed concern over the size of the acquisition.[74] And while the clinical-trial data looked promising, evidence of the drug's efficacy against hepatitis C's most common global variant (or genotype) was still pending. Under the headline "Gilead's Risky Revival Procedure," the *Wall Street Journal*'s "Heard on the Street" column worried: "With the Pharmasset deal, Gilead has transformed itself into a much riskier company. While all the signs suggest Pharmasset's drug is on a successful path, if something goes wrong, the value of the company could disintegrate."[75] In other words, Gilead had exchanged the technical risks associated with earlier-stage drug development for the financial risk of betting over $11 billion on a single company.[76]

Yet while Gilead faced significant financial risks as a company, its shareholders—who would ultimately receive the lion's share of the rewards from innovation—had not been the source of its risk-taking capital. To come up with the $11.2 billion for the acquisition, Gilead spent $5.2 billion of its approximately $10 billion HIV cash stockpile, saving the rest to pay down previous debt or finance future acquisitions and share buybacks. The company also raised about $6 billion in capital through new debt—a combination of bank loans and corporate bonds—for the remainder of the acquisition.[77] Rather than issue new shares, then, Gilead borrowed money—itself a function of the good credit status derived from its accumulated capital. Rather than providing capital for the drug development process, Gilead's shareholders continued to trade in the company's stock on the anticipation of sofosbuvir's phase III clinical trials. Though they had not risked their own capital, they stood to garner massive rewards.

This process highlights what Lazonick describes as one of the roles of stock markets: to facilitate "combinations" like that of Gilead and Pharmasset. Such acquisition deals, he writes, "may enable the combination to build productive capabilities

TABLE 4 Sofosbuvir-related clinical trial costs for Pharmasset and Gilead, 2007–2014

Trial sponsor	Phase	Reported cost for sofosbuvir specifically	Total firm R&D costs during period of sofosbuvir development
Pharmasset	Preclinical to Phase II trials	$62.4 million	$281 million (2001–2011)
Gilead	Phase III combinations* (actual)	$880.3 million	$4.02 billion (2012–2013)
	TOTALS	$942.7 million*	Total costs: $4.3 billion

*Includes clinical trial costs for combination treatments that used sofosbuvir as a backbone compound with Gilead's other antivirals to create more effective regimens.

SOURCE: US Senate Committee on Finance (2015: 23–24).

that support value creation"; indeed, the creation of a safe and highly effective all-oral tablet, made possible through Gilead's bet on Pharmasset, represented a pivotal improvement for patients with hepatitis C.[78] Yet, he goes on, "with the added cash flow that an acquisition brings to the acquiring enterprise, those who control the new combination will have much greater scope for value extraction."[79] In facilitating this acquisition, the stock market would be less a financier of a speculative bet, and more a mechanism used to derive financial gains for shareholders.

In the process, price and value became tethered to the stock market, and would bear no relation to Pharmasset or Gilead's actual R&D costs. To the Senate, Gilead reported spending in the amount of $880.4 million on final-stage clinical trials of sofosbuvir and its combination therapies.[80] Pharmasset had spent $62.4 million on developing the PSI-7977 compound that would go on to become sofosbuvir. Using this self-reported data, the total direct costs would be $942.5 million. The total research investment *across all therapeutic areas* during the main hepatitis C development periods for both Pharmasset and Gilead was approximately $4.3 billion (Table 4). Uncoupled from the sums spent in laboratories and in clinical trials, the speculative cost of acquiring sofosbuvir was instead tethered to the financial market's expectations and predictions regarding Gilead's potential profits from hepatitis C.

With the backbone sofosbuvir compound now in hand, in 2012 and 2013 Gilead fashioned a clinical-trial strategy bearing the imprints of its HIV approach: bringing multiple compounds together to create a single daily oral pill. Like many established companies, Gilead had had recent success in developing compounds for the NS3/4 protease and NS5a polymerase targets; yet each of these compounds had little value on its own. With sofosbuvir, Gilead now completed the hardest part of the puzzle by finding the backbone compound necessary for a simplified treatment regimen. For the new "combination strategy," Gilead brought together sofosbuvir and its internal secondary compounds in a series ("waves") of phase III trials. Each of these trials confirmed Gilead's confidence in the PSI-7977 compound, with cure rates near 100%.[81] In late 2013, Gilead received FDA approval for the first in a series of sofosbuvir-based treatments.

THE CANNIBALIZING COMPANY:
FOLLOWING GILEAD'S HEPATITIS C MONEY

Coming out ahead in this competition, Gilead Sciences launched sofosbuvir (branded as Sovaldi) in December 2013, and a next-generation sofosbuvir combination (branded as Harvoni) ten months later. The toxic interferon treatments would soon be retired from clinical use, as patients were cured at rates exceeding 90% by taking a single pill daily for just three months. The treatments produced jaw-dropping financial results: before the COVID vaccines, this was the fastest, most profitable drug launch in history, earning over $10 billion in just the first year.[82] Lipitor, previously the most profitable drug, had taken four years to reach this mark. Gilead's executives would have significant decisions to make over how to use this money. While I dissect the drug prices that would be responsible for these record-breaking revenues further in the next chapter, here I trace the flow of capital from hepatitis C to uncover the spectacular levels of *value extraction* that can occur in financialized drug development.

Paying Forward or Buying Back?

The flow began as a geyser. From their launch in December 2013 to the end of 2016, Gilead accumulated $46.4 billion in worldwide revenue from sofosbuvir-based regimens. In just three years, Gilead's total revenues as a business tripled, from $11.2 billion in 2013 to $32.6 billion in 2015.[83] Hepatitis C sales drove this escalation in revenue, accounting for 60% of all sales in 2015 and 50% in 2016, with the remainder coming largely from their steadily growing HIV sales.[84] With the relatively low cost of production for its HIV and hepatitis C medicines, the company's gross profits were 87% of revenues, totaling $75.9 billion between 2014 and 2016.[85] Where did these earnings go? Of this $75.9 billion in gross profits, Gilead's executives stockpiled $32.4 billion in cash and cash equivalents[86] by the end of 2016 (compared to $2.6 billion in cash at the end of 2013) for potential acquisitions and distributions of capital to shareholders.[87] The company also directed $32.6 billion toward share buybacks and dividends in those three years.[88] By contrast, the company reported spending $11 billion, or 14.4% of gross profit, on R&D.[89] The rest went to taxes and general operating expenses. Gilead's revenues and gross profits, as well as its capital allocation strategies, are depicted in Figure 5.[90] The bottom line: Gilead's leadership translated nearly 86% of its gross profits over three years into a cash stockpile and distributions of capital aimed at shareholders.[91] This flow of capital demands closer attention.

Rents and Value Extraction in Financialized Drug Development

To Gilead's senior leadership, share buybacks were part of a strategy to "maximize shareholder value." In an earnings call with investors in 2015, Robin Washington, Gilead's CFO, said that share buybacks would be the company's primary strategy "for shareholder return," reassuring Wall Street that, "if you look over the past several years, we've returned about 50%."[92] In this framing, shareholders are conceived

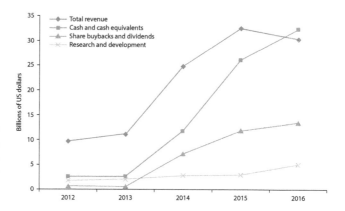

FIGURE 5. Gilead's revenues and capital allocation decisions, 2012–2016 (in billions of dollars). Source: Gilead's SEC filings.

of both discursively and materially as the source of risk capital to whom a surplus must be "returned." Yet this is an inversion of what actually occurs. For example, between 2006 and 2017, a net amount of $412 billion flowed *from* US businesses *to* shareholders *annually*.[93] In the case of sofosbuvir, Gilead's shareholders were *not* the primary source of risk-laden capital; they traded on the company's stock price to pursue capital gains. But the flow of capital to Gilead's shareholders illustrates the scale of *value extraction* possible under the conditions of financialized capital. This value extraction, in turn, is connected to the economic concept of *rent*.

As Mariana Mazzucato described in her book *The Value of Everything* and subsequent publications, rents were an important category of analysis by classical eighteenth-century economists like Adam Smith and David Ricardo. To them, rents represented *unearned income*. This concept of rent reflected a normative theory of value linked to the division of labor in the economy. As Mazzucato et al. write, "We need to recognize, as Adam Smith did, that there is a difference between profits and rents. . . . The first is a reward for taking risks that improve the productive capacity of an economy; the second comes from seizing an undue share of the reward without providing comparable improvements to the economy's productive capacity."[94] Economic activity defined as "rent" was epitomized, in David Ricardo's view, by landowners who collected rent without contributing to the productivity of land; he deemed them economic parasites.

In her book, Mazzucato traces how with the advent of neoclassical economics in the nineteenth and twentieth centuries, this normative theory of value—and along with it the notion of rent as unearned income—dropped from view. Instead, prices in markets came to be seen as an outcome of the preferences of economic agents maximizing their utility, with any income defined as "value" and a measure of economic productivity. Financialized capitalism has supercharged this view of value, as share prices in stock markets are seen as commensurate with the value and productivity of businesses.

But if we revive the earlier conception of rent in the context of contemporary economic processes like drug development, as Mazzucato urges, three key insights emerge. First, rents are made possible from intellectual property monopolies granted via patents, in which socially produced knowledge is turned into a scarce asset from which its owners can derive financial value. Second, the particular *flow* of rents is configured via a system designed to maximize shareholder value, in which shareholders are purported to have claims on capital even though they are *not* the primary source of risk capital for businesses. Third, the combination of intellectual property monopoly and the strategy of maximizing shareholder value enables economic actors—in this case corporate shareholders—to appropriate value produced elsewhere in the economy. In this case, Gilead's shareholders collected large financial rewards, even as the company's hepatitis C assets materialized from a social, collective process with significant public sources of finance.[95]

This understanding of rents has two important implications. First, it challenges the dominant view of "value," in which prices reflect the preferences of customers in a neoclassical sense. The theory of value advanced by Mazzucato and the classical economists allows us to conceive of value as a dynamic flow, involving processes of value *creation* as well as value *extraction*. With this dynamic theory of value, we can understand the drug prices and flows of capital that emerge from the prevailing system of financialized drug development as a product of specific political-economic relations of power.

Second, once this view of value is made visible, we can apprehend what processes—alongside intellectual property—make the contemporary scale of value extraction possible. As Birch has said, the "capture of monopoly rents is a proactive process"—one that we can observe in the flow of capital from sofosbuvir-based treatments.[96] Studying the flow of capital that emerged from Gilead's ownership of sofosbuvir-based assets—in particular share buybacks, executive compensation, and tax avoidance—reveals the processes of value extraction intertwined with financialized drug development as well as the magnitude of that extraction.

Disinvesting and Distributing Capital: Buybacks, Executive Pay, and Tax Avoidance

Gilead's share buybacks, conceived as a way to maximize shareholder value, illustrate a central strategy of value extraction in the financialized drug development process. The scale of buybacks shows that rather than stock markets financing businesses, the reverse has been true: businesses—and thus their customers and government buyers—have been funding the stock market. A Reuters investigation into the rise of buybacks across large publicly traded US businesses provided an apt name for this strategy: the "cannibalized company."[97]

Of the $30.7 billion that Gilead's executives distributed to shareholders in its first three years of hepatitis C treatment sales, $26.3 billion went to share buybacks (or "repurchases"), along with $6.3 billion in dividends.[98] By buying back shares, Gilead's executives aimed to raise the value of the remaining ones, promoting trading in the stock, and pushing up its price.[99] The main way to increase share price using buybacks is by artificially boosting a company's earnings-per-share ratio, a key financial indicator used by stock traders: reducing the share count reduces the denominator of this ratio, making the stock more attractive to traders in the near term.[100]

But share buybacks are not a natural feature of corporate strategy and financial markets. Before the 1980s, companies purchasing their own shares in such quantities would have been deemed to be engaging in illegal and manipulative stock trading. In 1982, however, the US Securities and Exchange Commission (SEC) introduced Rule 10-b-18, which gave companies "safe harbor" against charges of manipulation in pursuing such transactions.[101] This gave companies another way, besides dividends, to direct earnings to shareholders. In subsequent decades, share buybacks have grown as a corporate practice. Between 2005 and 2014, the nineteen pharmaceutical companies on the S&P 500 spent a total of $226 billion on buybacks—equivalent to 51% of their combined R&D expenditures.[102]

The rule change came as part of the Reagan administration's deregulatory agenda, with a former brokerage executive, John Shad, heading the SEC at the time. Shad described his agenda plainly to the *New York Times*: "to facilitate the accumulation of capital by corporations by removing regulations."[103] Yet as the pharmaceutical sector and Gilead's case illustrate, the rule change would have a paradoxical effect: though corporations could accumulate more capital, it did not stick around.[104] The buyback rule facilitated the *distribution* of this capital to shareholders via the purchase of a company's own shares. In contrast to the "retain and reinvest" strategy that prevailed in the US economy of the mid-twentieth-century, Lazonick and O'Sullivan term this approach "downsize and distribute." Here, maximizing shareholder value required the distribution of capital from firms to shareholders.[105] Lazonick has a more colorful description: "the legalized looting of the U.S. business corporation."[106]

The use of this buyback strategy to extract capital relied on a second dynamic: linking the strategic interests of senior executives with those of shareholders. In the 1990s, institutional shareholders increasingly tightened the link between the interests of shareholders and senior executives by pushing corporate boards to significantly increase the proportion of executive compensation coming from stock options and awards.[107] Regulatory changes in the early years of the Clinton administration aimed to limit the tax deductibility of salaries over $1 million for the top five executives in a company—unless the additional pay was linked to performance. The most popular "innovation" resulting from this regulatory shift was to use stock options as a primary method of "performance-based" compensation so that executives would have strong incentives to increase share prices. The rise in executive pay over the last three decades—with senior executives

TABLE 5 Compensation for Gilead's top five executives, 2014–2016 (millions of US dollars)

	2014	2015	2016*
John Martin (CEO, now retired)	192.80	231.96	98.15
John Milligan (COO, then CEO, now retired)	89.50	103.35	58.10
Gregg H. Alton (EVP)	56.20	22.57	8.50
Norbert Bischofberger (head of R&D, now retired)	50.70	95.53	7.00
Robin L. Washington (CFO)	26.60	21.97	5.53
Percent from stock-based pay	95%	95%	80%
Total compensation†	415.80	475.37	177.28

SOURCE: Gilead's SEC 14-A proxy filings, 2014–2016.
* As described in chapter 3, the lower 2016 figures reflect Gilead's falling share price in light of slower growth from curative hepatitis C treatments.
† Total of all three years: $1,068,450,000.

today earning 949 times as much as the average worker—has been attributed to this shift to stock-based compensation.[108]

Gilead's senior executives fit this now-common pattern.[109] Between 2014 and 2016, for example, Gilead's top five executives made a total of $1.07 billion in compensation (Table 5). In 2014 and 2015, 95% of that came in the form of stock options and awards; in 2016, 80% did.[110] As Gilead's shares rose on the strength of hepatitis C drug sales, and as its executives directed $26.3 billion to share buybacks, they also exercised their options and grant awards to make sizeable gains from Gilead's ascending share price. As shareholders themselves, Gilead's senior executives have been structurally incentivized to distribute capital to shareholders and to stockpile cash for potential acquisitions.

Value extraction was enabled not only by financial market rules on share buybacks and executive compensation, but also by corporate tax rules that reduced the state's ability to collect rewards it helped produce. Gilead's maneuvers with intellectual property (IP) protections of sofosbuvir are a prime example. In a February 2013 earnings call, Robin Washington, Gilead's CFO, told investment analysts, "The IP of 7977 [sofosbuvir] is domiciled in Ireland, so as we commercialize that, there is opportunity for our tax rate to decline over time."[111] Gilead had transferred the ownership of sofosbuvir to one of its six Irish subsidiaries, and created a licensing arrangement, letting it report lower US profits.[112] Though two-thirds of Gilead's hepatitis C sales were in the US, the company's US tax rate fell by 40%, from 27.3% in 2013 to 16.4% in 2015.[113] A report by Americans for Tax Fairness found that just in 2014 and 2015, Gilead had avoided $10 billion in US taxes by "domiciling" sofosbuvir in Ireland.[114]

This strategy is enabled by legal loopholes in the US tax code, by which companies routinely avoid paying corporate taxes (at that time, 35%) by holding earnings overseas.[115] Companies have argued that this rate hinders domestic investments, making such "tax planning" maneuvers a matter of survival. Yet when, in 2005, Congress and the Bush administration temporarily lowered the tax rate on profits to be repatriated from 35% to 5.25%, companies directed 92% of their $300 billion in repatriated profits toward the type of share buybacks and executive bonuses described in this section.[116] This was repeated with the Trump tax cut of 2017, which lowered the US overall corporate tax rate to 21%, and the rate for repatriated capital below 15%. US corporations proceeded to spend an unprecedented $1.1 trillion on share buybacks in 2018.[117] In sum, Gilead's strategies show the interconnected ways in which share buybacks, executive compensation rules, and tax avoidance are used to extract value via the financial market, with value flowing from a collective drug development process to Gilead's shareholders.

FROM R&D TO M&A AND BUYBACKS

Two years after the launch of its sofosbuvir-based medicines, Gilead Sciences' then freshly minted CEO John Milligan summed up the company's view of its strategy. "For us it's fairly simple," he told investment analysts. "We have the flexibility to do both things; that is, return shareholder value through stock repurchases and dividends and of course continue to be opportunistic in M&A" (that is, mergers and acquisitions). In reassuring Wall Street, Milligan distilled Gilead's *raison d'être*—it was a financialized business oriented toward distributing capital to shareholders. By tracing sofosbuvir's trajectory, this chapter uncovers three dynamics of this financialized business strategy and the pricing and value logics it entailed.

First, the financialization of American businesses—a function of the rise of maximizing shareholder value as corporate ideology—incentivized Gilead away from long-term research toward being *acquisition specialists* in the drug development process. Meanwhile, a set of scholastic fashions and political-economic forces present from the 1970s onward shifted the core purpose of business from profits to *growth* in profits—with this growth distributed to shareholders through maneuvers like dividends and buybacks. Yet meeting the double-digit growth expectations of shareholders runs counter to the long-term and risk-laden drug development enterprise. And with its pipelines drying up for lack of long-term investment, Gilead Sciences sought to generate growth by buying it, in the form of drug assets with promising future revenue streams. The prime example: its $11 billion acquisition of Pharmasset and the large revenue streams sofosbuvir promised.

This leads into a second key dynamic in sofosbuvir's trajectory. Gilead's capitalization of Pharmasset's hepatitis C asset revealed the relations of power at play in the pricing and value of medicines. In making its bet, Gilead valued sofosbuvir as an asset that could make the company tens of billions of dollars—far exceeding Wall Street's growth expectations for the business. This valuation would rest on Gilead's ability to turn its prediction of sofosbuvir's "value-based price" into a realized outcome. Gilead's power to project this future drew on two sources: its anticipation of acquiring Pharmasset's intellectual property and gaining monopoly power over prices; and its confidence that health systems could be compelled to pay more for a better drug. Capitalizing drugs, in turn, required capitalizing politics. Gilead's and the pharmaceutical lobby's sizable "investments" in political lobbying related to drug pricing and intellectual property regulations exemplify this influence. Buying the compound for $11 billion would also require another related power: large stockpiles of capital, much of which the company had accumulated from its prior sales of high-priced HIV medicines.

Gilead's eventual financial windfall from sofosbuvir reveals the third key dynamic in financialized drug development: the role of financial markets in extracting value for shareholders. The company made over $46 billion in revenue in its first three years of sales of sofosbuvir-based regimens, and it spent three times as much on buybacks and dividends as it did on its own R&D. This scale of value extraction is connected to the concept of economic rent, or unearned income. Gilead's shareholders garnered significant financial rewards by trading on an asset that was the product of collective public and private efforts, even as they had risked little of their own capital in the process.

Though Gilead Sciences had prided itself since its origins on being a techno-scientific company—as represented in its very name—Milligan had revealed a tension at the heart of financialized drug development. Soothing the "ups and downs" of finance that Gilead's founder, Riordan, had warned his employees about many years ago required a balm of its own sort, one not discovered in its laboratories but driven by Wall Street. It was to specialize in acquiring growth and extracting value for shareholders. But this approach would pose a threat to health systems and patients—and to future breakthroughs as well. We trace these consequences next.

3

Capitalizing Health

The Struggle over Value and Treatment Access

It is crystal clear to me that the body is an accumulation strategy in the
deepest sense.

—DONNA HARAWAY[1]

As soon as the drugs appeared, they've been snatched from our grasp.

—BRIAN EDLIN, INFECTIOUS DISEASE PHYSICIAN[2]

In the winter of 2015, I accompanied a liver specialist in the United Kingdom's
National Health Service as he counseled a patient with hepatitis C on the new sofosbuvir-based treatment. After reviewing the printed dosing instructions, the physician closed with a sobering piece of advice: "Guard these medicines with your life."

His words struck me. Life, in this formulation, needed to guard the medicine—
rather than the other way around. Indeed, many health systems, including the
National Health Service, were paying a significant sum for each bottle of pills.
Gilead Sciences, and the pharmaceutical industry at large, had told health systems
that paying high prices upfront for these medicines would mean billions in economic value for society, thanks both to improved quality of health and to downstream savings from averted liver transplants and hospitalizations. Health itself,
it appeared, could be capitalized—framed as the financial value of future healthi-
ness—and flowing as a stream of earnings to a pharmaceutical company.

This chapter traces Gilead's attempt to capitalize health from two angles. First,
we follow how in setting its prices, Gilead not only used its coercive political power
and gatekeeping role over intellectual property but also sought to establish a hegemonic influence over the very definition of "value" in drug pricing debates. A crisis
of treatment access ensued as Gilead charged "value prices" in financially valuable
territories such as the US and many other high- and middle-income countries.
But the company also licensed access to sofosbuvir-based medicines in a specific
set of less financially valuable territories where public health programs could be a

possibility. This strategy engendered political contestation in various forms, from patent disputes to government action to reduce drug prices. Analyzing the struggle over Gilead's pricing and patent licensing strategy reveals the ways in which the logics of value in financialized capital colonize debates over public health policy, and also the shape of resistance to the prevailing political economy of biomedicine.

Second, we trace Wall Street's response to the tenuous status of sofosbuvir as a financial asset. Because they cured the disease, sofosbuvir-based regimens would, over time, shrink the "market" of hepatitis C patients. Thus the treatment threatened the future growth on which its value as an asset in financial markets depended. As Wall Street soured on Gilead's declining growth prospects, the company responded with a series of financial machinations to generate accumulation for shareholders. These moves would echo strategies described in chapter 2, including price increases, patent extensions, and drug acquisitions. Taken together, these two areas of analysis—Gilead's pricing strategy and Wall Street's response to a curative asset—take us into the extractive strategies that underpin financialized drug development, as well as the system's multiple pitfalls and vulnerabilities.

HEALTH AS A FINANCIAL ASSET: SETTING AND JUSTIFYING A $1,000-A-DAY PRICE FOR A CURE

As sofosbuvir-based treatments advanced in clinical trials, Gilead turned to the looming question of the treatment's price tag. Because of the Senate Finance Committee's investigation, which reproduced hundreds of pages of internal corporate documents, we are offered a window into the company's approach to drug pricing. Gilead's pricing strategy was tethered to the financial market expectations that had driven the chain of speculative capital behind sofosbuvir. Internal documents show how Gilead set prices for sofosbuvir by adding a "value premium" to the prices of existing standards of care, anticipating that health systems could be compelled to pay more for better treatment.

As Gilead encountered political resistance to these high prices, it used not only its coercive political power but also its hegemonic influence to shape the definition of "value" in drug pricing debates. Along with its industry allies and even many health policy experts, Gilead pitched the notion of paying high prices for the "value" of better future health as a commonsensical, taken-for-granted idea. Drawing on a combination of moral-economic discourses and valuation practices, Gilead sought to shift the responsibility to governments: if public officials valued the health of patients with hepatitis C—and the improvement that future cures could bring—they should be willing to pay the price for that value. Yet this configuration of "value" was a kind of veil, hiding the dynamics of financialization which enabled significant *value extraction*. In sum, Gilead's strategy for setting prices and framing "value" illustrates how the speculative and extractive logics of financialized drug development shape drug pricing and public health policy.

Setting a Price for a Cure:
Floors, Ceilings, and the Value Logics of Financialized Capital

The Senate Finance Committee's report describes how, as clinical trials for sofos-buvir-based medicines proceeded in 2013, a senior leadership group within Gilead called the Global Pricing Committee met with IMS, a healthcare consulting group, to set the prices for these new medicines. These deliberations give insight into Gilead's "value pricing" strategy in the US and other high-income countries—a strategy which involved assessing the upper bounds of what health systems could be compelled to pay.

To seize the opportunity it had seen in hepatitis C, Gilead based its pricing strategy on the premise that new treatments would be easier for patients to take and lead to better health outcomes than previous medicines. This improvement would carry significant "value" for health systems that could be translated into a price point. To perform this translation, the company considered two primary factors: the prices of existing medications, which served as a kind of pricing *floor*; and estimates of the upper limits of what health systems could bear, which offered a kind of pricing *ceiling*. These factors pointed Gilead to an eventual price of $94,500 for their sofosbuvir-based combination therapy.[3] As is typical practice, this would become the US "list" price, from which Gilead would derive mandated or voluntarily discounted "net" prices, depending on the specific health system.

From the outset, Gilead used the prices of the existing standards of care as a *pricing floor* for its sofosbuvir-based regimens.[4] One example from Gilead's delib-erations highlights this approach. In a March 2013 briefing presentation with senior vice presidents, Gilead reviewed the pricing landscape of the standard-of-care therapies. Two "first-generation" antiviral therapies had been launched in 2011 that were used in combination with the original interferon-based regimens: Vertex's telaprevir and Merck's boceprevir.[5] Telaprevir had fewer side effects and more widespread use.[6] In their model, Gilead took telaprevir's price as $55,000 based on a scan of the prices Vertex was charging at the time (early 2013). Telapre-vir still required an average of nine months of ribavirin plus injectable interferon as part of a complete regime. Adding this nine-month cost of interferon and riba-virin ($28,000) to the price of telaprevir meant an average total price of $83,000 for the existing standard of care at the time.[7] This pricing floor can be viewed as the cumulative effect of previous increases in prices for hepatitis C medicines and the "pricing escalator" described in chapter 1.

As a slide from Project Harry illustrates (Figure 6), Gilead's executives con-sidered this $83,000 price point as a "baseline," compared to which sofosbuvir's "value premium" could command a higher price. They highlighted four key fea-tures of sofosbuvir that could be used to justify this premium: higher cure rates (sustained virologic response, SVR), increased tolerability (fewer side effects than

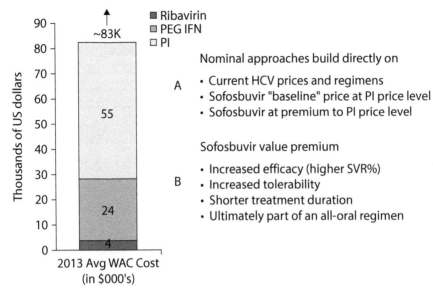

FIGURE 6. Gilead's initial pricing was based on the existing standard of care. Gilead's initial pricing approaches (A) "build directly on current HCV prices and regimens." Taking these as a baseline, sofosbuvir's higher quality would suggest (B) a "value premium" (letters added). "PI" here refers to the protease inhibitor medicines that were the standard of care at the time. Source: US Senate Committee on Finance (2015: 1348).

interferon), shorter treatment duration (only three months, compared to an average of nine months), and no need for injections (an all-oral regimen).[8]

Gilead's executives then sought to estimate the upper bounds of what this "value premium" could be by asking IMS to survey US health systems regarding how much they would pay for improved therapeutic outcomes. These surveys, which involved 90 officials in public and private health systems, helped Gilead estimate the price ceiling for sofosbuvir-based medicines. While their research clearly showed that lower prices would increase access to sofosbuvir, the surveys also gave Gilead confidence that a price range of $85,000 to $95,000 could be acceptable across a wide variety of health system payers, from commercial insurance plans to Medicare and Medicaid.

IMS's final recommendations also noted, however, that other, "softer factors must be considered."[9] Specifically, multiple stakeholders had pointed to the potential for public outcry due to the large number of hepatitis C patients waiting for better treatment. In addition to the survey, IMS prepared a "heat map" of the social and political responses Gilead might face from multiple key groups, such as patient activists and the US Congress, to different price points (Figure 7). This chart helped Gilead estimate the bounds past which "public outcry" or Congressional action would be likely.[10]

Stakeholders	Wave 1 Regimen / Wave 1 SOF product (12 wks) / Wave 2 FDC (8 wks or 12 wks?)	$60,000 / $50,000 / $70,000	$70,000 / $60,000 / $80,000	$90,000 / $80,000 / $100,000	$105,000 / $95,000 / $115,000	$125,000 / $115,000 / $135,000
Payers	Likelihood of applying directly observed therapy due to high price	Unlikely	Possible	Possible	Likely	Likely
Physicians	Likelihood of delay treatment of GT-1 TN patients due to pricing	Unlikely	Possible	Possible	Likely	Likely
	Likelihood of losing some KOL endorsement/support as price too high	Very Unlikely	Unlikely	Possible	Likely	Likely
	Likelihood of getting rejection on TE patients and delay treatment for all due to misconception of restriction for SOF	Possible	Possible	Possible	Possible	Possible
Patients and Advocacy groups	Likelihood of AHF, FPC and other advocacy groups reacting negatively to price, and affecting public opinion	Likely	Likely	Very Likely	Very Likely	Very Likely
	Higher out-of-pocket costs (not offset by patient support) could drive patient choice away from SOF, especially AbbVie has great patient support programs	Very Unlikely	Very Unlikely	Unlikely	Unlikely	Possible
	Likelihood of AHF, FPC and other advocacy groups promote AbbVie product due to the relationship and lower price	Unlikely	Unlikely	Possible	Possible	Likely
Treatment Guidelines	Likelihood of AASLD develop treatment pathway to prioritize (staging) patients (per KOLs or/and professional community request)	Possible	Possible	Possible	Possible	Possible
	Likelihood of a "price mention or asterisk" in AASLD (per KOLs or/and professional community request)	Unlikely	Unlikely	Possible	Possible	Likely
Others	Likelihood of public outcry if SOF revenue exceed $28 as government trying to control healthcare cost	Possible	Possible	Possible	Likely	Very Likely
	Likelihood of a letter from congress on SOF price	Possible	Likely	Likely	Likely	Likely
	Likelihood of a congressional hearing if SOF revenue exceed $28	Unlikely	Unlikely	Unlikely	Unlikely	Possible

FIGURE 7. Gilead's assessment of potential stakeholder responses to sofosbuvir's pricing. Gilead attempted to assess the severity of negative responses at the upper limits of the pricing range. For example, they anticipated "likelihood of a letter from congress on SOF price" at even $70,000 for sofosbuvir. Source: US Senate Committee on Finance (2015: 30).

Gilead's meeting with the Fair Pricing Coalition previewed this public pressure. A patient group that provided input to pharmaceutical-company executives on drug pricing, the coalition believed that sofosbuvir's price should reflect the great number of patients expected to receive it. The coalition's director, Lynda Dee, had already communicated this view at the FDA review meeting on sofosbuvir: "I mean, if the price of telaprevir and boceprevir I think is already exorbitant. I mean, if you could price it even close to what those drugs are, I think that you would be reasonable under the circumstances, and you'd still make a fortune. The volume that you're going to get for this is I think it's outstanding."[11] In their direct meeting with Gilead, the group communicated their hope that Gilead would set a price of $60,000, which roughly matched the price of telaprevir without interferon or ribavirin.

These appeals, however, were countered by a set of expectations from a powerful set of players: Wall Street investment analysts. In late October 2013, as Gilead prepared to launch sofosbuvir, Mark Schoenebaum—known then as one of the top biotechnology investment analysts on Wall Street—sent an email to Robin Washington, Gilead's CFO (and a member of the company's pricing committee) at the time, with the results of his own research. Schoenbaum had asked 203 investment analysts "Where do you think GILD [Gilead] will price 12 weeks of single-agent sofosbuvir?" The average answer was $85,400.[12]

On November 23, 2013, just two weeks before the FDA's decision date and the likely approval of sofosbuvir, Gilead's senior leadership arrived at their US launch price: $84,000. In an email to the senior leadership team, CEO John Martin noted that the per-bottle price of $28,000 (one bottle lasting a month, making the total $84,000 for a three-month treatment) would be "easy from the press release, from 28 days and $28,000."[13] Gilead's other senior leaders concurred on the email chain, figuring that $1,000 a day for a cure would make for an easy marketing push. Instead, this easily digested figure became a target in the latest political battle over drug prices.

Ten months later, Gilead would launch its sofosbuvir-based combination therapy (which eliminated the need for interferon in all hepatitis C patients) at a price of $94,500. Gilead arrived at this figure by following the logics of the "value premium" described above, adding about $11,500 from Vertex's prior interferon-containing standard of care.

The launch prices of sofosbuvir-based treatments, then, served as a culmination of the pricing escalator that had been intertwined with financialized capital. Wall Street and drug companies predicted that health systems would pay high prices for the "value" of better treatments; drug companies had the patent-protected power to set those prices. Gilead's launch price also underscored the company's role in the chain of speculative actors that were a part of sofosbuvir's trajectory: that of an acquisition specialist betting on hepatitis C assets, with the power to turn expectations of future prices into a realized outcome. Gilead's efforts would now turn to the political process of getting health systems to pay high prices for the purported value of future health.

Justifying a Price: Health as Financial Asset with Future Value

Gilead's pricing approach triggered a crisis in treatment access and a contentious public debate over the value of new breakthroughs, landing the company on the front pages of the news media.[14] National network television in the US ran with stories of treatment restrictions faced by veterans and patients with Medicaid insurance due to sofosbuvir's price. Activists at the 2014 World AIDS Conference in Melbourne held a "die-in" to protest the company. By the summer of 2014, the Senate Finance Committee had launched an investigation into Gilead's pricing strategy.

In this politically contested space, the company's leadership shifted the discussion to what they believed would be favorable ground. Gilead executive Gregg Alton told a journalist, "Price is the wrong discussion. . . . Value should be the subject."[15] Value, from this perspective, meant the economic value of future health made possible by curing patients with hepatitis C. Paying the prices for these medicines, in Gilead's framing, was well worth this value. While I focus on the United States in my description here, such debates over pricing and value resembled those taking place in many other high- and middle-income countries where Gilead sought to charge "value prices"—lower than in the US, but still at the upper bounds of what health systems could afford.

To pursue this strategy, Gilead mobilized its overt political power, seeking to directly influence public officials and politicians. After the advent of sofosbuvir, Gilead's lobbying expenses more than doubled, from $1.59 million in 2012 to $3.48 million in 2016.[16] Gilead also made direct political contributions to public officials, including Richard Burr, the ranking Republican senator on the Senate's VA committee. In a Senate hearing, Burr echoed Gilead's argument, calling the focus on prices "misplaced" and urging his colleagues instead to "examine the long-term benefits groundbreaking therapies bring to our veterans and to taxpayers."[17]

But Gilead's strategy of "value" was not one of straightforward coercive dominance over public officials. Rather, Gilead's influence can be understood in terms of Sunder Rajan's work on *hegemony* and the pharmaceutical industry, in which he shows how corporations create a new "common sense" over the very terms used in health policy debates.[18] To establish a hegemony over value, Gilead pursued two strategies: enacting a moral-economic discourse to shift responsibility to health systems, and drawing on technocratic valuation practices that garnered credibility in influential policy and academic circles. In the new sensibility they sought to inculcate, high prices were the investment society needed to make to realize future health.

First, Gilead enacted this moral-economic discourse across its public communications as it launched sofosbuvir-based treatments. In a press statement regarding Harvoni's launch, for example, Gilead argued that the price "reflects the value of the medicine," emphasizing that "unlike long-term or indefinite treatments for other chronic diseases, Harvoni offers a cure at a price that will significantly reduce hepatitis C treatment costs now and deliver significant savings to the healthcare system in the long term."[19] John Milligan, the company's chief operating officer, would echo this refrain of value at a Brookings Institution policy forum: "We were providing more value, better outcomes, shorter duration, better patient experience at the same cost as the standard of care."[20] In their narrative, the "cure" secured substantial gains in health that translated into economic value—value for which health systems should pay.

This strategy aimed to shift responsibility to governments and public health systems—not for reducing drug prices but for appropriately valuing a curative treatment by paying the prices Gilead was charging. In 2015, Gilead put its rhetoric into practice by limiting enrollment in its "patient assistance program" for hepatitis C drugs, which had previously helped some patients gain access to the sofosbuvir-based treatments. By limiting enrollment, a *Wall Street Journal* article explained, "Gilead appears to be counting on patients to complain to payers about a lack of access."[21] One of Gilead's executives said, "We believe that payers should take the responsibility to provide coverage for their insured patients based on the treatment decisions of their healthcare providers."[22] In this framing, public health systems—which covered other expensive treatments that offered less benefit—needed to pay up for a curative medicine.

The access restrictions put US states under pressure from advocacy and civil society groups. As Robert Greenwald, a professor at Harvard Law School and faculty director of the school's Center for Health Law and Policy Innovation, put it, "If there were a cure for breast cancer or Alzheimer's or diabetes, people would be storming the White House to make sure those medicines were available to everyone, you can be sure of that."[23] He continued, "But we've responded completely differently with the cure for hepatitis C because of the stigma associated with that disease." In an effort to redress this situation, patient and civil rights groups launched a string of lawsuits against US states, with courts determining in most of these cases that state Medicaid and prison systems could not legally withhold access. States like Michigan, Missouri, Pennsylvania, and Florida all changed their access requirements or reached settlements due to these lawsuits.[24]

To buttress this moral-economic narrative, Gilead's "value pricing" strategy drew on a set of valuation practices from clinical medicine, health technology assessments, and epidemiology. These practices translated the value of health gains into quantifiable, future-oriented economic terms—terms that could then be used in influential policy and academic circles to bolster claims of value. This knowledge amounted to a kind of "valuation science," a set of methodologies that have been used, particularly in Europe, in the vexing public task of allocating budgets "cost-effectively." A prime example is the UK's National Institute for Clinical Excellence, which evaluates the costs and benefits of treatments and makes recommendations on whether the country's National Health Service should pay for a given treatment.

Though the US health system has eschewed the mandated use of such assessments—in large part due to historical industry opposition—such valuation practices have increasingly become part of the public debate over healthcare. In the realm of drug pricing, some progressive reformers have urged the use of valuation practices—similar to those used in Europe—to assess whether a treatment demonstrated its value at the price being charged by drug companies.[25] Reformers have plausibly presented "value assessments" as a rational approach to balancing incentives for innovation while also regulating prices in a way that directs industry capital and public budgets toward the treatments that yield the most health benefits. Such reforms may be making headway in the US, as signaled by legislation passed in the summer of 2022 which includes a limited use of value assessments as part of government negotiation of drug prices.

The emergence of the Boston-based Institute for Clinical and Economic Review (ICER) as an influential body in drug pricing debates reflects this growing focus on "value."[26] ICER assesses the cost-effectiveness of drugs and releases public reports that can be used by health systems to determine whether a given treatment is worth the price. The pharmaceutical industry has continued to be largely opposed to the mandated use of such assessments in the US, for fear they could curb prices in their largest revenue market. Yet on the other hand, the industry has trumpeted "value-based" approaches to buttress its much broader moral-economic discourse of value.

Gilead's strategy on hepatitis C drew on pharmacoeconomic assessments to legitimate its prices in influential policy and academic communities. In a 2014 call with Wall Street investors, Gilead's chief operating officer, John Milligan, pointed to "publications out there, not by Gilead, but by respected people in the field," who can "start these conversations" regarding value "in more of an academic, collegial way." In referring to these studies later in the investor call, the company's chief scientific officer said that Gilead was working on "putting all of this together into a bigger pharmacoeconomic argument".[27] This "pharmacoeconomic argument" rested on a combination of three sets of knowledge practices which positioned sofosbuvir-based treatments as valuable for health systems.

First, clinical medicine methodologies developed in the postwar era, such as long-term tracking studies and randomized clinical trials, enabled assessment of the potential population-level effects of treatments on downstream disease. As Joseph Dumit has traced in his book *Drugs for Life*, these knowledge practices abstracted health from a "felt illness" model of disease into "statistical health."[28] Pharmaceutical consumption, in this model, enables health by reducing the risk of future disease progression. In the field of hepatitis C, long-term studies by the CDC and NIH found that liver dysfunction and mortality were long-term consequences of the virus.[29] Randomized clinical trials of successive generations of hepatitis C treatments found potential benefits of treatment with respect to these consequences.[30] The potential to reduce future disease risk through early treatment, in turn, became a locus of potential financial value for pharmaceutical businesses.

This locus of value was made visible by a second set of epistemic practices: a burgeoning field within economics of "health technology assessment," which has sought to assess the future benefits versus the costs of a given treatment in comparison to an existing standard of care.[31] With the prices of new medicines typically many times the median wages of individuals, this cost–benefit assessment falls to health systems. As buyers of medicines, health systems weigh how to generate the most health improvement for their populations with the money they have, a process known as "comparative cost-effectiveness research."[32] In this research, new treatments are tested for whether they can create more health in the future than other interventions—the unit of health being *quality-adjusted life years* (QALYs). These benefits are then weighed against the costs of the new treatment, and this ratio is compared with the benefits and costs of comparative interventions. with health systems using a "value threshold"—the upper limit of what they are willing to pay for one more unit of health—to determine whether they will approve funding for a new treatment. This threshold varies between health systems. In the UK it ranges from $30,000 to $40,000 per QALY; US economists use $100,000 to $150,000 per QALY.[33]

In the hepatitis C case, a series of eight health economics papers published in the two years after sofosbuvir's launch (with authors including prominent hepatitis C experts like John Ward, then the CDC's chief of viral hepatitis) each affirmed the pricing of sofosbuvir-based treatments as "value-based" using cost-effectiveness methodologies.[34] One study summed up the commonly held finding: "Treating HCV infection at early stages of fibrosis appeared to improve outcomes and to be cost-effective."[35]

Manufacturers and health policy experts have also turned to a third practice: using epidemiological studies to quantify "prevention value," which models comparative treatment strategies for their *population-level* health and economic benefits. For an infectious disease like hepatitis C, such studies have computed the economic value of reduced disease transmission and improved health for cured patients. These studies have also calculated the savings from averted liver transplants and hospitalizations. One study published in *Health Affairs* and funded by Gilead Sciences, for example, estimated that giving sofosbuvir-based treatments at all stages of hepatitis C could generate $610 billion to $1.2 trillion in value in the US, with an additional $139 billion in savings over fifty years.[36] These valuation practices framed health as an asset—an economically valuable state achieved through therapeutic consumption of a curative medicine.

Drawing on the very knowledge practices and even the discourses used by healthcare reformers, this valuation regime supported Gilead's aim to create a new "commonsense view," not just within the industry but also among decision-makers and influencers in academia and public policy. In a 2014 *Harvard Business Review* article, "It's Easier to Measure the Cost of Health than Its Value," Amitabh Chandra, an economist and the director of health policy research at Harvard's Kennedy School of Government, wrote with his colleagues that while focusing on the price of sofosbuvir made for "good theater," it missed crucial points about the "value of the treatment," including the future savings from averted liver transplants.[37] Chandra and his coauthors all cited industry funding, including from Gilead Sciences. This view would be echoed by other peers within academia, such as Mark Roberts, chair of the University of Pittsburgh's Department of Health Policy and Management: "The most important thing to remember about cost-effectiveness is that something that is really expensive can still be cost-effective if it is really, really effective. . . . And these drugs are very, very effective."[38] Wall Street logics of value had become mainstream perspectives in health policy circles.

This position reinforced the idea of holding governments responsible for valuing curative medicines. And the logic extended not only to hepatitis C treatments in the present but also to potential future cures. In summing up an interview with a group of health economists at the American Economics Association's annual meeting in 2014, journalist Sarah Kliff found a common thread: "Sovaldi, many of them argued to me, is exactly the type of drug we should reward with high prices."

While acknowledging the tension around access to medicines, these economists shared a common view that "when push comes to shove . . . many prefer that we err on the side of higher prices as a way to encourage other big, blockbuster drugs in the future."[39] In their *Harvard Business Review* piece, Chandra and colleagues warned that driving down prices would represent an overreaction from the government and that "future generations [would] suffer from the depletion in innovation" that could result from such efforts.[40] By not paying high prices, in their view, health systems were endangering not only patients with hepatitis C but all patients who might benefit from curative medicines in the future.

The Veil of Pharma Value

This hegemonic view of value, however, is a kind of veil, hiding the many other possible conceptions of value. By themselves, value assessments can be a useful way for health systems to allocate funding to better treatments. Yet the "pharma version" of value advanced by Gilead and echoed by many health policy experts appropriated this rationality in a way that naturalized ever-higher prices demanded by a financialized system of drug development. Specifically, the pharma version of value hides three processes intertwined with financialized capital: rising drug prices over time, the power of monopoly protections, and the dynamics of value creation and value extraction.

As I described in chapter 1, each new generation of treatment sets a new pricing floor, leading to a "pricing escalator" for many diseases. In 1998 interferon regimens cost $19,000, but by 2002 they were $32,000 (for a modified version).[41] With the advent of telaprevir in 2011, the price of hepatitis C medicines leaped again, and by 2013 it exceeded $70,000 per patient.[42] Physician and policy analyst Peter Bach has pointed out the challenge this raises for analyzing prices using existing value frameworks: "Expensive drugs can still seem deceptively cost-effective, because of the long upward spiral we have seen."[43] Combined with the larger number of eligible patients that might stand to benefit from an improved treatment, such price trends create significant budgetary challenges for health systems. This fiscal challenge is why groups like ICER have called for "budget impact" to be one of the considerations in assessing the price and value of any new treatment.[44] But such calculations present their own moral dilemmas. When ICER assessed Gilead's initial prices in 2014 as too high, based on their potential budget impact given the large population of hepatitis C patients, it received pushback not only from industry but also from many in the health policy and hepatitis C treatment communities. These communities felt that such negative evaluations of a curative treatment's pricing would threaten widespread access and restigmatize an already marginalized patient population as not valuable enough to treat.[45] The turn to restrictions in treatment access in the early years of sofosbuvir-based treatments gave ample grounds to those fears.[46]

A second aspect hidden by the pharma view of value is that the rising trend in prices is less about future health benefit and more about monopoly power in financialized markets. With many goods, a higher price would result in a lower demand for the monopolists' product. Yet with medicines, what economists call the *price elasticity of demand* is much smaller, because people's health is at stake.[47] Higher prices are thus a manifestation of "what society can bear" in the face of monopoly power. Without the threat of viable competition, intellectual property protections enable companies like Gilead to charge prices at the upper bounds of what health systems can be compelled to pay.

These two points feeds into a third elision in the pharma view of value: the ways value is *created* and *extracted* in financialized drug development. While the industry describes "value" as its reward for taking risks, reward actually flows, via mechanisms of *value extraction*, to the financial actors that take the least risks: corporate shareholders. The scale of Gilead's share buybacks, for example, shows that financial markets in contemporary drug development are a vehicle for extracting capital from the large pharmaceutical companies charging high prices to health systems. Furthermore, financial markets offer a mechanism by which companies like Gilead can buy growth by acquiring promising assets like sofosbuvir. Such assets are the product of *value-creation* processes that are collective and cumulative in nature, building on public contributions to the drug development process.

The dominant industry narrative veiled these alternative considerations of value. Instead, Gilead sought a *hegemony* over value, in which prices ostensibly reflect the "value" that curative medicines have for health systems. In the process, Gilead attempted to naturalize the financialized political-economic order as a taken-for-granted system. But the account presented here illustrates that this dominant orientation to value enabled significant value extraction—which in turn would drive crises of treatment access and political resistance in a contentious terrain.

RATIONING VERSUS PUBLIC HEALTH: THE POLITICS OF VALUE AND THE CRISIS OF TREATMENT ACCESS

At a health center in south Los Angeles in the summer of 2015, I huddled with Paul, a clinical coordinator for HIV and hepatitis C patients. As he reviewed the roster of patients for the day, he spoke of an anger that had been smoldering for many months. Seventy of the clinic's patients with hepatitis C had yet to receive treatment. More than eighteen months had passed since the launch of sofosbuvir-based treatments. Yet California's public insurance program for low-income patients, MediCal, had set an array of hurdles between patients and treatment. Like many health systems across the US and the world, MediCal did this due to the price tag of sofosbuvir-based treatments. Posted on the wall next to Paul's workspace were large sheets displaying a labyrinthine set of instructions, forms, and lab tests that clinic staff needed to pursue to see whether a patient could get approval for the new medicines. To this point, only one patient had been approved.

Such delays and denials of care stood in stark contrast to the promise of the new hepatitis C treatments. With cure rates nearing 100% in many clinical trials, the new class of direct-acting antivirals conjured visions of curing not just individual patients but entire communities. "Viral elimination" became a tractable possibility. In 2016, all 194 member states of the World Health Organization (WHO) adopted the goal of eliminating hepatitis C as a public health threat by 2030 (defined as 90% reductions in new infections and 65% reductions in mortality from the 2015 baseline).[48]

Yet this would depend on widespread access to treatment, which in turn would be shaped by the political struggle over Gilead's intellectual property and pricing strategy across the world. The divergent trajectories of drug pricing and treatment access that unfolded in the years following the launch of sofosbuvir-based treatments illustrate how Gilead's position as a global gatekeeper over valuable pharmaceutical assets enabled it to maximize financial accumulation, as well as the opportunities for governments and civil society movements to challenge this dominant position. For low-income countries, Gilead selectively licensed its intellectual property to Indian generic manufacturers to produce medicines priced at about $1,000 per treatment. In high- and middle-income countries, Gilead charged "value prices," which produced a crisis in treatment access as health systems rationed treatment. In countries like Egypt and Australia, which had different approaches to intellectual property and drug pricing negotiations, sofosbuvir-based medicines were provided at a fraction of their US launch prices as part of public health strategies aimed at eliminating the virus.

The concept of *countervailing powers* sheds light on these disparate outcomes. Coined by John Kenneth Galbraith in 1952 as he observed an economy dominated by large financial interests and corporations, the term refers to competing sources of power that could be used to bring fairness and balance.[49] This power could reside in government policy, union organizing, social movements, or even a competing large corporation. In the realm of drug pricing, countervailing power can be exercised by governments and civil society actors to the extent that they counter the dominance of drug companies. My aim here is not to offer an exhaustive account of the treatment-access struggles that ensued. Rather, my empirical goal is to show how Gilead's global strategy and the responses of countervailing actors led to sharply contrasting outcomes: some health systems paid "value prices" and rationed care, while others paid a fraction of these prices and created public health programs. These divergent outcomes illuminate the contours of financialization's impact on global public health as well as the sites of struggle and resistance that open alternative possibilities for valuing medicines.

Resorting to Rationing: Public Health Systems in the United States

In March 2017, a commission of viral hepatitis experts convened by the US's prestigious National Academies of Sciences, Engineering, and Medicine concluded that eliminating the virus by 2030 was a possibility with the "prompt, large-scale treatment of hepatitis C." However, the commission would explain, "the price of these drugs is a major obstacle to unrestricted treatment, especially for institutions of limited means such as the prison system and state Medicaid programs."[50] This stark warning was founded on three years of observations of a patchwork approach in which rationing of treatment played a prominent role.

Officials estimated that at the launch of sofosbuvir-based treatments, the US had over 4 million patients with hepatitis C. Some were uninsured; some were covered by a fragmented network of private and public health systems. Public systems were responsible for about half of this population, as these systems finance and deliver care for multiple populations disproportionately affected by hepatitis C—patients over the age of 65 (Medicare), low-income or disabled patients (Medicaid), veterans (Veterans Affairs), Native Americans (Indian Health Service), and the incarcerated (such as state prison systems).[51] This patchwork of health systems is one of the reasons the countervailing power of the US health system is limited: the government cannot maximize its role as a buyer for the entire nation. Though current health policy mandates certain pricing discounts from list prices for specific health systems, such as Medicaid, Gilead could still use its position as a monopolist over sofosbuvir-based treatments to pursue a "value pricing" strategy and charge the most each health system could bear.

These health systems had to grapple with the significant expense of trying to treat even a small fraction of patients with hepatitis C, let alone all those who could benefit. One prominent study estimated that the drugs to treat all hepatitis C patients in the US would cost $136 billion over five years, of which $61 billion would need to be paid by the government.[52] For comparison, federal spending by the US Medicare program on *all* drugs amounted to $120.7 billion in 2014.[53] While this same study found that sofosbuvir-based medicines provided good "value," these projected figures also exposed how the financialized logics of price and value challenged health systems' budgets.

In the face of these remarkable financial considerations, US health systems faced one of three scenarios, each with its own political constraints: reduce drug prices, find more money, or ration the treatment. Reducing drug prices was a possibility open to US policymakers. The approach that would have led to the most significant price reductions required breaking the patent monopoly Gilead had been granted over sofosbuvir-based treatments. Section 1498 of the Code of Federal Regulations, for example, gives the government the power to procure generic versions of patented drugs in exchange for royalties to the patent-holding company. Drawing on prior precedent, a group of policy experts allied with Louisiana's secretary of health to advocate applying Section 1498 to sofosbuvir-based drugs.[54] The Obama administration, however, did not pursue this path. This reluctance to license intellectual property to generic manufacturers illustrates the limits of the countervailing power of the US state in the face of the political influence of the pharmaceutical industry.

Another strategy for drug price reductions would be direct negotiations between health systems and drug companies. Yet given Gilead's initial monopoly over hepatitis C treatments, buyers had little power or leverage. Gilead's prices later dropped below $50,000 for many US health systems with the entry of competing hepatitis C regimens from AbbVie and Merck. Facing legal action and with the opportunity to pay lower prices, some state Medicaid programs loosened their treatment restrictions. Yet the US national hepatitis C commission concluded that even a $40,000 price per patient would be a barrier to developing a public health program aimed at treating patients already with the disease and substantially reducing new cases.[55] At that price, the commission found, only 240,000 patients on Medicaid could be treated (over twelve years, at a cost of about $10 billion)—far short of the nearly 700,000 Medicare members with hepatitis C at the time. "It is unlikely," the commission found, "that market forces alone will lower the prices of these drugs sharply or quickly enough to meet the targets set."[56]

The US Medicare program, which finances drugs for patients over 65, faced a different challenge: the 2003 legislation that inaugurated Medicare's prescription drug plan explicitly barred the program from negotiating with drug companies.[57] The program spent nearly $14 billion on hepatitis C treatments between 2014 and 2015, with its total prescription drug spending rising 17% in 2014 from the prior year due in part to this spending.[58]

Medicare's funding increase for hepatitis C points to the second approach health systems could take: finding more money to pay for treatment. As a hybrid public–private program, Medicare's prescription drug spending in turn falls on a mix of private insurance plans and "patient-beneficiaries." With greater prescription drug spending, these beneficiaries have experienced rising copays and premiums. For health systems like the VA and Medicaid, finding more money is a thorny political task, reliant on congressional approvals and individual state decisions. For example, even with discounted prices, in 2015 the VA ran out of funding for hepatitis C drugs in the second half of the year after spending nearly 17% of its entire pharmaceutical budget on sofosbuvir-based treatments.[59] In early 2016, public pressure, stemming in part from two national news broadcasts devoted to the VA challenge, led Congress to allocate $3 billion for hepatitis C treatment.[60]

The Medicaid program, which is run by individual states, also faced challenges. Spending on drugs rose by 24% in 2014, in large part from Gilead's launch of sofosbuvir-based treatments. Yet with the program reliant on a mix of federal and state financing, public officials had to weigh the impact of hepatitis C treatments on their budgets. These impacts involved opportunity costs across multiple areas of health and social spending. The Drug Pricing Lab at Memorial Sloan Kettering worked with the state of Louisiana, for example, to develop a web-based tool to let users see for themselves how paying for hepatitis C treatments, even at a discounted price of $28,000, would force difficult budget decisions and additional legislative processes to allocate funding.[61] Ultimately, the US Medicaid program spent $4 billion in 2014 to 2015 to treat only 7% of all its hepatitis C patients.[62]

A major reason for this small number is that Medicaid programs responded to Gilead's prices with the third option: rationing.[63] At least thirty-three states, including states with large numbers of hepatitis C patients, such as California, Texas, and New York, restricted patients by the stage of their liver disease, giving access only to patients with advanced fibrosis.[64] Many states also required that patients be alcohol and drug free in the month (or even the six months) leading up to treatment. Most observers concluded that these guidelines, which had no clinical basis, were set up purely as obstacles by which to delay access and contain costs.[65] Researchers at the University of Pennsylvania found that about half of Medicaid patients in a national sample were denied access.[66] These denials disproportionately fell on those populations at the most risk for worsening hepatitis C as well as transmission of the infection: low-income patients and those with a history of injection drug use.

Beyond the Medicaid system, these restrictions impacted another vulnerable population: incarcerated patients. The US prison system, which accounts for an estimated 15–25% of the entire hepatitis C population in the US, provided treatment to less than 1% of its patients by 2016.[67] State prison systems are not mandated to receive a discount from Gilead, making their access challenges even steeper than other public systems.[68] Restricting access in this population has been a major squandered opportunity for tackling the epidemic, as prisons are often the only stable source of healthcare for these patients; after release, they are also at higher risk for transmitting the virus in the community.[69] In total, approximately 230,000 patients were given sofosbuvir-based treatments across US public health systems over the first two years of their launch—a sizable number, but still a small fraction of the estimated 1.6 to 2.4 million hepatitis C patients with publicly funded insurance.[70]

With rationing, the US health system had deferred what new hepatitis C medicines promised: a public health plan to eliminate the threat of the virus. Having examined the landscape for over two years, the national commission of hepatitis C experts painted a bleak picture. Though "eliminating the public health problem of hepatitis C is feasible," the group concluded, it would "require near universal access to treatment, something that appears unfeasible given the current pricing and policy environment."[71]

For Gilead, as for much of the pharmaceutical industry, the US represents a significant share of global revenue. But Gilead also recognized that pricing "for value," as the company had, would make rationing likely. A group of economists funded by Gilead, for example, cautioned in a study published in *Health Affairs* that rather than providing universal access, "new treatments must instead be meted out over time."[72] By their analysis, "limiting access to new therapies to a subset of diagnosed patients prolongs disease transmission and generates less value, but it is more realistic given system capacity constraints."[73] Rather than explore the option of lower drug prices, the authors promoted a strategy of treating 5% of patients with hepatitis C annually.

Investment analysts on Wall Street even openly wondered about the "positive" implications of such rationing for Gilead's long-term growth potential. Michael Yee, a leading investment analyst for the Canadian investment bank RBC Capital Markets, summed up this possibility in a note to his clients in May 2014:

> If payers prioritize or ration patients and limit use to only F3–4—would this be bad because F3–4 is only 30% of the market? Our conversations with investors over the last week is peak revenues might be less near-term but long-term tail is much longer ... so this is much more attractive. ... *So if anyone including Medicaid starts to limit to only sicker patients, this wouldn't dramatically worry us and could be better long-term.*[74]

Here Yee invokes a grim epidemiological calculus. Referring to the F0–F4 system for staging liver disease (with F3 and F4 representing more advanced disease), Yee suggests that the "long-term tail" of revenues in a rationing approach might be "better," because the virus could be transmitted to more patients and linger for longer in the population.

While this chilling calculation would not faze Wall Street, such rationing of treatment would exact a deep medical and psychic toll from patients and their providers. In the later stages of disease (such as F4), New Mexico physician Sanjeev Arora noted, the liver is as "hard as a rock."[75] He would go on, "treating someone for hepatitis C after they have developed cirrhosis is a little bit like closing the barn door after the horse has left." Without timely treatment, patients can develop a dreaded outcome: end-stage cirrhosis. Recalling experiences with her patients, nurse practitioner Laura Bush told an *Atlantic* writer, "At the end you die not knowing who you are, your belly looks 12 months pregnant, you're malnourished, and you're bleeding to death."[76] At the time of her interview in 2015, Bush had twenty patients waiting for sofosbuvir-based treatment at her community health center in New Mexico. While treatments were helping reduce mortality rates from the virus, delayed access combined with injecting drug use associated with the surging opioid epidemic led to a spike in new hepatitis C infections in the US between 2015 and 2018, from 33,900 to over 50,000.[77]

In sum, Gilead's Wall Street–backed pricing strategy, in the years following the launch of its treatments, conceived of the US not as part of a public health program to eliminate hepatitis C but as a financially valuable territory within which to execute its "value pricing" strategy. "Value," in this framing, was tethered to financial growth for Wall Street, which in turn was connected to epidemiological visions of ongoing disease and infectious risk. With its fragmented health system and limited use of countervailing public powers, the US provided Gilead a route to significant accumulation.

Segmenting the World and Strategies of Countervailing Power:
From Rationing toward Access

As of 2015, the WHO estimated that about 71 million people worldwide were infected with hepatitis C, and that it killed about 290,000 globally every year.[78] For pharmaceutical companies like Gilead, part of the financial allure of hepatitis C was the opportunity to sell medicines across the entire world, as the disease could be found in almost every country. Yet the new treatments for hepatitis C were arriving in the wake of the global HIV/AIDS struggle, in which patients in poor countries were denied access to medicines in the 1990s and well into the 2000s.[79] This triggered a decade-plus-long social movement of civil society and treatment activist groups that managed to bring significant political pressure on global pharmaceutical companies. And this pressure coincided with the mobilization of a generic drug manufacturing sector in places like India and Brazil that could produce medicines at far lower prices than global multinational corporations.

Amid the global HIV/AIDS struggle and in response to activist pressure, some multinational corporations developed access strategies for low-income countries. As a leading manufacturer of HIV/AIDS medications, for example, Gilead pursued a two-pronged "global access" program: first, the company worked with eleven distributors to sell their branded medicines on "tier pricing" terms (with prices according to the income level of a given country); second, they licensed their technology to generic manufacturers to produce the drug at a cheaper price for low-income countries hit particularly hard by the HIV/AIDS pandemic.[80] The two prongs led to treatment access for about six million patients with HIV, with medicines priced as low as $100 annually.

Playing out on this global terrain shaped by the struggle over HIV/AIDS medicines, Gilead's pricing strategy for hepatitis C would result in at least four different trajectories for sofosbuvir and treatment access outcomes. These divergent trajectories illustrate how Gilead's role as a gatekeeper over access to intellectual property in the global system allowed it to accumulate the scale of capital expected in financial markets—as well as the countervailing powers that governments and civil society groups can apply to drug pricing and access to medicines.

First, in "less financially valuable" territories—low-income countries like Rwanda, for example—the medicines were licensed to generic manufacturers who could sell them closer to the cost of manufacture. At a September 2014 press conference in Delhi's Taj Palace Hotel, Gilead announced that it would issue a license for its sofosbuvir-based treatments to seven Indian companies, enabling them to provide cheaper versions of the treatment in ninety-one low-income countries.[81] With this strategy, Gilead aimed to bring a treatment priced at about $1,000 per regimen, about 1% of the cost of the same regimen in the US at the time, to countries that would otherwise not be able to afford the medicine. Under the license, the Indian generic producers would pay a royalty to Gilead but still make a profit on a medicine that was estimated to cost only about $100 to make. These medicines, in turn, could be used as part of public health campaigns. Yet middle-income countries such as Ukraine, Thailand, Argentina, Georgia, and Brazil—home to some 40 million hepatitis C patients—were excluded from this initial licensing agreement.[82]

This exclusion would be part of carving out a second, more lucrative trajectory for Gilead: middle- and high-income countries where large patient numbers offered the chance for significant capital accumulation. Given their resource limitations, such a configuration would be particularly problematic for middle-income countries and the millions of hepatitis C patients there requiring treatment.

This selective licensing strategy highlights Gilead's position as a global gatekeeper over intellectual property and access to medicines. This position was a function of decades of lobbying by multinational companies and advocacy by US and European governments to "harmonize" intellectual property rules across the world. The effort to create a global intellectual property regime favoring multinational pharmaceutical companies accelerated with the 1995 creation of the World Trade Organization. The WTO emerged from multilateral so-called "free trade" negotiations aimed at regulating global trade. From these negotiations, intellectual property rules for national governments were enshrined in the TRIPS (Trade-Related Aspects of Intellectual Property Rights) Agreement.[83] In simple terms, this agreement gave the WTO the power to enforce uniform intellectual property regimes, similar to those in the US and Europe, all over the world. As some observers have noted, this process enabled intellectual property law to serve as a kind of neocolonizing force, guaranteeing the protection of foreign property in regions made to be dependent on this property.[84] Joining this global trade regime required many low- and middle-income countries to forgo their own previous national governance over intellectual property, which in cases like India had historically not granted product patents for pharmaceuticals.

For Gilead, a globalized intellectual property regime posed a financial opportunity in middle-income countries with large numbers of hepatitis C patients. Even though the prices charged in these countries would be significantly lower than in high-income countries, treatment access would be limited without significant new public funding. The group I-MAK (Initiative for Medicines, Access and Knowledge) estimated that if Gilead charged $7,500 per patient—as it proposed in Brazil—it would cost nearly $270 billion to treat patients in middle-income countries.[85] Without action to challenge intellectual property or devote significant new sums to hepatitis C treatment, rationing would be the norm in these countries.

In many high-income territories, like Canada, Australia, and across Europe, Gilead charged "value prices"—lower than those in the US, but still the most a given health system could be compelled to pay for the purported "value" of future health. In the United Kingdom, for example, where an estimated 214,000 people were living with hepatitis C, the National Health Service initially restricted access to select sites, before opening up access over time. Annual treatment rates doubled between 2014 and 2016, from 6,000 to 12,000 annually, but prices per regimen were in the range of $40,000.[86] It would take almost five years of lengthy negotiations and a court battle for the NHS to procure treatment from three companies, including Gilead, at the scale needed for hepatitis C elimination.[87]

This divergence between high- and middle-income countries on the one hand and low-income countries on the other, however, led to a third trajectory for treatment: the phenomenon of "buyers clubs," a movement of "personal importation" to access medicines across borders. Living in a polarized world of rationed patented medicines versus generic access, patients waiting for treatment pursued desperate measures, including importing sofosbuvir-based medicines themselves. Through buyers clubs found on the Internet, patients get advice on accessing specific treatments. Profiled in the *New York Times* in 2017, Gregg Jefferys was an early example of "personal importation" with hepatitis C. An Australian patient suffering from progressive disease and without access to the treatment in his country, in 2014 Jefferys traveled to India and brought back a full twelve-week regimen for $1,000.[88] After he began blogging about his experience online, he began receiving hundreds of requests. For those who could not travel to India, Jefferys would organize a shipment of generic medicines in exchange for $1,000, an identification form, and a prescription or medical report showing they had hepatitis C. Hundreds of such buyers clubs launched with the advent of the new class of hepatitis C treatment, a stopgap measure only accessible to those who could afford it. Such desperate measures are a direct result of configuring medicines as a scarce asset subject to the conditions of financialized capital and pharmaceutical-company gatekeepers.[89]

Finally, with the emergence and action of countervailing powers in various forms—activist pressure and patent opposition, government action, and the entry of competing corporations—a fourth trajectory developed: the use of sofosbuvir-based treatments in public health campaigns aimed at eliminating the virus. In the wake of sofosbuvir's launch in high-income countries in early 2014, activists from across the world seized on Gilead's pricing. For example, at the 20th International AIDS Conference, in Melbourne, Australia, a consortium of groups held a "die-in" to protest the company.[90] With lessons learned from the HIV movement, civil society groups pursued one of three options in their campaigns: pressure Gilead to offer voluntary licenses to its patents; challenge governments to give compulsory licenses to generic producers; or directly oppose the patents in the legal arena.[91]

When in the fall of 2014 Gilead provided a voluntary license for low-income countries—an approach that the precedent-setting activism for HIV antiretrovirals made possible—civil society groups focused their attention on the many middle-income countries left out of the licensing agreement, as well as high-income health systems struggling to provide access. While activism centered on pressuring high- and middle-income governments to issue compulsory licenses, only some middle-income countries (like Malaysia) followed suit. Patent opposition became a central strategy.

In this effort, groups like I-MAK took a leading role in contesting the patentability of compounds like sofosbuvir-based medicines under a given country's laws on intellectual property. I-MAK's legal claims in the case of hepatitis C rested on calling into question the "inventiveness" of sofosbuvir's underlying patents, given that much of the science behind the compound was drawn from collectively and already known science at the time of its development and thus, by their view, did not merit the patent protections the medicines ultimately garnered. In 2015 the group joined with local civil society and patient advocacy organizations to dispute Gilead's patents in multiple middle-income countries, and would later succeed in getting authorities in Ukraine, Argentina, and China to reject key patents on sofosbuvir-based medicines.[92] Though the creation of public health programs would require further political leadership and investment, the successful patent challenges opened the door for generic medicines as well as price concessions from Gilead in these countries. Efforts to replicate this success in high-income countries have yet to bear full fruit, but a partial revocation of Gilead's patents in 2016 by the European Patent Office, won by Medicines du Monde and Medicines Sans Frontiers, along with I-MAK's victories in some middle-income countries, signals a vulnerability in prevailing patenting systems that can be used to "de-assetize" and thereby definancialize medicines.[93]

In territories where sofosbuvir-based medicines were taken less as financial assets and more as essential medicines in need of distribution, hepatitis C treatment was scaled up as part of national public health programs. Egypt is perhaps the most notable example. In the 1960s and 1970s, unsterile needles were used in a public health campaign against schistosomiasis, infecting six million Egyptians with hepatitis C. By 2014, 10% of the country's population, or nine million people, were chronically infected.[94] As Egyptian authorities began price negotiations with Gilead, the country scrutinized the drug company's application for a patent—and subsequently declined to issue one. Ultimately, Gilead agreed to sell its sofosbuvir-based regimens in Egypt for $10 a pill, or about $900 per three-month regime.[95] This allowed Gilead to still garner sizable profits, given the modest manufacturing cost and large patient numbers, while also supporting a flagship public health effort. With affordable medications, the government launched an aggressive national campaign to screen, diagnose, and treat the millions of patients with the disease. At its current pace, the country is on a path to cut the disease's prevalence in half by 2023 and could even eliminate it in the near term with additional investments.[96]

In high-income countries where intellectual property protections remained in place, restrictions gave way to access when governments deployed their countervailing powers as the primary buyer of medicines. This power was eventually aided by the entry of pharmaceutical company AbbVie, which offered a formidable alternative to sofosbuvir-based medicine, at a 2017 list price of $26,400 in the US. Gilead later launched a "generic" version of sofosbuvir-based treatment at $24,000 in the US. With two competing treatments, governments had a stronger position from which to negotiate lower prices. This instance of price competition may be more the exception than a rule in drug markets, as illustrated by Gilead's HIV treatments.[97] Out of these negotiations emerged the concept of the "Netflix model" of treatment, which frames medicines as assets to which buyers—in this case health systems—pay a "subscription fee" for unrestricted access for a defined period, much like a Netflix subscription lets one watch any show Netflix carries.

Australia is a prime example, having used its power as a national buyer to bargain with Gilead for a better deal. At Gilead's initial prices, the county could not afford to scale up treatment. In 2015, however, Australian authorities negotiated an agreement with hepatitis C drug manufacturers, including Gilead, in which the country would pay AUD 1 billion (USD 766 billion) for unlimited access to hepatitis C treatments.[98] For Gilead, this deal provided a guaranteed lump-sum payment for a territorial jurisdiction that had otherwise capped the number of patients who could receive treatment—which in turn also capped the company's revenue. For Australia, the agreement incentivized the health system to diagnose and treat at-risk patients as early and as much as possible to reduce transmission in the population. A research institute in Australia estimates that the country is now on pace to eliminate the virus by 2026, four years ahead of the WHO's targets. One study estimated that the country had also saved nearly USD 5 billion, compared to treating the same number of patients at Gilead's previous per-treatment price.[99] In the US, some states have pursued an approach similar to Australia's, negotiating with Gilead and its competitor AbbVie for universal access to treatments in exchange for fixed payment over a number of years.[100] Louisiana and Washington, for example, struck such deals with hepatitis C manufacturers in 2019.

By mid-2017, Gilead estimated that sofosbuvir-based regimens had treated 1.5 million around the world.[101] The WHO estimated that by the end of 2018, five million people globally had been given curative hepatitis C treatments, with a significant share coming from sofosbuvir-based treatments (Gilead's branded or generically licensed treatments).[102] While this is significant progress, the WHO estimates that about 71 million are still chronically infected. Drug prices are just one of the barriers to wider treatment: health system investments in diagnosis and delivery programs, as well as political commitment to caring for vulnerable populations (such as people who inject drugs), will be critical to reaching WHO's 2030 targets. Yet the unmistakable link between lower drug prices and greater access also indicates the global implications of a financialized drug development system, in which Gilead's position as a gatekeeper over intellectual property allowed it to carve sharply divergent trajectories for treatment access in different places to maximize accumulation for shareholders.

Gilead has publicly supported viral elimination efforts, but Wall Street's expectations for growth are in conflict with this promise. Asked by investment analysts about the company's revenue projections for Egypt, a Gilead executive cautioned against large financial hopes: "Given that this is a *public health initiative*, obviously, the revenue number is small per patient" (italics added).[103] This response begged the question, if "public health" was happening in Egypt, what was happening everywhere treatments were being rationed due to their price? This distinction made it clear that maximizing shareholder value—not the "value" of future health—made rationing an acceptable strategy, and the one Wall Street preferred.

THE PATIENT CLIFF:

THE LIMITS OF A CURE AS AN ASSET

Gilead had success, by every financial metric, after its launch of sofosbuvir-based medicines. Its revenues tripled in two years, from $11 billion in sales in 2013 to over $30 billion in 2015, mostly on the strength of its hepatitis C medicines. In 2015, these medicines alone brought $19 billion in total sales.[104] Investment analysts couched this success in historic terms. In 2014's first-quarter call, one of biotech's leading investors, Mark Schoenebaum, congratulated Gilead's senior leadership on the "best launch of any drug of all time, that I'm aware of at least." A fellow analyst, Brian Skorney, added: "Let me congratulate you and maybe even one-up Schoenebaum by saying I think this was actually the biggest single quarter for a pharmaceutical product in U.S. history."[105]

The Wall Street celebration came with major gains for Gilead's shareholders, who could anticipate near-term revenue growth in each new quarter. When Gilead bought Pharmasset in late November 2011, its share price stood at $19. By June 2015, it had leapt to $122 (Figure 8). As I noted in chapter 2, Gilead's senior executives, as significant shareholders themselves, were major winners from this share price boom. This honeymoon, however, would be short-lived.

Even with revenues exceeding $20 billion, the company's share price fell by almost 50% from its peak in mid-2015 to April 2017 (Figure 8).[106] The problem: from a purely financial point of view, curative sofosbuvir-based treatments cut into the very market on which their value as an asset depended. For Gilead, this

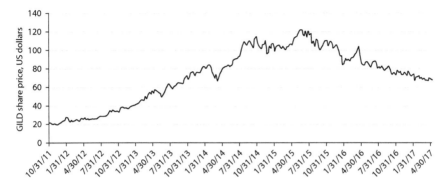

FIGURE 8. Gilead's share price, November 2011 to April 2017. The price climbed from $11 in November 2011 (before the Pharmasset acquisition) to $122 in June 2015 on the strength of hepatitis C–driven growth. But with the treatment being curative and growth slowing, by May 2017 the share price had sunk back into the mid-60s. Source: Google Finance, GILD.

meant forecasts of slowing growth and ultimately declining revenues. To respond to this decline, Gilead turned to a series of machinations that would reinforce and intensify the processes of value extraction made possible by the intellectual property protections and financial markets highlighted in chapter 2. The process would lay bare the threat that financialization poses to drug affordability but also to future medical breakthroughs.

The Patient Cliff for Hepatitis C

Sofosbuvir-based treatments revealed a clash between public health and the conditions of shareholder-oriented growth: while universal treatment and cure would end an epidemic—the best possible public health outcome—it would also shrink the number of patients needing treatment. Rather than a patent cliff, sofosbuvir would lead to a *patient cliff*: gradually eliminating the disease would in time also eliminate the market for Gilead's product. I use the stylized image of the patient cliff to illustrate a key point: even though tens of millions of patients continue to have hepatitis C, what matters under the conditions of financialized capital are the possibilities of growth. As Joseph Dumit has described in his book *Drugs for Life*, such growth is strongest with chronic and recurring treatment over a life course.[107] In the absence of such growth potential, what financial markets see is a danger similar to the loss of intellectual property protections—an eroding of the future financial value that serves as the basis for value extraction.

Analysts on Wall Street had run epidemiological models of hepatitis C under different pricing, treatment, and competition scenarios. Bloomberg financial analysts considered, for example, three hepatitis C "market scenarios" for Gilead.[108] All three had one trend in common: a downward revenue trajectory. Gilead's predicament came in part from the population-level dynamics of hepatitis C that had been triggered by the launch of sofosbuvir-based medicines. Before 2013, a sizeable proportion of patients had delayed treatment for many years due to the toxicity and lower response rates of interferon-based therapies. With Gilead's treatment approved in late 2013, these patients-in-waiting turned up in higher numbers than the company originally estimated.[109] The large numbers of patients eligible for treatment, even under restricted access guidelines, combined with the company's launch pricing to fuel a surge of revenue growth in 2014 and 2015. Yet this high growth rate appeared to be impossible to sustain with a curative therapy.

With Gilead's hepatitis C sales starting to plateau, Wall Street analysts focused on the limits to the potential growth of these curative medicines.[110] When Gilead "disappointed" with second-quarter sales of $7.7 billion in 2016, a 19% decline compared to the same quarter in 2015, the company's share price fell by nearly 10%.[111] Deutsche Bank analyst Gregg Gilbert noted, "While management pointed to increasing screening volumes and confirmed its prior estimate of about 1.5 million people in the US who are yet to be diagnosed, it also anticipates a gradual decline in new patient-starts going forward, especially in mature markets such as the US, Germany, and France."[112] These gloomy predictions led to a progressive drop in Gilead's share price: from its peak of $122 per share in June 2015, it fell below $70 per share by late January 2017 (Figure 8). One trader, Bret Jansen, summed up Wall Street's view of Gilead in late 2016:

> Being a shareholder in biotech juggernaut Gilead Sciences over the past two years has been akin to being stuck in the classic *Waiting for Godot* as one feels like he is waiting for something that will never happen. Despite seeing a ~600% increase in earnings from FY2013 through FY2015 driven by the blockbuster success of hepatitis C cures Sovaldi and Harvoni, the stock has gone nowhere as investors have worried that hepatitis C sales will continue to decline in the United States as the sickest patients have been treated and new competition will continue to emerge in this lucrative space.[113]

Gilead's rate of profitability, 55% in 2015 and 45% in 2016, became almost insignificant under this calculus of shareholder-oriented growth.[114] Yet as I described in chapter 2, the velocity and magnitude of growth demanded by financial markets run counter to the long-run risk-taking needed for new breakthroughs. To meet growth expectations, then, Gilead turned to a set of business strategies that further illustrate the mechanisms and consequences of financialized drug development.

Playing the Game for Growth: Patent Controls, Price Increases, and Acquisition and Buyback Cycles

In a January 2016 *Financial Times* piece, "Gilead Risks Becoming Victim of Its Own Success," the company's executive vice president at the time, Paul Carter, admitted, "There's this sort of pressure now we are a $30 billion a year revenue company. People are asking where the next 8 or 10 percent of year-on-year growth is going to come from."[115] In other words, the faster the company had grown in the recent

TABLE 6 Strategies to maximize growth and extract value for shareholders

Strategy	Execution	Examples from Gilead
Extend length of control over chronic-treatment assets	Focus on late-stage clinical trials that will extend patent protection for medicines for long-term patient use	Late-stage clinical trials for HIV that will create new patent protections for Gilead into the late 2030s
Boost revenue from existing chronic-treatment assets	Raise prices of current chronic-treatment medicines; Identify new indications that require long-term therapeutic consumption	Price increases on HIV drugs; Launch of PrEP treatment based on government-funded research
Buy assets and stocks in financial markets	Stockpile cash to acquire drug assets via the financial market; Use capital to buy back shares	$40 billion spent on multiple acquisitions between 2017 and 2020; $23 billion in share buybacks between 2014 and 2016

past, the faster it would have to grow in the near future. As Gilead searched for this growth, it turned to a familiar set of strategies: extending its control over the patent life of its treatments for chronic HIV/AIDS; raising the prices and broadening the indications for existing treatments; and executing a financial cycle of acquisitions and share buybacks. Studying these strategies (summarized in Table 6) reveals the ways in which financialization reproduces itself, and even intensifies—producing even larger financial gambles, flows of capital to shareholders, and ongoing machinations for drug price increases and patent extensions.

Controlling Patents for "Chronic Market" Treatments

As Gilead sought to sustain growth for its immediate future, the company would initially turn to its most familiar business, treatments for HIV/AIDS. An exchange at Morgan Stanley's annual healthcare conference, in September 2016, between an analyst and Gilead's CEO, John Milligan, illustrates Gilead's approach to growth.

Matthew Harrison (Morgan Stanley): It feels like the default investor viewpoint is that Gilead has to be a growth company. So do you think that's reasonable, do you think that's accurate?

John Milligan (CEO, Gilead, italics added): We had an unprecedented rate of growth through 2015, essentially tripling revenue in three years. *That's a very challenging thing to grow off of.* . . . *So that* [hepatitis C] *doesn't lead to the continuous growth that you would want.* Still great economically, still great in cash flow and will be a very important product category for us for the next decade or beyond. But I separated [hepatitis C and HIV] at the beginning for a reason. *If you look at where we can focus and what we can do, it's really off that base HIV business.* I think what we'd like to see is that business continue to grow and really ultimately eclipse the HCV business through new products and growth out of our pipeline, which we certainly have the potential to do in the coming decade.[116]

In this response, Milligan outlined Gilead's predicament of near-term shareholder-driven growth, and how the company sought to respond. As he reminds us, the predicament is two-fold. First, *growing off growth* is itself a challenge; the launch of hepatitis C treatments had set a high bar of growth that would be nearly impossible to sustain. Second, a curative therapy "doesn't lead to the continuous growth that you would want." Both the magnitude and the rate of growth expected by shareholders posed a threat to Gilead. To address this threat, Milligan shifted the attention of the audience to where Gilead had placed its near-term hopes: "If you look at where we can focus and what we can do, it's really off that base HIV business." Gilead's HIV medicines are not curative; patients with HIV must take them as a lifelong treatment. This lifetime demand makes these treatments particularly valuable intellectual property for Gilead.

To seize this financial possibility of growth through HIV treatments, Gilead maneuvered to extend the patent life of its HIV franchise by making incremental improvements to one of the key compounds in its existing treatments. Gilead's intellectual property protection for one of its two backbone HIV compounds, tenofovir disoproxil fumarate (TDF), was set to expire in 2017.[117] This would expose its two main HIV/AIDS regimens, Complera and Stribild, to generic competition—threatening approximately $11 billion in revenue—because both contained TDF.[118] But the company had a play to avoid this fate: it pursued approval of a "new" HIV compound with incremental but clinically significant improvements, tenofovir alafenamide fumarate (TAF).[119] The original TDF therapies had adverse side effects such as kidney dysfunction and bone loss in some patient populations, but the new TAF therapies showed milder effects by means of a smaller dosage based on a minor change in chemistry.[120] Though some scientists have challenged the extent of these clinical improvements, the TAF therapies received approval from the FDA in 2015.[121] Critically for Gilead's future growth, the intellectual property rights for their new HIV regimens (Odefsey and Genvoya, both containing TAF) will last into the late 2020s and early 2030s. And with list prices over $30,000 annually, Gilead will make hundreds of thousands of dollars *per patient* during the fifteen or so years that the company has patents over these medicines.

The story behind TAF has drawn public scrutiny and is at the center of multiple lawsuits, in which patient groups have alleged that Gilead deliberately delayed further clinical trials of the new compound for several years to extend its intellectual property protection for as long as possible.[122] Legal filings show that as early as 2001 Gilead scientists had published findings describing a less toxic formulation of tenofovir than TDF, and in 2002 they even performed a small trial, with thirty patients, demonstrating this result.[123] But Gilead's leadership halted further study of the compound until 2010, and the results of the small trial were not published until 2014. As clinical trials of TAF were initiated after 2010 and accelerated in 2014–2016, a Gilead executive reported to analysts that the new alternative could add "a great deal of longevity" to its HIV business.[124]

In 2018, the company accrued $14.6 billion from its HIV franchise (up from $12.9 billion annually just two years before), which helped offset flagging earnings from its hepatitis C franchise. The centrality of HIV as a recurring revenue source for Gilead's business strategy is one of the reasons one business analyst lamented that "the cold, hard truth is that developing a cure for HIV could be detrimental to Gilead over the long run."[125] Unlike hepatitis C cures, which formed a new source of revenue, a curative treatment for HIV would eat into, or even eliminate, its main source of growth.

Price Increases and Wider Indications for "Chronic Market" Treatments

To maximize this source of growth from HIV treatments, Gilead engaged in two other moves: regular price increases; and marshalling government-funded research to identify a new patient population for its HIV medicines.

Price increases for HIV treatments were critical to sustaining the antiretroviral business as a continued growth vehicle for the company. As has become common practice across the industry, Gilead raised the prices of a range of its products at the beginning of each year. Between 2006 and 2011, the company raised the list prices of its HIV medicines from $13,800 per year to $25,874 per year.[126] Gilead has continued to raise the prices of Complera and Stribld—for example, by 7% each in July 2016, after 5% and 7% increases on those two drugs in January 2016.[127] In 2017 and 2018, they were increased by 6.9%, to over $30,000 annually. These price increases are now so regular that even an increase that is smaller than expected generates headlines like "Gilead HIV Drugs' Price Increase 30% Lower than Prior Years, Says Piper Jaffray."[128]

Beyond price increases, Gilead also used government-funded research to seek a new "indication" for existing HIV assets with the launch of their pre-exposure prophylaxis (PrEP) treatment. Taking a daily medicine called Truvada—which contains Gilead's older TDF compound—has been shown to *prevent* HIV infection in those at high risk, such as men having sex with men, heterosexual men and women with multiple sexual partners, and injection drug users. The genesis of this regimen lay in research first conducted by the CDC in the mid-to-late 2000s, in which Truvada's main components were seen to prevent transmission of the virus in monkeys. Approximately $50 million in federal funding from NIH, and an additional $17 million from the Bill and Melinda Gates Foundation, supported human clinical trials that showed that a daily dose of Truvada prevented healthy people from contracting the virus.[129] According to the CDC, 1.1 million Americans could stand to benefit—creating a whole new "market" of potential patients for the company.[130] In 2012, Gilead received regulatory approval from the FDA to extend

Truvada's initial indications from suppressing the virus in people with HIV to also reducing the risk of acquiring HIV sexually.

Gilead's PrEP treatment has grown steadily since its launch in 2012, with over 200,000 patients in the US now using the regimen (up from 22,000 in 2014). But one reason why even more people have not started on PrEP is the price: nearly $2,000 a month in the US by 2018. Though the CDC has patents on Truvada's use as PrEP due to its pivotal early work, the US government has yet to exercise its ownership rights, such as by demanding royalties or lower prices.[131]

The long history of price increases for HIV drugs is one of the central factors blamed for the relatively slow uptake of PrEP.[132] A report by HIV activists known as the PrEP4All Collaboration estimated that it would take more than twenty-two years for the pill to reach all who might benefit from prophylactic treatment if prescriptions continued at their current rate.[133] In countries in which Gilead's patents for Truvada have expired, a one-month supply of the generic treatment costs less than $10 a month. Rapid adoption of this generic treatment in Australia, for example, has raised hopes the country might be able to make new infections a rare occurrence—and potentially eliminate HIV.[134] Yet even price increases and broader indications for existing HIV medications would not provide the rate of growth necessary to satiate the expectations of financial markets. Despite its new approach to its existing medications, Gilead's quarterly growth projections continued to shrink as 2016 rolled into 2017.

Acquisition and Buybacks

To meet shareholder expectations, Gilead turned to a third strategy, reprising a familiar financial cycle described in chapter 2: acquisitions and buybacks.[135] As the company pursued new revenue, Gilead's internal pipeline lacked value in the eyes of Wall Street, with Brian Skorney of the investment bank RW Baird seeing "few opportunities for such growth in the company's existing pipeline as is" in a note after Gilead's earnings call in early February 2016.[136] Piper Jaffray's Joshua Schimmer went further: "We have little enthusiasm for most of what we consider to be a highly speculative pipeline and nowhere close to the level we would expect from such an important and sizeable company. . . . There is not a single program which we even find worth highlighting."[137] Growth, in other words, appeared less likely to come from Gilead's own R&D.

Acquisitions remained Gilead's, as well as Wall Street's, favored vehicle for new revenue growth. In December 2015, when the *Financial Times* caught up with Norbert Bischofberger, the company's *head of R&D*, for an interview, he did not focus on the company's internal R&D prospects but on the company's acquisition strategy.[138] Under the headline "Cash Rich Gilead Hits the Acquisition Trail," Bischofberger positioned its approach to Pharmasset as a model moving forward: "Philosophically, we prefer to wait for more certainty and pay more money, which is what we did with Pharmasset, rather than getting something cheap with uncertainty."[139] He was echoing the mantra described in chapter 2: instead of research and development, Bischofberger saw Gilead's role as *search* and development. When asked what the company was going to "do with all its money," Bischofberger continued, "Well, we have our eye on the external world—we have incredible cash flows and we are looking for opportunities."[140] Indeed, Gilead had accumulated over $20 billion in cash by early 2016, much of it from hepatitis C sales.[141]

This stockpiled cash positioned Gilead for a major acquisition. Leading biotechnology analyst Mark Schoenbaum probed Gilead's senior leadership in an earnings call: "The biggest question on everyone's mind for Gilead is, 'Who are you going to buy? Who are you going to buy? Who are you going to buy? Who are you going to buy?' Every day this is what we talk about in investment circles."[142] Though the company's senior leadership continued through 2016 and into 2017 to scan the market of pharmaceutical assets for their next Pharmasset, they would not have an immediate answer for Wall Street.

While speculation about acquisition possibilities continued, Gilead's senior leadership pointed investors to the other component of their financial strategy: directing capital to shareholders. The company's chief research executive, Bischofberger, shared the company's strategy on an earnings call in 2016:

> If you look back at the last six years, it has been remarkable. *We have done many, many deals*—CGI, Arresto, Calistoga, Pharmasset, Galapagos—and yet, *we were able to return 70% out of free cash flow to shareholders.* So I think that is a good way to think about the future, to in-license through collaborative efforts while at the same time *returning money to shareholders.*[143]

Indeed, as I documented in chapter 2, Gilead announced a series of major share buybacks with their new hepatitis C revenue. These aimed to boost the company's critical earnings-per-share ratio, making the stock more attractive for speculative trading by shareholders. In just the first six months of 2016, for example, Gilead bought back $9 billion in its own shares, about three times their entire R&D budget for the year.[144] Gilead used $23 billion in capital—a mix of its cash and debt—to purchase its own shares between 2014 and 2016.

Yet the share price still fell. The failure to generate ongoing growth with a curative therapy cost the company $41 billion in market capitalization between mid-2015 and the end of 2016. Buybacks, with their transient, short-term effects, could do little to influence this downward trajectory.[145]

From that perspective, the share buyback program *destroyed value*—both by limiting reinvestments into R&D and by failing even to boost the company's share price for its shareholders. In a *Bloomberg Business* piece, "Gilead Mismanaged Its Gold Mine," reporter Max Nisen described the buyback strategy as a "more efficient way to destroy value than an acquisition, with none of the upside."[146] The lack of positive share price performance after share buybacks among pharmaceutical companies (including Gilead) has even caught the eye of some prominent financial analysts. Studying six large biotechnology companies, including Gilead, between 2014 and 2017, Geoffrey Porges, a longtime Wall Street biotechnology analyst, found that buybacks "destroyed more than $12 billion in value." Of the six companies he analyzed, only two generated any gain in their stock price; the group averaged a loss of 6%. "We believe investors should view buybacks with caution," Porges concluded, "and possibly regard them as value destroying."[147]

The long-awaited acquisition would finally come late in the summer of 2017, when Gilead bought a small biotechnology company, Kite Pharmaceuticals, for $11.9 billion.[148] While Kite had no approved products, the company had developed a novel cancer-fighting method which uses the body's own immune system to attack malignant cells. The company's most promising treatment, for non-Hodgkin's lymphoma, was already under FDA consideration, and was expected to receive approval later in the year. Using a sizable chunk of its hepatitis C capital in the acquisition, Gilead hoped that Kite's pipeline of cancer treatments would provide a new growth source.

Yet the basis for this promising class of treatments recalled Gilead's earlier HIV and hepatitis C franchises: public investments. In a 2017 *New York Times* story, "Harnessing the U.S. Taxpayer to Fight Cancer and Make Profits," Kite's founder and CEO Arie Belldegrun said that the company had tapped into "six years of monumental work" by NIH. He continued, "We shouldn't underestimate the value and the importance of N.I.H., not only to Kite, but to the whole field of engineered T-cell therapy."[149] Entering into the fray with their 2017 acquisition, Gilead now looked to Kite to develop oncology treatments and generate its newest source of growth. With its first cancer treatment, Kymriah, coming to market, Gilead set the price at $373,000. Gilead would make three more large deals by the end of 2020, betting an additional *$31 billion* to gain control over already approved or promising treatments. While it waited for gains from these acquisitions to materialize, in 2020 Gilead reported a 10% growth in revenues over the year before, largely thanks to nearly $3 billion in sales of remdesivir, the antiviral treatment for COVID-19 I mentioned in the preface.[150]

PHARMA(VALUE)

"Success in biotech comes with a curse," a writer in the *Wall Street Journal* observed in 2011: "the further a company goes, the harder it becomes to keep its growth story alive."[151] He was describing Gilead's position as it pursued Pharmasset, but he could have well been describing its position in 2017, after its hepatitis C growth story had faded. This almost continual search for growth marked the circulation of financialized capital that underpinned sofosbuvir's path. In tracing sofosbuvir's trajectory through the political struggle over treatment access, this chapter reveals the influence of financialized drug development on drug pricing and value in three key ways.

First, Gilead's justification for its pricing attempted to capitalize health itself—monetizing the value of future health into a present earnings stream that could generate the growth expected by financial markets. This strategy reproduced the logics of speculative financial markets, in which the locus of value was configured around the notion that health systems would pay more for better treatments. Yet through an array of political lobbying, moral-economic discourses, and techno-cratic valuation practices, Gilead also sought to establish a *hegemony of value*— with higher prices representing the value of health as a commonsensical idea, one that society should adopt to realize future health.

Second, Gilead's pricing strategy illuminated its ability to use its position as a global gatekeeper over intellectual property to maximize financial accumula-tion and shape divergent trajectories of treatment access. Operating in a politi-cally contested space, Gilead charged "value prices" in high- and middle-income countries, where treatment would be rationed. The company also selectively licensed its intellectual property to many low-income countries for use as part of public health programs. Countries excluded from this licensing agreement would either face a crisis of treatment access or exercise countervailing powers—at times buttressed by treatment activism, patent opposition, and the entry of corporate competitors—to lower drug prices and use sofosbuvir-based treatments as part of public health strategies aimed at eliminating the virus.

Third, capitalizing a curative medicine revealed a crisis at the heart of finan-cialized drug development: the cure depleted the potential for ongoing growth. With Wall Street souring on Gilead's growth prospects, the company turned to an array of financial maneuvers—from patent extensions and drug price increases to acquisitions and buybacks—to generate fast accumulation and extract value for shareholders. These turns in the story of sofosbuvir both describe the mechanisms by which financialization shapes drug pricing and chronicle its outcomes. What emerges is a portrait of a political-economic system in which the financial logics of value can powerfully structure public health policy but also are vulnerable both to Wall Street demands and to social contestation.

The political struggle over treatment access shows that value is always plural— and human *values* are also at stake. Amid sofosbuvir's restrictions in his state, a Kentucky-based infectious diseases physician Dr. Fares Khater lamented, "It's very hard to see the patient, and just tell them, 'I can't treat you.'"[152] In this kind of encounter, it is not just abstracted future economic value but rather the values of the therapeutic relationship, the lived experience of neglect or care, that also hang in the balance. Because these values remain precarious, it becomes an urgent political task to empirically lay out the mechanisms of financialization that refigure, appropriate, or push aside these values—and how we might chart a different course.

4

From Financialization to Public Purpose for Health

Every system is perfectly designed to get the results it gets.
—ATTRIBUTED TO MULTIPLE PEOPLE, INCLUDING DONALD BERWICK
(1996), FORMER HEAD OF THE US CENTERS FOR MEDICARE AND
MEDICAID SERVICES[1]

The social history of our time is the result of a double movement: The one is the principle of economic liberalism, aiming at the establishment of a self-regulating market; the other is the principle of social protection aiming at the conservation of man and nature as well as productive organization.
—KARL POLANYI, *THE GREAT TRANSFORMATION*[2]

In March 2016, pharmaceutical-industry executives and lobbyists huddled in a Boston hotel conference room as they grappled with the rising public attention on drug prices. They were there to hear from a powerful group of people, the largest institutional shareholders of their companies—mutual funds, including Fidelity, T. Rowe Price, and Wellington Management. Leaders from these funds had come with a warning and a directive: the pharmaceutical industry needed to better defend the prices of its drugs. How should pharmaceutical companies mount this defense? By educating the public about the value of their medicines. Otherwise, these Wall Street leaders cautioned, the government would impose price caps. In covering the meeting, a Bloomberg journalist observed, "The drug industry, just as eager to bolster slumping biotech shares, appears receptive to the message."[3]

Gilead Sciences had already taken up this charge over the previous two years, arguing that the value of its sofosbuvir-based hepatitis C medicines—quantified as the economic value of future health and averted health care costs—justified their launch prices in the United States and other high- and even middle-income countries. These prices had triggered a significant crisis in treatment access in the US and across the world. Health systems had rationed care to only those with advanced disease, leaving millions of patients without treatment for a deadly and infectious disease. And yet even amid this crisis and the highly contentious debate over the price of new medicines, the launch of curative medicines for hepatitis C had shifted the terms and focus of the struggle.

Though the focus on drug prices had yet to recede, many in the drug industry and public policy circles had heeded Gregg Alton's exhortation that "price is the wrong discussion. . . . Value should be the subject." Across the pharmaceutical sector, companies were adopting the frame of "value"—with many policymakers, public officials, and other health sector stakeholders also taking up this rationale for the prices of new medicines. Value became a common refrain with the launch of new medicines, from Novartis's $2.1 million treatment for a rare disease in infants, to Gilead's remdesivir treatment for COVID-19.[4]

This book has pursued an alternative course in considering the subjects of both price and value. Unprecedented drug prices are creating crises in treatment access for patients, and certain representations of value appear to be legitimating these ever-higher prices. Guided by sociological and political-economic scholarship on capitalism and biomedicine, I have investigated the practices and strategies of pricing and valuation intertwined with the making of sofosbuvir-based medicines. Rather than weigh existing justifications, this book offers a new etiology for high drug prices: *the financialization of biomedicine*. Over the last three chapters, I have traced the mechanisms of this political-economic system through the twists and turns of the development of sofosbuvir-based medicines—from the conversion of public science into financially valuable assets, to the extraction of capital through speculative bets, and onward to the influence of financial logics over health policy and trajectories of treatment access.

In this chapter, I apply the key findings from this analysis to answer the two central questions motivating the book. First, what is the influence of financialization on pricing and value in the drug development process? This descriptive inquiry provides insights to apply to the second question: how has financialization shaped the outcomes for public health and future innovation? Berwick's observation rings true here: the financialized system out of which sofosbuvir-based medicines emerged was *designed* to produce unprecedented drug prices as well as significant value extraction, all naturalized under the banner of "value."

Bringing in wider industry examples to complement the analysis of hepatitis C, the evidence here debunks key claims regarding price and value in drug development and reveals the deleterious impact of financialization on our current and future health. The prevailing financialized approaches to drug development and pricing have been met with rising public discontent and inspired calls for alternative systems of biomedical research. Heeding Polanyi's insight, that counter-movements play a critical role in shaping a social economy, the second half of the chapter considers what a drug development system that intentionally prioritizes access and affordability would look like, and how it might already be within our reach.

WHEN MEDICINES ARE FINANCIALIZED:
MECHANISMS, MYSTIFICATIONS, AND OUTCOMES

Writing at the dawn of the biotechnology revolution, science and technology scholar Edward Yoxen described the emerging intersection of finance and genomics as a new kind of "technology controlled by capital . . . a specific mode of the appropriation of living nature—literally capitalizing life."[5] But this appropriation was not latent in "living nature"; it has been *made* by the political-economic system described in this book: the financialization of biomedicine. The primary strategy of this system is to extract financial value through speculation on health assets in stock markets. Hepatitis C and sofosbuvir-based treatments provide powerful examples of how this plays out for the development and pricing of new medicines. As the last three chapters described in detail, setting drug prices and extracting value in this financialized drug development process rested on capitalizing science, drugs, and health itself. After taking up the mechanisms by which financialization influences pricing and value, we will turn to its impacts, showing how access, future breakthroughs, and democratic governance all become jeopardized in the process.

Powered to be High: Prices Tethered to Financialization

When Gilead set the launch prices for its sofosbuvir-based medicines for hepatitis C, it was making a basic calculation. As the US Senate investigation shows, Gilead reckoned that health system buyers would be compelled to pay more per treatment course for a superior therapy. But this expectation was not Gilead's alone; it is central to the entire circulation of capital in the drug development process. From Pharmasset's early venture backers to Gilead Sciences' shareholders, financial actors used their position in the drug development process to collect speculative gains based on this anticipation—in time horizons far shorter than the decade-plus time it took to develop sofosbuvir-based medicines. Rather than being tied to some tangible cost of research or production, pricing was almost entirely tethered to financial market expectations. Three mechanisms making up financialized drug development illuminate this link: capitalizing collectively produced knowledge into financial assets through patents; capitalizing drugs via short-term bets on growth in financial markets; and capitalizing health by compelling health systems to buy medicines at "value-based" prices.

First, the entire speculative process of drug development rests on the transformation of collectively developed knowledge into monetized assets. Long-term public investments supported the development of the nucleoside base for sofosbuvir. Later, Pharmasset's scientists turned to the publicly developed "prodrug" strategy to allow one of the company's existing compounds to better attack the hepatitis C virus. In granting Pharmasset its first patents for the compound in 2008, the US government converted this cumulative knowledge into an intangible asset with specific political-legal properties.

Patents are popularly conceptualized as a legal contract governing an exchange between an inventor and society, particularly the potential users of a given unit of knowledge. In the realm of drug development, patents are supposed to be a way for drug companies to "recoup" the costs of R&D. In a US Senate hearing on drug pricing, for example, senator Jon Cornyn voiced the commonly held view: "I support drug companies' recovering a profit on their R&D of innovative drugs."[6] The rationale of the patent, by this view, refers to what Sunder Rajan has called "the figure of the inventor-industrialist"—risk-taking drug companies that are positioned as the "inventors" of medicines.[7]

As I have shown, this conception is at odds with how financialized drug development actually operates. Patents allow knowledge to be repackaged into intangible assets, giving their owners specific control, such as the power to appropriate value or to transfer ownership. This control takes on financial meaning in the speculative markets in which these intangible assets are the objects of valuation and transaction. Through a relay race of financial actors, invention itself then comes to be about, in the words of Sunder Rajan, "the production of capitalized value rather than the production of the product itself."[8] In other words, patents become disconnected from the sources of their original innovative labor, and instead are transformed into financial assets in the circulation of capital.

This dynamic is connected to the observation made by industrial economist F. M. Scherer in a 2004 *New England Journal of Medicine* article on the role of patents in confounding debates over R&D costs.[9] In practice, he argued, patents in contemporary drug development *do not* function as vehicles to recuperate R&D costs; they are a lure for speculative capital. Given this reality, it becomes easier to see why the pharmaceutical industry has so fiercely resisted attempts at greater transparency into their R&D costs.

As the sofosbuvir case shows, at no point in the "relay race" are prices reflective of these costs. Though Pharmasset had spent $62.4 million on sofosbuvir and $271 million *in total* on R&D over its existence as a company, the company was valued in the billions—mostly driven by the asset that would eventually become sofosbuvir. Gilead's $11 billion bet on Pharmasset in 2011 was almost *three times as large* as Gilead's $3.96 billion in R&D costs *for the previous four years combined* (2008–2011). When the Senate later asked Gilead to enumerate its R&D investments in sofosbuvir-based regimens, Gilead gave a figure of $880.4 million. Even the R&D costs for *all* of its drugs during this time—over $4 billion—pale in comparison to the over $46 billion Gilead made on its sofosbuvir-based treatments in the *first three years*. Patents, in this system, are severed from logics of invention and production and instead tethered to the valuations that are possible in speculative financial markets.

This leads into the second mechanism: structural changes in the economy have shifted how capital circulates in drug development, from R&D-focused businesses to a relay race of economic actors betting on drug assets in financial markets. As

William Lazonick has shown in his work on maximizing shareholder value, gone is the era in which companies "retain and reinvest" their capital in their own R&D process.[10] As a consequence of a series of regulatory changes in financial markets and executive compensation beginning in the 1970s, business strategy has become increasingly oriented toward distributing earnings to financial actors that are external to the firm, from venture capitalists to shareholders in stock markets. For these financial actors, value comes less from the *profitability* of actual drugs, and more from trading on the anticipation of future *growth* in profitability. For pharmaceutical companies, this growth expectation usually hovers in the low double digits, just above what financial actors can expect to garner from the stock market otherwise. This produces a set of structural conditions that are inextricable from the drug pricing outcomes we witnessed with hepatitis C.

For large pharmaceutical companies like Gilead Sciences, with established products and revenue, striving for growth at the 10% clip (or more) that shareholders in financial markets expect means a near-continual hunt for new revenue streams. And, as Sunder Rajan has shown, this leads to an array of problematic strategies, from continual drug price increases to attempts to lengthen patents on existing medicines.[11] In the absence of sufficient growth, for example, Gilead turned to these strategies in its HIV business, pursuing annual price hikes as well as new patents for their treatments. Across the industry, price hikes are now almost a January ritual. At the beginning of 2019, the *Wall Street Journal* reported that pharmaceutical companies had hiked the prices of over 100 drugs by an average of 6.3%, with another round of increases expected in the second half of the year.[12] The practice is so baked into the business model that some companies have even taken it as a badge of honor to keep price increases *under* 10% per year. Then-CEO of Allergan, Brett Saunders, for example, said that he had limited price increases to under 10% per year as part of a "social contract" with patients.[13] The company later stuck to its pledge—by setting most of its price hikes at between 9% and 9.5%.

But this hunt for short-term growth also creates another problem: it reduces companies' appetite for making the long-run and risk-laden investments needed to create breakthrough medicines. Instead, large pharmaceutical companies prioritize maximizing growth for shareholders. To do that while mitigating risk, these businesses position themselves less as life sciences companies developing critical medical breakthroughs, and more as *acquisition specialists*—betting on the flow of capital in the drug development process by purchasing drug assets with the potential to bring in significant revenues. Gilead's pursuit of Pharmasset exemplifies this dynamic. Despite annual profitability of 20–30% in the 2009–2011 period, Gilead's share value *plateaued* on a perception of limited growth prospects.[14] Without the internal research pipeline to generate new growth, Gilead bet $11 billion on Pharmasset—with the anticipation that sofosbuvir-based medicines could generate many more billions in revenue growth.

On the other hand, for the smaller pharmaceutical and biotechnology ventures like Pharmasset, that often have no products or revenue, the *potential* of future growth is the lure for finance capitalists. In the summer of 2011 Pharmasset would come to be valued at over $4 billion, despite having no approved products, no sales, and having lost $330 million over its twelve-year existence.[15] This valuation was entirely based on its hepatitis C drug assets, which were anticipated to become big sellers once approved. Hepatitis C medicines in use at the time already cost upwards of $50,000. Newer treatments were expected to fetch even higher prices, and have more eligible patients. Yet the capital such valuations helped lure was not meant to bring the treatment across the finish line. Rather, for Pharmasset's financial backers, these valuations were an opportunity to make speculative bets with an end in mind—either through an IPO, a stock trade, or acquisition. Given this short-term dynamic, a small biotechnology company like Pharmasset is often seen less as a durable business and more as a *disposable* one, designed to be "exited" by its financial backers and ultimately bought out. Pharmasset, the epitome of such a business, was started with the explicit purpose—as signaled by its very name—of being a vehicle to develop assets for larger pharmaceutical companies.

Finally, financialized capital in drug development is predicated on a third key feature: the power of drug companies to capitalize health itself. The chain of speculative capital, from a small venture-backed firm to a large pharmaceutical business traded on the stock market, operates on the expectation that one day in the future buyers will be willing to pay more for better health outcomes. This expectation, in turn, rests on the power of businesses to transform predictions of future prices into a realized outcome. In other words, it is less that health systems will be *willing* to buy medicines at a given price, and more that they can be *compelled* to do so.

The power of pharmaceutical companies is thus contingent on their structural position, which lets them maintain patents and charge prices based on what the "market will bear"—and thereby is also vulnerable to political contestation and social resistance. The struggle over Gilead's pricing strategy in the three years after the launch of sofosbuvir-based medicines vividly illustrates this dynamic. In its pursuit of the growth expected by financial markets, Gilead took a territorially targeted approach. With the power of its patents, the company charged what it deemed "value prices" in financially lucrative countries, particularly in the US but also across Europe. It then licensed access to its sofosbuvir assets to low-income countries that could not have afforded anything near the "value prices" being charged elsewhere, but also used its control over patents to exclude dozens of middle-income countries from the license. Gilead's "value pricing" in high- and middle-income countries yielded significant treatment rationing—and capital accumulation. Yet this strategy, which relied on blatantly testing the upper limits of what societies could tolerate, was in turn met with resistance, as exemplified by civil society responses—notably in the form of patent opposition—as well as governments' use of their negotiating power. Along with the entry of corporate competitors, this resistance opened spaces for public health programs in which pricing and value were more tethered to access and care, rather than the growth logics and imperatives of financialized capital.

Anticipating this deeply contentious terrain of drug pricing, Gilead tried to deploy not only its coercive political and market power, made possible by patent controls, but also a hegemonic conception of "value" that could satisfy both Wall Street and health policy elites. Through a moral-economic discourse, Gilead and the pharmaceutical lobby argued that it was a kind of duty for health systems to pay more now, to secure the economic value of better health in the future. This discourse attempted to shift the responsibility to governments—not to reduce drug prices, but to value the lives of hepatitis C patients by paying the prices Gilead was naming. To buttress this discourse, Gilead also drew on a set of valuation practices from clinical medicine, health economics, and epidemiology that quantified this future economic value of health and deemed sofosbuvir's price to indeed be "cost-effective" and "value-based." These valuation practices are viewed by many public and health policy experts as a rational way for public health systems to weigh how to most effectively allocate resources, so that more money goes to medicines with greater evidence of benefit. However, by wielding this evidence in the public sphere, Gilead appropriated the rationality of such valuation practices and attempted to turn its high prices into a new "common sense."

The attempt to frame drug prices in terms of financial value, in turn, highlights a key observation by anthropologist Danya Glabau: "Price in the pharmaceutical industry today is a highly orchestrated accomplishment with no natural referent."[16] Even as business leaders, health policy experts, and public officials search for such a natural referent—citing the costs of research or the quantified value of health—we see that the pricing of sofosbuvir-based medicines was in reality the orchestrated outcome of a financialized drug development process. The absence of some underlying fact that might serve as a natural referent is part of what makes drug pricing so hotly contested and why questions of power in its various forms must continue to be central to understanding the dominance and potential vulnerability of prevailing systems. Without political contestation, and short of alternative models of R&D financing, drug prices become tethered to the structural power and expectations of shareholders and financial markets. "Value," in this narrative of "value pricing," buttresses this structural power; in the process, this narrative elides the way value is created and extracted in contemporary drug development. Confronting these omissions reveals the possibility and importance of conceptualizing value in a different way, one that makes visible the pitfalls of the hegemonic view and legitimizes new forms of power and models of biomedical innovation.

*The Dynamic of Value: Collective Value Creation, Public Value,
and Value Extraction*

After the launch of Novartis's $2.1 million Zolgensma treatment, John Arnold, a hedge fund manager turned philanthropist and drug-pricing activist, took to Twitter. "Successive therapies," he wrote, "should be better, which will be used to justify even higher prices. But certainly there must be a price that is too high. 5 mil? 20 mil? 100 mil?"[17] In asking this question, Arnold was pointing out the basic challenge of "value-based" assessments under the conditions of financialized capital: each increase in drug prices sets the floor for the price of the next treatment, a dynamic which is used as a lure for speculative capitalists.

This phenomenon is not limited to hepatitis C. A group of neurologists found, for example, that while the first-generation multiple sclerosis drugs of the 1990s were priced between $8,000 and $10,000, those treatments now are priced north of $60,000.[18] In a *Wall Street Journal* piece on this study, one of the main authors observed that "These companies didn't have to price them at a lower level, because the prices for the older drugs were steadily being increased. What they're doing is feeding off each other in terms of how the prices are set."[19] The primary justification for these increases? The better clinical outcomes observed with the newer drugs.

Over time, financialization can turn the basic rationale of prevailing value assessments of treatments into almost a kind of absurdity. What would the "value-based" price have been, we might ask, for a polio vaccine? Within a decade, Arnold wonders, will we be comparing treatments with prices in the tens or hundreds of millions? This dystopic possibility signals the pragmatic and moral pitfalls of such frames of value, in that they normalize an upward spiral of prices, thrusting financial, ethical, and bodily challenges onto health systems, physicians, and patients.

In her book *The Value of Everything*, Mariana Mazzucato puts this kind of value thinking in a much larger historical context within the field of economics. She argues that at the core of economics, as conceptualized by classical thinkers like Adam Smith and David Ricardo, was a theory of value that was tied to the dynamics of production and the division of labor. In contemporary economics, however, value has become narrowly defined as the preferences of economic agents, who signal their preferences with prices in markets. Thus "price has become the indicator of value: so long as a good is bought and sold in the market, it must have value."[20] What drops from view, however, is a much more dynamic theory of value which was once at the heart of economic thinking—a political-economic analysis of how goods are actually made and produced.

Mazzucato revives and updates this theory for contemporary capitalism. She formulates a way of analyzing value as a dynamic entity that is central to the sofosbuvir story: both in terms of *value creation* as a collective process among public and private actors, as well as the *value extraction* that occurs due to financialization. Value, in this conceptualization, is not a static entity, but rather involves questions of how value is created, shared, and distributed in the economy. This dynamic concept of value offers a counterpoint to prevailing discourses that legitimize significant value extraction under the banner of "value." "Returning value" to shareholders, and businesses as "value creators," are popular turns of phrases that pervade our thinking and direct the attention of policymakers. Thus, Mazzucato writes, "We have made it easier for some to call themselves value creators and in the process extract value."[21] In addition to unpacking the way financialization impacts drug prices, part of my empirical task was to cut through this hegemonic discourse and instead lay out the dynamic creation and distribution of value.

In Mazzucato's formulation, value is *co-created* by multiple kinds of actors, in public agencies, businesses, and civil society. A critical feature of studying value creation is the question, *For what ends?* In other words, innovation by definition has not only a rate but also a *direction*: potential new outcomes that are made possible through a novel product, market, or service. In the realm of drug development, the direction is better health through medical advances. But the hepatitis C case shows that public investments are critical to shaping this direction across the drug development process. The most prominent example is the public financing of the replicon, which transformed the possibilities of hepatitis C drug development and enabled the discovery of compounds which eliminated the virus.

To be sure, private business also created value in the sofosbuvir drug development process. However, our challenge is understanding how this private value creation occurs. Pharmasset's initial venture capitalists and the public shareholders involved in the IPO provided risk capital that enabled the business to further develop hepatitis C compounds. Gilead's pursuit of Pharmasset, in turn, required a major speculative bet and further private investments to create a curative regimen. Competing companies, like AbbVie and Vertex, also spent significant sums on hepatitis C clinical trials.

But these investments only came *after* and *alongside* critical public investments. Pharmasset, for example, was a company built on decades of public investments in nucleoside science with roots in government-funded HIV research. In its early launch phases, the company also received direct grants from the US government through the SBIR program. Later, when scientists at Pharmasset sought to improve their hepatitis C compounds, they relied on prodrug techniques—knowledge available in the public domain and the outcome of publicly financed science in the US and Europe. Through these developments, along with the replicon, the public sector co-created the market for potential hepatitis C investment and shaped the direction of this investment toward realizing potential curative medicines.

While the public sector plays this critical role in value creation, we lack policy and economic thinking that accounts for it. A conception of what Mazzucato calls "public value" would help consider and measure progress toward social goals that are pursued through an interaction between public and private actors.[22] The state, in this configuration, would see as part of its charge not only financing innovation but also fostering a set of relationships that allow collective value creation to be directed toward these social goals—such as the elimination of an infectious disease and reinvestment of a large share of profits back into research, wages, and worker training. Prevailing policy thinking does not flow from this view. Instead, the state is relegated to the role of "fixing market failures"—such as financing "basic science"—with almost any other action deemed market "interventionism." Ironically, such pronouncements occur even as private corporations lobby governments for frequent intervention on their behalf, such as ironclad government protections for patents.[23] This setup leads to significant government failures in stewarding public value (including value that the state helps create) toward positive social outcomes. NIH, for example, does not take a stake in the companies it helps develop, nor does it garner significant royalties. The US tax code routinely allows companies to avoid taxes through loopholes, often by offshoring intellectual property that public investment helped create. The US intellectual property system grants broad patent protections, even for products that resulted from significant public investment. These examples encourage us to also pay attention, then, to how the benefits that emerge from innovation are distributed. In other words, a theory of public value needs to account for both the creation of value and how it may or may not be shared.

Under the current conceptions of "value," financialized drug development can lead to massive value extraction. Take the hepatitis C case. Between just 2014 and 2016, Gilead accumulated $46 billion in revenue from sofosbuvir, and distributed $30.7 billion to shareholders in the form of buybacks and dividends. Yet these shareholders were *not* the primary source of the risk capital in Gilead's investments in the drug development process and were even less crucial when taking the full pipeline of development into consideration. In fact, the accumulated capital for Gilead's $11 billion bet on Pharmasset came in large part from prior sales, not shareholder investment.

The flow of capital to Gilead's shareholders can best be understood through the economic concept of *rent-seeking*, in which a group or individual with special privileges (such as intellectual property claims or stock ownership) can extract a large share of wealth that would have been produced without their input.[24] Yet this extractive mode of capitalism is not unique to Gilead. Between 2008 and 2017, Lazonick found that the largest pharmaceutical companies spent *more than 100%* of their combined profits on payouts to shareholders.[25] This structure of value extraction echoes Mazzucato and Lazonick's reflection on inequality in contemporary capitalism:

> Although risk-taking has become more collective . . . the reward system has become dominated by individuals who, inserting themselves strategically between the business organization and the product market or a financial market, and especially the stock market, lay claim to a disproportionate share of the rewards of the innovation process.[26]

Beside financial actors on Wall Street, an important example of individuals occupying this strategic position are the executives of pharmaceutical companies, who—as major shareholders—garner earnings increasingly out of balance with their role in the drug development process. For Gilead's five leading executives, this meant collecting over $1 billion in earnings in the three years after the launch of sofosbuvir-based medicines. Making executives into shareholders with pivotal stakes in a company's share price has been a critical mechanism for embedding the ideology of "maximizing shareholder value" into the operations of the economy.

But this dogma of maximizing shareholder value has always itself been built on a set of economic, legal, and business myths. First, defenders of financialized drug development will claim that given the importance of the stock market for Americans' pensions, higher share prices (made possible by higher drug prices) end up flowing back to people. But such a claim runs up against the facts of unequal and diminished stock ownership—in 2019, for example, the top 10% of Americans controlled 84% of all of Wall Street's stock value, while the bottom 50% owned only 1%.[27] Meanwhile, many older citizens, even those with pensions invested in the stock market, struggle to afford medications.

Second, the legal scholar Lynn Stout, in her book *The Shareholder Value Myth*, has uncovered the ways in which corporate leaders do *not*, as is often claimed, have some fiduciary responsibility to "maximize shareholder value."[28] Reviewing case history, she shows that courts have *rarely* held corporate boards of directors liable for this purpose. Rather than being the "owners" of a company, and thus entitled to corporate earnings, Stout shows that shareholders are engaged in contractual relationships with corporations—a subset of many such relationships that corporations must navigate, such as with suppliers, buyers, and workers.

Finally, business scholar William Lazonick has demonstrated that investments in workers and knowledge creation—through wages, training, and R&D—create the conditions for long-term value creation within businesses. The irony of the ideology of maximizing shareholder value, Lazonick argues, is that the "shareholders held up as the only risk bearers do not typically invest in the value-creating capabilities of corporations at all."[29] Putting the perils of shareholder primacy in blunt terms, he says that maximizing shareholder value is "a theory of value extraction without a theory of value creation."[30] Indeed, the commitment to this dogma, and the system of drug development underpinned by it, has led to systemic crises.

The Triple Crisis of Financialization: Jeopardizing Access, Future Breakthroughs, and Public Governance

At the 2014 gathering of the American Society of Health Economists in Los Angeles, the topic *du jour*, particularly for health economists, was sofosbuvir-based treatments.[31] Dana Goldman, a health economist at USC, echoed a common view among his colleagues: "We'd love for pharmaceutical companies to come up with a treatment that cures diabetes rather than just treats it. I want to pay them enough so it's possible they'll start working on cures rather than treatments." Lacking an analysis of financialization, Goldman subscribed to the view that rewarding the innovation system behind sofosbuvir-based treatments could incentivize more future cures. But the evidence from the sofosbuvir case belies this view. Instead, the financialization of biomedicine poses a three-fold threat. First, financial markets *penalize* the development of curative breakthroughs, even if prices are set high, because by curing people, these medicines can prevent ongoing revenue *growth*. Second, the occasional breakthroughs that *are* produced are priced at levels that pose an affordability challenge to patients and health systems. And these are intertwined with a third threat: the withering of democratic governance.

A 2018 report from Goldman Sachs, "The Genome Revolution," illuminates the threat that financialization poses to future breakthroughs. In the report, Goldman's analysts considered the potential for "one-shot cures" one of the "most attractive aspects" of medicines made via new gene-editing technologies.[32] But the author, Goldman's Salveen Richter, added a note of caution: "Is curing patients a sustainable business model?"

He had an example in mind. "GILD is a case in point," Richter wrote, using Gilead's stock-ticker abbreviation, "where the success of its hepatitis C franchise has gradually decreased the available pool of treatable patients." Though the company had made over $46 billion in revenue in the first three years of sales, Wall Street treated it like a transient sugar rush, because sales *growth* slowed and then plummeted.[33] After a peak near $120 per share in 2015, by early 2017 Gilead's market value had dropped by almost half.[34] Contrary to hopes that its high drug prices would enable the company to invest in further curative innovation, Gilead stockpiled money to acquire future treatments, while it doubled down on cornering patent protections and raising the prices of their HIV drugs.

In *Drugs for Life*, Joseph Dumit captures this dilemma. "In too many drug studies," he writes, "cures get in the way of repeat revenue."[35] A cure for HIV, for example—a medical breakthrough that could simplify treatment for millions of people around the world—would, over time, decimate a key earnings stream for Gilead. Better than cures, for the financial valuation of a publicly traded company, are recurring treatments for chronic pathologies—like lifelong treatment for HIV. "Mitigator" treatments can bring in the kind of recurring revenue and growing accumulation expected by shareholders. A *Bloomberg Business* story on Gilead's tribulations with hepatitis C captured Dumit's view: "Wall Street wants the best patents, not the best drugs."[36] The best patents, in turn, are financial assets with the most durable growth potential—which curative drugs do not provide.

In addition to *penalizing* curative medicines as an obstacle to future growth, this financialized model threatens breakthrough treatments in another way: it disincentivizes and undercuts long-run investments. As we have seen, to maximize shareholder returns, pharmaceutical businesses direct significant portions of their capital to shareholders, instead of making long-run investments in research.

And for the capital businesses do reinvest internally, a priority is placed on late-stage clinical trials, often of medicines surer to meet regulatory approval. This has produced a raft of "me-too" medicines, as businesses pursue lucrative markets by making drugs that are similar to existing treatments or represent an incremental advance.[37] To be sure, drug companies also use their stockpiled capital to speculate and acquire promising compounds. Occasionally, one of these compounds will end up being a breakthrough treatment, as sofosbuvir did. But when this financialized process does produce occasional breakthroughs, they are priced at levels that represent a second crisis: affordable access to medicines.

High prices for new medicines are rationalized as reflecting the "value" of better future health. But what they instead represent is the power of pharmaceutical companies to use their intellectual property protections to price their products at the upper bounds of what health systems can be compelled to pay. These prices are intertwined with a financialized drug development system in which expectation of higher prices for drug assets is the primary fuel for speculative capitalists.

With each progression in treatment setting the pricing floor for the next one, however, even a "value-based" price for a new medicine presents fiscal challenges for health systems. The leaders of these health systems are encouraged to "think like investors," as Birch and Muniesa put it, because paying for a given treatment *now* may optimize a "return on investment" in terms of savings and quality-adjusted life years *later.*[38] But the leaders of public health systems have a different job from Wall Street investors. When large numbers of patients stand to benefit from a high-priced medicine, as in the case of sofosbuvir, officials either have to engage in a political process to find significant new funding, use legal measures to lower the price, or make fraught ethical decisions about who can get access. Meanwhile patients' lives are left hanging in the balance.

The health systems in high-income areas, such as the US and Europe, that paid Gilead's "value prices" rationed treatment and delayed the public health planning that might have been possible if the treatments had been more affordable.[39] In countries and health systems like Australia's that took a bolder political stance toward Gilead and negotiated prices that would permit greater access, this planning began in earnest. In low- and middle-income countries, access to sofosbuvir depended on Gilead's "benevolence" in including countries in licensing agreements that enabled generic production and pricing of medicines closer to their manufacturing cost. Middle-income countries like Brazil and Ukraine were initially excluded from this licensing, so their health systems were essentially barred initially from deploying public health programs aimed at widespread treatment of hepatitis C.

To be sure, the pursuit of a lucrative market drew in competitors, as observed with AbbVie's successful entry into hepatitis C. With Gilead and Abbvie competing in an oligopoly market, lower list prices (in the range of $20,000–30,000) helped open up access in many high-income countries. Yet such price competition often does not occur, even with multiple treatment options. Gilead dropped the price of its hepatitis C medicines, but continued with annualized price hikes on its HIV treatments—even with multiple competing HIV treatment manufacturers. This dynamic may reflect the peculiar political-economic features of a curative treatment, further illustrating the growth and accumulation logics of financialized biomedicine. One hypothesis might be that the political-economic dynamics of a curative treatment—in which Wall Street did not see long-term financial growth potential—led companies to engage in price competition (with prices still more than twenty times the cost of production) to pursue whatever sales and accumulation they could within a finite market. With "chronic treatment" assets like diabetes, insulin, or HIV medicines, drug companies have sought long-term financial accumulation and used their intellectual property protections to keep prices high for the life of their patent. In addition to Gilead's HIV price increases, for example, a 2021 paper in *JAMA* found "lock-step" price increases by manufacturers of specific classes of diabetes and anticoagulant treatments even with multiple competitors.[40]

This crisis of access and affordability is not limited to medicines for diseases affecting large populations. If drug prices continue at their current pace, new medicines even for smaller patient populations will represent a growing challenge. New "million-dollar" drugs are beginning to receive FDA approval on the basis that they present significant benefits for populations that previously had few viable options. Novartis's $2.1 million treatment for spinal muscular atrophy, Zolgensma, is one example. Some 400 gene therapies are currently in clinical trials. If even a fraction of these are approved and then priced based on the purported "value" they provide, they may drive rising insurance premiums and struggles for access in the US and around the world.[41]

The story of cancer drugs provides a preview. The mean launch price for new cancer treatments approved in 2018 was $150,000 in the US; all of them were over $100,000.[42] In low- and middle-income countries, cancer drugs are routinely priced at a fraction of the US prices but still many times the median wage in a given country. Xtandi, for example, a breakthrough prostate cancer treatment developed with major public investments and priced at $140,000 in the US, was priced at $65,000 in India, or 40 times the annual income of the average person in that country.[43] The consequences of the prices in the US are also staggering. Twenty-seven percent of insured adult cancer patients reported medication non-adherence due to cost.[44] Forty-two percent of insured cancer patients report a significant or catastrophic financial burden.[45] Oncologists have coined a phrase for this grave comorbid condition in their patients: "financial toxicity."[46]

These two crises of financialization—penalizing investment in curative medicines and making medicines unaffordable—are intertwined with a third one: the withering of public governance. With their large stockpiles of accumulated capital, pharmaceutical companies can mobilize significant political power by financially supporting political campaigns, and also through the direct influence of corporate lobbyists on the policymaking process. But the interests of financialized capital also operate in a more subtle way, as I described earlier, by monopolizing the epistemic categories in which political struggles are conceptualized. The industry, backed by Wall Street, trumpets concepts like "risk" and "value" through marketing campaigns and also in scholarly discourses in academic fora. We saw this with hepatitis C, as many policy experts and academics came to view the $90,000 price point as a justified—and even morally good—outcome. These discourses gain their power, in part, through elision—for example, by keeping the scale of public investment and private value extraction out of view.

Through these strategies, pharmaceutical businesses attempt to make a given political-economic system—financialized drug development—into a naturalized system, free from democratic accountability to citizens and unburdened by public imaginations of alternative possible futures. Many scholars have warned of the danger of public goals being captured by private purpose; in drug development, we see this purpose being not only privatized but financialized.[47] This financial capture operates in at least two directions. On the one hand, it can the dominate the goals for which biomedical innovation might otherwise aim. We observe this, for example, in the way Gilead's "value pricing" strategy led to rationing in certain territories rather than the public health programs that materialized in others. On the other hand, this capture works by taking advantage of some of the internal tensions of the state to activate certain versions of public action on behalf of financialized capital while suppressing and denaturalizing others that could have been taken on behalf of citizens and patients. This is exemplified by the ongoing reluctance of the US government, for example, to curb intellectual property protections—even amid a global pandemic—for fear of blunting private incentives to commercialize publicly funded research.

In this conception of a multifaceted state, however, lies the seeds of alternative possibilities—a chance to imagine and mobilize a different version of what people do together through their government and publicly sanctioned courts of law. The struggle over access to treatment for hepatitis C indicated the willingness and even momentum for such action. Multiple groups—from the G7 to the European Union to the United Nations—recognized in the wake of hepatitis C that the prevailing order that produces such high drug prices needs to change. Civil society groups directly challenged patents on collectively and cumulatively produced knowledge and won in several legal arenas. Public authorities negotiated new types of deals, as in Australia and in certain US states. And despite the failure to enact such lessons in the global response to COVID-19, the massive government investments in vaccines to fight the pandemic have the potential to accelerate a push for new models of biomedical research. Public purpose, rather than financialized purpose, is within our imaginative *and* real-world reach.

TOWARD A PUBLIC-PURPOSE SYSTEM

A transition to a different model of biomedical R&D is possible—a model intentionally designed for equitable and affordable access *and* investment toward the future medicines we need. The nucleus of such a vision can be found in the struggles over the US R&D system after World War II. At the heart of these struggles was the role of government in financing and governing science and technology. Reviving and updating this lost vision can offer a guide for where we go next.

As the country sought to win World War II and to build the economy that would follow, policymakers debated the federal government's role in innovation. In a 2020 piece titled "Whose Drugs are These?" technology scholar Bhaven Sampat chronicles two competing visions that emerged from these debates, each championed by significant figures in science policy at the time.[48] Harvey Kilgore, West Virginia's powerful senator and a New Deal–era Democrat, proposed an ambitious government role: public financing across the early and applied stages of R&D, and a patent system that would protect these investments from the threat of monopoly power. Kilgore feared that without major public investments and coordination, private corporations would fail to address key problems at the speed required; he also feared that monopolists would abuse the patent system. At stake, in Kilgore's view, was the nation's technological competitiveness, as well as whether new technologies would be used in the public interest.

Yet Kilgore's legislative push in the early and mid-1940s was strongly opposed by policy leaders as well as industry and trade groups, all of whom feared that the government would crowd out and repel private investment. One of Kilgore's primary rivals would be a better-remembered figure in postwar science and technology policy: Vannevar Bush, FDR's chief science advisor and head of the wartime Office of Scientific Research and Development. He advocated a position that ultimately won out: the government would finance "basic research," with patents stimulating industry to do the needed "applied" research of turning science into usable products. Bush's primary fear was that, without profit opportunities for private industry, the massive new government investments in science would fail to be commercialized into technologies. Public policy, in his view, should solve this "commercialization problem" by providing incentives for private industry to take up the work.

In the subsequent decades, US science and technology policy has almost entirely heeded Bush's call for commercialization while ignoring Kilgore's prescient warnings against private and monopoly power. Yet the *way* this knowledge has been commercialized—increasingly under the conditions of financialized capital—has produced and exacerbated another problem: unaffordable medicines. This problem is one reason for the rising public discontent with the pharmaceutical industry, with polling in the US showing the worst favorability of any industry.[49] Reforming this system has posed a significant challenge. The pharmaceutical lobby is among the most powerful in national capitals around the world, and particularly in Washington, DC. Defenders of the current system meet any drug pricing regulation with the claim that such moves would cause drug development to implode. After House Democrats in Congress proposed a reform bill in 2019, for example, the trade group Pharmaceutical Research and Manufacturers of America warned that a "nuclear winter" would befall the sector and endanger future medicines.[50]

Such claims are too strong. The pharmaceutical industry is significantly more profitable than other major industries, and lower prices would still leave the sector in a strong financial position.[51] But as I have shown, it is also plausible that in a financialized system powered by high prices, such regulations—without any other changes—would reduce some amount of speculative capital from entering the sector. Given the scale of the current drug affordability crisis, this trade-off may well be worth it. Consider the House bill proposed in 2019, which would give the US government negotiating power over as many as 250 high-cost brand drugs using benchmarks for drug prices in other countries.[52] The Congressional Budget Office estimated this policy would save Medicare $345 billion between 2023 and 2029, but would also result in perhaps eight to fifteen fewer new drugs over the next ten years.[53] This calculation assumes a static government which does not expand its investments in public R&D. Yet policies that only target drug prices after a medicine has launched would fail to address the larger systemic problem: the way medicines are financialized.

Kilgore's vision points to a path out of this financialized quagmire: a *public-purpose* system, in which government explicitly finances technology development and also governs the fair distribution of the rewards that flow from these investments. His 1942 Technology Mobilization Act, for example, called for the creation of a public innovation agency to lead such efforts. Contemporary activists and policy entrepreneurs offer a vision that follows in Kilgore's spirit, calling for a "public option" for drug development. In this alternative to a financialized trajectory, a public-option model would position the government to take a "full-cycle" approach to developing drugs, including financing clinical trials, and ensure they are sold at a price closer to their manufacturing cost. This public enterprise, in turn, would introduce valuable competition into the prevailing financialized model of biomedical R&D—with key governance lessons that could steer this prevailing model toward public purpose.

A Public Option for Medicines

Imagine the year 2030. Not long ago, a federal Health Innovation Institute was launched with the express intent to translate scientific advances into usable and affordable treatments for patients. The program began as a pilot soon after the end of the COVID-19 pandemic. The government's significant investments in vaccines, including clinical trials and manufacturing capacity, had proven to the public and policymakers that an entrepreneurial state was capable of taking on sizable risks and accelerating science at a pace and in a direction that private industry alone could not have managed.

Instead of paying for high-priced medicines whose benefits flow to shareholders, the institute invests money in early and late-stage clinical trials, currently the most expensive part of R&D and the *raison d'être* for many large pharmaceutical businesses. The institute conducts clinical trials in various ways, from partnering with private companies through prizes and grants, to running the trials itself. Having taken on the risks of this process, the institute then ensures that treatments are priced in a way that guarantees a modest profit over and above the cost of making and distributing the product—either through public manufacturing corporations or through licensing to private manufacturers. In working with private manufacturers, the institute keeps its intellectual property in the public domain. Any royalties made in the process are reinvested in the institute, providing a sustainable stream of financing to complement other tax revenues.

Such a scenario is not far-fetched. It would offer a kind of "public option," as described by Sitaraman and Alstott, in which governments develop publicly financed alternatives that coexist alongside private businesses but operate with explicit public-purpose aims.[54] Public options have long been the practice in many other familiar arenas, including public libraries and the US Postal Service. In the realm of drug development, iterations of this idea have been proposed by various groups and scholars, from economist Amitabh Chandra's call for a "NASA for drug development," to the Democracy Collaborative's "public pharmaceutical sector" strategy.[55]

To be sure, there are thorny issues that would need working out—including which therapeutic and disease areas to direct investment to, the institute's organizational setup, and questions about global collaboration and access. For its first experiments, this institute might attend to areas where private innovation has failed to meet a significant health need, such as vaccines for future pandemics, new antimicrobials, or treatments for Alzheimer's disease. It could also focus on treatments where drug prices are creating acute crises—such as insulin, whose price has tripled over the past decade and led one in four people with diabetes in the US to ration or outright skip doses.[56] The institute could spearhead the development of a new insulin technology, or it could work with generic manufacturers to rapidly mobilize public production to bring patients an urgently needed affordable option. (In a preview of such an approach at the state level, in 2022 California announced a $100 million plan for public development and manufacturing of low-cost insulin products).[57] The institute could be an independent agency and draw on the expertise of other public agencies, such as DARPA and ARPA-E, that have experience in effectively managing high-uncertainty projects.[58] Though President Biden proposed an agency modeled on DARPA focused on biomedical innovation (called ARPA-H) as part of his Build Back Better agenda, whether it would operate with the principles enumerated here is an open question.[59]

On issues of global concern, such as antibiotic research, the institute could help spearhead international efforts in collaboration with other governments. Such endeavors can take inspiration from precedents like the International Space Station, which receives $3–4 billion annually from NASA and is part of a $150 billion international investment.[60] Intellectual property that arises from such investments could go toward international patent pools, like the UN-backed Medicines Patent Pool, and thereby be licensed to manufacturers around the world. This would build regional manufacturing capacity while avoiding the sharply divergent trajectories in treatment access observed with hepatitis C, and even more prominently with HIV treatments and COVID-19 vaccines. Countries could in turn tailor public health programs to their populations soon after the launch of a new technology, rather than waiting for years.

This public option would present its own challenges, including financing and maintaining political independence. Yet the benefits would far outweigh—and could even directly address—these risks. Any complaint about the price tag of this public option, for example, would need to consider current public spending on prescription drugs. The US government spent about $130 billion in public funds on prescriptions in 2015, which covered 43% of all drug spending in the country.[61] Spending even a *fraction* of this $130 billion on technology development (NIH's budget in 2020 was north of $40 billion) would yield significant savings and would allow new investment to address unmet health needs that today's financialized model neglects. And concerns over political gaming and influence over the agency and innovation policy would have to be weighed against the sheer scale of private influence that today corrodes public trust in both the political system and the pharmaceutical industry.

In sum, a public option is the most systemic way to address the many negative consequences of financialization. Rather than pursuing a variety of piecemeal reforms that could be rolled back, this strategy would develop durable public capabilities and be part of a renewed US industrial policy. To be sure, the prevailing model of financialized drug development and pricing would remain even with a public option. But the public option offers another opportunity: a proof of concept for the key principles that should undergird all biomedical R&D: mission-oriented innovation, socialized risks and rewards, collective learning and intelligence, and equitable access. With this competing public-option model, government policy could be used to steer the wider and currently financialized system toward public purpose.

Mission-Oriented R&D

Innovation has not just a rate but also a direction—the social outcomes that are made possible by new products, markets, or services. In the realm of biomedical R&D, such directions are new treatments that address significant unmet health needs. Yet the present financialized model still privileges "me-too" medicines and therapeutic areas that are highly profitable while penalizing the development of curative medicines (as seen in the aftermath of sofosbuvir) and other treatments for conditions with low financial value. The public option would instead be clearly geared toward what Mazzucato has called a "mission-oriented" approach, in which a publicly funded innovation institute would collaborate with other public and private actors to take on important unmet health needs.[62] But governments can and should use this approach to shape the direction of the wider biomedical R&D system.

Rather than leaving the directions of innovation to be set by commercial interests, public organizations should take an active role, along with civil society and business. For example, in the US such directions could include addressing racial health inequities by taking on conditions like sickle cell disease and breast cancer. Across many industrialized countries, aging and dementia-related diseases and cancers present major public health threats. Globally, future pandemic disease and growing antibiotic resistance loom as challenges that require proactive public investments.[63] Setting these as purpose-led missions can create entirely new technological horizons while also addressing crucial health needs for patients. These missions would be defined with the goal of not only producing new technologies but also ensuring their widest and most equitable deployment for health.

Policymakers can use multiple tools to steer the hybrid public–private model of biomedical research toward such missions. In selecting potential directions, governments can help set ambitious but reachable goals that attract and coordinate investment. Governments can also provide financing through prizes and loans, using them to attract bottom-up innovation. But for such a configuration to succeed in realizing social goals, public policies would also need to ensure that the fruits of public investments are mobilized for these goals. This would require rethinking our prevailing approach to the distribution of risks and rewards in the innovation process.

Socializing Risks and Rewards

The existing system allows private shareholders, particularly of large pharmaceutical companies, to take the lion's share of the rewards from drug development, though they are far from being the primary risk-takers. Instead, the public pays twice, both for the significant investments made in the most uncertain stages of research, *and* for the high prices charged by companies at the end of the process. In this scenario, the risks of innovation are socialized (with significant public risk taking), but the rewards are privatized (accumulated by financial actors). The public-option strategy addresses this directly, by socializing the risk through investments across the technology development process, but also sharing in the rewards, through manufacturing drugs at generic prices and reinvesting any royalties that come out of the process.

This general principle can guide policy more broadly. First, governments should seek a more direct return on public investments by setting clear and

transparent conditions to ensure that technologies are used to fulfill public pur-
poses. In the COVID-19 vaccine rollout, for example, the US and European governments failed on this crucial front. Even with significant government investments,
US and EU contracts lacked basic mechanisms to protect government-funded
intellectual property, guarantee delivery timelines, or prevent future price-
gouging.[64] Governments could also earn direct returns via royalties and equity
stakes in businesses in which they invest, though there would have to be a way to
guard against the public sector adopting the same short-term and growth-oriented
financial interests as Wall Street shareholders.

Second, policymakers should enact corporate governance reforms that limit
disproportionate extraction of rewards by Wall Street. They can follow in the
tradition of the COVID-19 legislation passed by Congress in the spring of 2020,
in which the CARES Act banned companies benefiting from the bill from buying back shares.[65] Buybacks were illegal until 1982; given their role in share price
manipulation and significant value extraction, they can and should be significantly limited through legislation and rulemaking. Furthermore, policymakers
can reform executive-compensation rules and limit the role of share ownership
in compensation packages. Senator Elizabeth Warren's proposed Accountable
Capitalism Act, for example, would prohibit executives and directors of US corporations from selling their shares within five years of receiving them, or within
three years of a company stock buyback, limiting the gains from short-term
speculative activity.[66]

On their own, these steps regarding buybacks and executive compensation
would not solve the problem of financialization. But they would be important
initial steps away from the era of maximizing shareholder value. This desire has
even been endorsed by corporate leaders, as exemplified by a 2019 statement by
the Business Roundtable, which broke long-held orthodoxy by holding that providing value to *stakeholders* (such as communities, customers, and employees),
rather than only shareholders, should be a core aim of business.[67] Yet whether
a more stakeholder-oriented version of capitalism emerges will turn less on the
statements of CEOs and more on whether voters urge, and political leaders craft, a
new set of rules for the economy.

Learning and Collective Intelligence

One set of rules we need to consider is those that govern how we share knowledge to accelerate and direct innovation toward social goals. For example, what
if a global network of scientists and medical experts could collaborate to develop
and update a vaccine for an emerging strain of a contagious virus and then share
this knowledge with companies and countries around the world? This is precisely
the purpose of the World Health Organization's Global Influenza Surveillance
and Response System.[68] For the past five decades, this network of experts and
laboratories spanning 110 countries has developed the annual flu vaccine. Funded

almost entirely by governments (with some foundation support), this system is a prime example of the power of "open science."

Whereas the financialized system is organized around patents, which allow their owners to package and control biomedical knowledge as financial assets, open science models privilege shared learning and collective intelligence. If research data and processes are available under terms that enable reuse, redistribution, and reproduction, scientists can use the collective intelligence of the knowledge commons to learn from failures, successes, and unexpected outcomes. An emphasis on open science methods could more efficiently accelerate knowledge production and potentially address the declining rate of productivity observed today in the private pharmaceutical industry, with fewer approved treatments approved per billion dollars spent on R&D over the past two decades.[69]

The public option could model these open science principles. The Democracy Collaborative has suggested, for example, that an innovation institute could be chartered in a way to ensure that its inventions are patented, so that private companies do not use them to raise prices; these patents could also be maintained in a pool and licensed to companies and third parties.[70] The institute would also begin discretionary sharing of its preclinical and clinical trial data. Such data sharing would reduce redundancy, allow researchers to replicate findings, assess drugs for preliminary safety concerns, and speed the development of new treatments.

Outside of this public option, patents would still play a role in the biomedical R&D toolkit, but they could be modernized to encourage innovation and public-purpose use. Public patent policy would require a paradigm shift: to receive a patent, the applicant should have to show they have invented something substantially better, thereby incentivizing true breakthroughs and promoting competition. I-MAK has found, for example, that in 2017, on average, *each* of the twelve best-selling medicines had 125 patents. Many of these are for slight variations in manufacturing processes.[71] Such "patent thickets" stifle competition and have attracted bipartisan concern in the US Congress.[72] Rather than raising barriers to generic production, policymakers need to raise the bar for patents. For such a reform to stick, patent-granting offices would need to be funded differently. Funding for the US Patent and Trademark Office, for example, is based on the number of patents it grants, which incentivizes lax patenting standards and less competitive markets.

Another area of reform would center on university licensing policies, via which private companies are often given ownership of publicly funded knowledge without public protections on future use and accessibility. Universities Allied for Essential Medicines is a group that has long fought for fair licensing rules between universities and private pharmaceutical companies, beginning with a battle to convince Yale and Bristol Myers Squibb to permit generic production of a Yale-discovered HIV/AIDS drug—a move that led to significant price reductions in sub-Saharan Africa. Efforts like this will continue to be vital, as transformative, publicly funded tools such as the gene-editing technology CRISPR are developed at universities across the world and commercialized by private companies for various health conditions and indications. A move toward "socially responsible licensing," such as the one spearheaded by Dutch university medical centers in 2019, can serve as a guide.

Equitable and Affordable Global Access

As the main buyers of medicines in the world, governments hold significant power to negotiate more affordable and equitable access to treatments. The public option would demonstrate this power in its fullest form, by protecting patents from being used in a financialized system and working with public or private corporations to offer new medicines at near the cost of production. While initially many if not most drugs would still be developed outside the public option, this strategy would bolster government efforts to negotiate better deals with industry, in part by providing a more visible role for the public sector in the value-creation process.

To improve access to key health technologies in low-income and many middle-income countries, US and European governments would need to promote and even mandate—particularly in health emergencies—the pooling of intellectual property and licensing to generic manufactures in these countries. Without this licensing, countries could be left with the option of unilaterally issuing a "compulsory license" to a generic manufacturer, which allows a government to override a patent holder's protections when there is a public interest in doing so.[73] Malaysia notably used this approach for hepatitis C, when it issued a compulsory license for sofosbuvir in 2017. This echoed Thailand's move in 2007, when authorities there rejected Merck's and Abbott's prices for antiretrovirals and instead approved generic versions from India, saving more than 50%. As observed with COVID-19 vaccines but also with hepatitis C remedies, the failure to take such measures sustains sharp inequities in access. In response to the absence of licensing for COVID-19 technologies, a promising and emergent strategy has been the creation of technology hubs in countries like South Africa and Brazil that are pursuing the development and manufacturing of vaccines and treatments.[74] While such efforts face challenges over intellectual property, their success could bolster local and regional innovation and production capacity outside North America and Europe and make technologies more widely accessible to low- and middle-income countries.

In high-income countries, value assessments like the ones performed by ICER and NICE would play an important role, since governments need to decide how best to spend their money on existing and new medicines. Yet such assessments would need to be differentiated from the "value" narrative advanced by the industry, which involves pushing the upper bounds of what governments and health systems might be compelled to pay even for diseases with large numbers of patients (as in the case of hepatitis C). Formal value assessments by public bodies would need to weigh incentives for private investments in drug development against the impacts of drug prices on public budgets and their consequences for treatment access.[75] Canada, for example, announced new policy in 2019 in which public health systems would pay for new drugs based on value-based assessments but also require discounts for additional units of drugs sold past certain thresholds of market size. This policy reduces the possibility of delays in access to treatment due to fiscal pressures for otherwise high-priced health technologies that may benefit large patient populations.[76]

Such valuation assessments could also consider the public role in the value-creation process—and potentially even the extent to which a given manufacturer engages in value-extracting activities, like share buybacks. This can create the space for more robust deliberation between governments and drug companies, leading to prices and deals that are anchored in health rather than a narrow conception of value flowing to private shareholders.

When formal assessments and negotiations fail to address an access challenge, governments should pursue alternatives. The US can take a page from the licensing strategies of low-income countries. Though the US government has not used licensing as a strategy for drug pricing reductions, representative Lloyd Doggett (D-TX) has developed legislation calling for "competitive licenses" to be issued to generic companies when pharmaceutical companies fail to negotiate affordable prices with public health systems.[77] This discursive turn is welcome particularly in the American context, given that the creation of competitive markets is an aim those of differing political orientations often share, at least rhetorically.

Finally, if public officials are not prepared to take action on drug prices or patents, then they should be prepared for the fall-out for failing to cover the price of new medicines, particularly for those that can benefit marginalized populations that rely on public insurance for access. The response chosen too often early in the story of sofosbuvir-based medicines—of restricting access based on criteria with little medical basis—injures patients and harms public health.

· · ·

In his seminal work *The Great Transformation*, the Austro-Hungarian economic historian Karl Polanyi argued that market societies comprise two opposing movements—what Polanyi scholar Fred Block calls a "*laissez-faire* movement to expand the scope of the market" and a "protective countermovement" that resists the "dis-embedding of the economy."[78,79] Laissez-faire movements defend a supposed "self-regulating market," free from the rules of public governance, in which the price mechanism automatically adjusts supply and demand. In Polanyi's analysis, such a pursuit is both dangerous and mythical, because the economy is embedded in social relations and politics—processes which depend on trust, deliberation, and contracts. "The idea of a self-adjusting market implied a stark utopia," he wrote—its existence contrary to the "human and natural substance of society."

Polanyi's insights are useful as we contemplate financialized drug development and what an adequate social response might be. Share prices and drug prices are used as metrics of efficiency, growth, and value; these are in turn used for the allocation of capital. To grease the flow of capital, the same defenders of "free markets" want governments to protect broad patent monopolies. This occurs even though public systems finance the creation of pivotal knowledge, and then are the primary buyers of high-priced medicines. Across the world, counter-movements are calling for alternative directions, in which biomedical R&D is "re-embedded" in human health and public purpose.

The politics of such efforts must consider, however, that the state—far from being outside questions of markets, drug pricing, and value—is deeply intertwined with the creation and design of the political-economic structures that shape biomedical R&D. In harkening back to the lessons of Polanyi's economic history, Block writes, "Real market societies *need* the state to play an active role. . . . It cannot be reduced to some kind of technical or administrative function."[80] The public-purpose system I have outlined in this chapter offers one possibility for such a role—a kind of blueprint some social movements are already employing in their quest for a fairer drug development system.

Conclusion

Reckoning with Pharmaceutical Value in Crisis Times

"Talking to the companies, I don't hear any of them say they think this [vaccine] is a money-maker," Francis Collins, director of the National Institutes of Health, said in a May 2020 interview with the Economic Club.[1] "I think they want to recoup their costs and maybe make a tiny percentage of increase of profit over that. . . . Nobody sees this as a way to make billions of dollars."

Yet billions of dollars were *already being made* as he was speaking, *well before* any COVID-19 vaccine had left a manufacturing plant. "Corporate Insiders Pocket $1 Billion in Rush for Coronavirus Vaccine," said a headline in the *New York Times* of July 25, 2020.[2] The story covered just a five-month span, in which company executives and investors in at least eleven companies with vaccine announcements had sold over $1 billion in shares. About a third of those sales were from three companies—Moderna, Inovio, and Vaxart—that had never successfully brought any drug or vaccine to market.

Not only were these companies making billions for their shareholders, but these financial gains all had a common source: investments by the US government—including NIH. By August 2020, US government investments alone in vaccine development, from research and clinical trials all the way into manufacturing and deployment of approved products, had topped $9 billion.[3] A risk-averse private sector, long eschewing vaccine research due to the absence of new and ongoing growth potential, was eagerly accepting billions in public finance in a race to capitalize on new patents on vaccine candidates. Though they were made possible by public investment, these vaccine candidates had become shiny new financial assets to showcase to Wall Street.

Collins's prediction of a benign pharmaceutical industry strategy relied on an almost mythologized version of capitalism valorized in textbooks. In this romantic picture, vaccines are a widget, and pharmaceutical companies are widget-makers trying to make just enough money to keep their business running. But the pharmaceutical companies in the vaccine chase, and particularly their executives and shareholders, were operating with a starkly different conception. Their pursuit of financial growth was tied to speculating on the future of their new vaccine "assets," no matter their ultimate outcome.

While drug companies were making public pronouncements about not profiteering on vaccines amid the immediate crisis, they were already positioning their vaccines as financial assets with long-term growth potential. Pfizer's chief financial officer, Frank D'Amelio, told investors, "As this shifts from pandemic to endemic, we think there's an opportunity here for us."[4] Speaking to Barclays, Moderna's president, Stephen Hoge, predicted that "post-pandemic . . . we would expect more normal pricing based on value."[5] Who would determine when the post-pandemic period would begin? Johnson & Johnson's executive vice president, Joseph Wolk, told investors: "I think when we look at it, it's not going to be something that's dictated to us."[6] By August 2021, even as the pandemic raged in many parts of the world, Pfizer and Moderna announced new price increases for COVID-19 vaccines in European countries.[7]

The anticipation of this "post-pandemic" period and the years of potential corporate control over vaccine patents were why Wall Street *did* expect companies to make billions in revenue. In fact, Pfizer and Moderna together were expected to make over $90 billion from COVID-19 vaccines—*in 2022 alone.*[8]

And whether or not these companies would realize that gain, the projection of a new vehicle for financial growth had already meant billions for traders on Wall Street. As the pandemic progressed during 2020, for example, Moderna's value had soared on the financial promise of a COVID-19 vaccine, with its share price more than quadrupling. Three of Moderna's executives—CEO, chief medical officer, and president—had made stock sales totaling over $100 million.[9]

Meanwhile, against the backdrop of massive financial accumulation, "global vaccine apartheid" became a grim outcome, as companies have acted as "gatekeepers" over vaccine assets, enforcing artificial scarcity, amid a pandemic.[10] In the first ten months that vaccines were available, over 80% of the 5.5 billion doses went to high- and upper-middle-income countries, and only 1% to low-income countries.[11] Only 2.5% of people in low-income countries on the African continent had been fully immunized.[12] And of the "donations" of two billion doses promised to poor countries, only 15% had materialized.[13] Multilateral efforts to open up access to vaccine patents through a WHO-led technology pool failed to gain momentum as companies hoarded their assets for lucrative futures and US and European governments declined to force them to share intellectual property and transfer technology to the manufacturers in low- and middle-income countries that stood ready to make mRNA vaccines.[14] Meanwhile, in an example of financialization *par excellence,* companies like Pfizer and Moderna sold highly profitable boosters to high-income territories—looking to secure immediate and ongoing growth—even as they failed to deliver first doses to the countries housing most of the world's population.[15] Scientists and public health experts warned that such inequities risked new variants and waves of preventable mortality.[16]

. . .

As these dynamics play out with terrible costs, a kind of blindness to financialization and its consequences for biomedical research and access to medicines persists. When the new sofosbuvir-based medicines for hepatitis C were launched, the crisis in treatment access was frequently billed as a result of industry price-gouging.[17] In the October 2020 hearings over rising drug prices led by the US House Committee on Oversight and Reform, the media coverage often focused on the extent to which individual companies had sought to "maximize their revenue."[18] But as the present account demonstrates, the crises we face are not just about maximizing revenue but about the wider system of financialization. In this system, companies have been repeatedly incentivized by public policy to use collectively developed knowledge to maximize *growth* and thus *shareholder value*. The tale of the hepatitis C medicines and the broader debate over drug affordability are emblematic less of an isolated crisis of drug pricing and more of intersecting and structural crises in contemporary political economy.

COVID-19 has only served to further crystallize these connected maladies in our political and economic order: "shareholder value" ideology, political capture by corporate and financial interests, and governments failing to respond to accelerating precarity. Even amid a public health crisis, pharmaceutical companies continued to raise the prices of hundreds of medicines.[19] Even amid record unemployment and growing hunger, stock markets soared to new heights.[20] Increasingly, life and health seemed to be not just *uncoupled* from conventional stock market metrics, but *inversely related* to them.[21]

But as the pandemic exacerbated and exposed these pre-existing conditions for suffering and inequity, it also forced a reckoning. The *Financial Times*'s editorial board declared, "Virus lays bare the frailty of our social contract."[22] In the *New York Times* of October 8, 2020, Mariana Mazzucato's opinion piece ran under the headline, "Capitalism is Broken. The Fix Begins with a Free Covid-19 Vaccine."[23] And in a widely circulated piece, author Arundhati Roy challenged readers to think in radically new ways: "Historically, pandemics have forced humans to break with the past and imagine their world anew. This one is no different. It is a portal, a gateway between one world and the next."[24] When it comes to making and deploying the fruits of modern science, might we indeed be at the gateway to a different kind of system?

In weighing this possibility, we can look to prior economic transitions for hopeful evidence. Through her seminal work in mapping the history of capitalism and technological change, the economist Carlota Perez has found patterns that may be instructive for our time. From the first Industrial Revolution, in the eighteenth century, she argues, financial capital has played a dominant role in every technological "epoch," which she defines as distinct "techno-economic" phases of capitalism (e.g., steam and railways, steel and heavy engineering, oil and automobiles, information and communication technologies). In the initial frenzy of a new technological paradigm (the "installation period"), financial speculation and laissez-faire markets push the economy to crisis. The railway boom, for example, was followed by financial panics in the mid-nineteenth century. The rise of the automobile, oil, and mass production in the 1900s into the 1920s was followed by the Great Depression.

But each period of crisis, Perez shows, provoked a societal response, whereby the technological possibilities of the time were rebalanced toward the concerns of the public rather than those of financial capital.[25] In this "deployment period," as in the Progressive Era and the New Deal, governments took a leading role in creating the social and economic conditions for investment that expanded access to and use of new technologies to more broadly improve standards of living. To be sure, these periods were often built on the exclusion and exploitation of others, via colonialism and structural racism, globally and in the United States. And yet these periods marked a significant—though vastly incomplete—expansion in the rewards of new technologies flowing beyond financial capitalists and instead to workers and families.

These "golden ages" did not come about via some automatic circuit breaker for capitalism; they required concerted efforts by political leaders, citizens, and social movements to make new sociopolitical choices. This latest technological era, marked by major advances in digital and genomic technologies since the 1970s, has led to a burgeoning set of hopes and possibilities. Yet it has also had its paroxysms of financial frenzy and political crisis, from the dot-com boom and crash to the global financial meltdown of 2007–08, and now the COVID-19 pandemic. In the specific domain of health, financialized capitalism has pushed the hybrid public–private system of biomedical research to a point of popular discontent and distrust—a reaction to ever-higher drug prices and ever-greater wealth extraction.[26] Science promises a golden age for health; yet our economic system taints this promise, and at its worst, places it at grave risk.

. . .

A transition to a public-purpose system is far from inevitable. Powerful people will try to protect and expand their interests. In a "status quo" scenario, a muddle of incremental reforms, with some perhaps aimed at bolstering public health systems' ability to negotiate with drug companies, will struggle against the political sway of industry lobbying. The broader financialized system of drug development—including a reliance on short-term, extractive financial actors and broad patent protections—will remain dominant. Health systems, clinicians, and patients will struggle perpetually with drug companies for access to the occasional new breakthrough, as escalating prices, justified in terms of "value," force care providers and policymakers to decide who should get such therapies first.

In a world where biomedical research becomes further intertwined with the dynamics of financialization, yet another scenario lurks: the mortgage model. Payment for new breakthroughs, in this case, would not be limited by a health system's finite budget but would be facilitated by access to loans, akin to buying a home. Through what a group of "financial engineers" at MIT have proposed as "health care loans" for curative medicines, patients—either through health insurance plans or individually—would gain access to treatments with a down payment, and then pay monthly or annual installments on the total cost (with interest) over some number of years.[27] The cost of cures, anticipated to be in the hundreds of thousands or even millions of dollars in this scenario, would be amortized over many years, with diversified pools of such loans "securitized" into financial products that can attract further capital—similar to the products that were at the heart of the 2008–2009 global financial crisis.

Yet literally mortgaging our future health in this way would represent a different form of rationing, with deeply unfair consequences. If the housing mortgage market is a troubling presage, patients' access to medicines would depend on their ability to qualify for a loan and thus potentially place specific patient groups at systematic disadvantage due to racial and socioeconomic factors. These new healthcare loans would only add to the long list of debts that have increasingly placed families and patients in crisis. Even the authors of the piece admit that "a law mandating full coverage for curative therapies and allowing for price negotiation would likely be economically more efficient, more sustainable, and socially more acceptable than a purely private-sector solution."[28]

In writing these words, they understand what has become increasingly apparent: the status quo—or worse, deepened financialization—will only trigger more widespread and popular momentum for alternative directions. Though no single law can be a silver bullet, a series of trials and changes—from large-scale public financing to laws underpinning a democratic reshaping of our economic systems—has the potential to produce a future that is more popular, more innovative, and more just. This final scenario of a public-purpose system, as detailed in chapter 4, is one within our reach. Just as in previous periods of crisis, it now falls to a new generation of scientists, business leaders, public officials, and civic entrepreneurs to forge this transition.

. . .

Underlying whichever scenarios come to fruition will ultimately be a social struggle over what we value most. When health systems refused to pay the prices for sofosbuvir-based medicines, patients with hepatitis C reasonably wondered why their lives were not worth the price tag. The director of a hepatitis C patient group told me that public officials did not really value the lives of the patients he had come to know. Though appalled by the scale of drug-company profits, he had become resigned to the idea that, with patients' lives at stake, society should be willing to pay the $90,000 price tag for a cure.

His wish speaks to the palpable desire to do whatever it takes for our health and the health of those we love. Restricting access to essential treatment is certainly not the answer to high prices. Health is a fundamental need. Yet it is precisely this vulnerability that can be exploited. And this exploitation illuminates the moral crisis at the heart of ever-higher drug prices. The question we are too often forced to answer—What is the maximum price society should be willing to pay to drug companies?—is the wrong one. This question treats extractive prices as natural and inevitable—when instead they are products of human-made systems that can be changed.

Indeed, our vital and shared need for health should urge us to answer and act on a question focused on a different orientation to value. Instead of capitalizing our vulnerability in search of the upper bounds of drug prices, how might we value equitable and affordable care for everyone, ensuring access to the medicines we have, and the ones we need? A moral imagination in pursuit of this question might yet yield the kind of future we deserve.

Acknowledgments

The research and writing behind this book were accompanied by large and humbling doses of support and encouragement. My journey with what became *Capitalizing a Cure* has lasted almost a decade—during which time I completed my doctoral training in sociology, medical school, and medical residency. By virtue of this circuitous process, my path intersected with many forms of inspiration and care to which I will be forever grateful.

The key object at the heart of this book—sofosbuvir-based medicines—would not be possible without the collective scientific labors of dozens of scientists and organizations carried out over decades. While I critique the economic arrangements that dominate contemporary biomedical research, I do so with the understanding that so many of the scientists I met want their individual labor to be used more assertively for social goals that advance health. This book carries their spirit with it.

I am deeply indebted to the doctors, health workers, and patients who let me into their lives to understand the lived experience of hepatitis C and the bureaucratic hurdles and moral questions brought forth by the pricing of new antivirals. As my research brought me into the worlds of Wall Street, corporate finance, and a US Senate investigation, their experiences served as an ongoing reminder of what was at stake.

In reflecting on these stakes, the work of the access-to-medicines movement taught me that the unequal rationing of medicines is not a natural given but the product of social forces that can be investigated, reimagined, and changed. Their abundant lessons—particularly amid the struggle over antiretrovirals for

HIV/AIDS—served as the larger context within which a book like mine could be written.

Producing a doctoral thesis required mentorship and accompaniment of various kinds. To my doctoral advisor, Lawrence King, I am grateful for many conversations and guidance on where to take the project, and for your reading and feedback of my work. Thank you also to my two examiners, Stuart Hogarth and Mariana Mazzucato, who took the time to thoroughly review my dissertation, engage with my ideas, and offer thoughtful comments during my viva. Stephen Kissler spent many afternoons and weekends outside his doctoral projects to build a Markov model that helped me understand the public health implications of treatment access for hepatitis C. Conversations with Trenholme Junghans were filled with ethnographic and anthropological insights within a spirit of friendship. To Brian Hanson, Jeff Richardson, and Art Winter, thank you for nurturing my sense of possibility at so many points in the past fifteen years, and modeling humility and grounded purpose in all you do. I also thank Beth Pardoe for encouraging me to apply for fellowships as an undergraduate at Northwestern, helping me find my voice, and in the process opening doors that have opened so many others.

In pursuing this path, my time at the University of Cambridge as a graduate student was pivotal, most of all for the community of relationships that I found there. Thank you to my Cambridge community as I navigated the dissertation process, and particularly to Isaac, Tara, Andrew, Ben, Julien, Andrea, Pete, Reid and Geo—our friendships made a medieval town feel like home. Tara, thank you especially for your generous guidance and care at critical moments in the process—from believing the project could be a book in the first place, to helping the manuscript get across the finish line. Simon, thank you for being my brother from Australia, always with wisdom when I need it. As I traveled back and forth from Cambridge to the US to pursue research, I was buoyed by Ankur, Pedro, Lindsay, Prajwal, Naman, Evan, Peter, Jon, Lauren, Bianca, Iram, and Brian—you all celebrated milestones with me, reflected together across time zones, and allowed me to crash on your couches.

I am appreciative of several organizations that provided support in many forms. For my summer in New York, the Paul & Daisy Soros Fellowships team offered me a welcoming home to jump-start my project. Northwestern's Feinberg School of Medicine—particularly Dr. Marianne Green's belief and mentorship—provided me with the security of knowing that I had a place to resume my clinical training even as my research took me on a winding journey. University College London's Institute for Innovation and Public Purpose, through Dr. Mariana Mazzucato's guidance and vision, enriched my post-doctoral path by offering a dynamic intellectual home as I pursued my clinical training. I thank Henry Lishi Li for helping me stay connected to it. Thank you also to Boston University's Department of Family Medicine, particularly Katherine Gergen Barnett and Suki Tepperberg, for trusting and encouraging me as I worked on revising my manuscript amid the rigors of residency. Along the way, King's College provided the funding to share my research and build relationships with peers. Grants from the University of Cambridge's Department of Sociology allowed me to pursue my research wherever it took me, from capitols, to corporate headquarters, to clinics. Finally, the Gates Cambridge Trust granted the belief and support that made it possible to come to Cambridge and begin this work. The values at the heart of this scholarship community—of building leadership committed to the lives of others—will continue to steer my future.

I am deeply grateful for the organization and people who helped turn my writing into a book—thank you to Naomi Schneider at the University of California Press for believing in this project, and to Summer Farah for accompanying the manuscript through the production process. Two academic peer reviewers and the faculty editorial board at the University of California Press provided thoughtful reflections and feedback on the manuscript. Barune Thape's crucial reading and revisions pushed my writing from a draft to a completed manuscript.

For reading the drafts of each of my chapters with close attention, for being a partner in dreaming, and for believing in me: thank you, M. To my family—my parents and my sister, Tina—I could not have walked this path without your unconditional love and support at every turn. Finally, I dedicate this path to my maternal grandfather, Dadu, who saw me off in India as I began my time at Cambridge, and whose memory and example as a physician and healer for over six decades in rural West Bengal will continue to remind me of what really matters for my patients.

Overview of Data Sources

The data for this sociological account of sofosbuvir's pricing and valuation dynamics came from several types of sources: documentary content (including scientific and medical journals, media accounts, organizational reports and websites, earnings-call transcripts, and a major US Senate investigative report), key funding and financial databases, semi-structured interviews, and observation at meetings. These were supplemented by secondary sources of published data relevant to my research questions. All the sources used in the account are cited directly in chapters 1, 2 and 3.

SCIENTIFIC, MEDICAL, AND HEALTH POLICY JOURNALS

To develop a timeline of milestones in science, drug development, and hepatitis C policy, I searched for journal articles from 1989 (the published identification of the hepatitis C virus) to 2018 (four years into the treatment access period) in the Web of Science and PubMed databases. I also used the archives of the *New England Journal of Medicine, Lancet, Hepatology, JAMA, Annals of Internal Medicine,* and *Health Affairs.* To narrow my search, I used highly cited scientific and historical review articles to construct the backbone of my timeline.

MEDIA ACCOUNTS

I searched for media accounts that documented the actors and events in the drug development process, focusing on replicon development as well as on Pharmasset and Gilead Sciences. I used LexisNexis to search for media accounts between 1997 and 2014 (which covered the key period of hepatitis C drug development). I also identified news stories in the *New York Times, Bloomberg, Financial Times,* and *Wall Street Journal,* as well as the industry-specific *FierceBiotech* and *STAT* between 2014 and 2020 to follow the ensuing struggle over treatment access and financial-sector reaction to Gilead's strategy.

ORGANIZATIONAL REPORTS AND WEBSITES

To build detailed organizational timelines, I used the SEC's EDGAR database to gather Pharmasset's and Gilead's annual financial (10-K) reports. I studied each of Pharmasset's reports from its 2006 IPO to Gilead's acquisition in 2011; and I reviewed Gilead's 10-K filings from 2007 to 2016. I also used the Wayback Machine, an internet archive, to access Pharmasset's website, which provided a timeline of key early events and public and private funding announcements that preceded their SEC filings. I also searched Apath's website to identify key milestones and sources of funding. To study global treatment access outcomes, I studied World Health Organization reports, in particular 2016 and 2018 progress reports, which provided country-by-country information.

US SENATE INVESTIGATION

The Senate Finance committee released both a summary report and appendixes reproducing over 1,500 pages of internal documents from Gilead Sciences and Pharmasset, including board meeting minutes, strategic plans, and internal corporate forecasts. I reviewed all of this. The report and appendixes also detailed Gilead's internal deliberations over how to price sofosbuvir-based treatments.

EARNINGS-CALL TRANSCRIPTS

To further analyze the relationship between Gilead and the financial sector, I reviewed transcripts of earnings calls between Gilead Sciences and Wall Street analysts from the third quarter of 2013 to the first quarter of 2017—that is, from right before the approval of sofosbuvir to well into the launch of the therapies and the ensuing political struggle over pricing. I used the S&P Capital IQ database and the Seeking Alpha website to gather these transcripts.

GOVERNMENT AND PRIVATE FINANCIAL DATABASES

To identify public funding amounts, I used NIH's RePORTER database to search for grants that were linked to the key technological and organizational developments behind sofosbuvir-based treatments, such as the discovery of the replicon, nucleoside research, and the emergence of Pharmasset. To supplement private financial data gleaned from SEC filings, I also used the S&P Capital IQ database, which included key corporate milestones and financial data in an easily accessible format. Finally, to understand the evolution of Gilead's lobbying efforts toward the US federal government, I searched the Open Secrets database from 2006 to 2016.

INTERVIEWS

I interviewed forty-one individuals, including hepatitis C scientists, venture capitalists, corporate executives, physicians, civil society leaders, and health policy experts involved in the sofosbuvir case. Because I did not use any direct quotes from those interviews in this book, I do not name them here (see the introduction for further explanation). My interviews were primarily useful for triangulating and corroborating other sources of data and sharpening my focus on specific events and episodes in the timeline, such as Gilead's acquisition of Pharmasset.

OBSERVATION OF PUBLIC MEETINGS

I observed nine policy and industry meetings—six in person and three online—during and after which I prepared field notes. These meetings allowed me to identify individuals and organizations for interviews, understand how debates over drug pricing and value were unfolding, and track developments in hepatitis C and drug pricing policy. Of these meetings, the three I cite are HEP DART (December 6–10, 2015), a scientific meeting on viral hepatitis organized by Ray Schinazi, founder of Pharmasset; a Brookings Institute forum, "The Cost and Value of Biomedical Innovation" (October 1, 2014), featuring Gilead's COO and leading health policy experts; and the National Viral Hepatitis Roundtable's World Hepatitis Day meeting (July 29, 2015), involving public health officials and physicians.

SECONDARY STUDIES

To supplement the data listed above, I also incorporated the findings of other researchers studying sofosbuvir and Gilead Sciences. Four studies were particularly useful. First, I reviewed a study by Harvard's PORTAL (Program on Regulation, Therapeutics, and Law) that identified all the traceable public funding behind sofosbuvir (Barenie et al. 2020). Second, I examined an analysis by Americans for Tax Fairness, an advocacy group, that was peer reviewed by a member of

PORTAL and showed the scale of Gilead's use of loopholes to avoid taxation (Rice and Clemente 2016). Third, I reviewed a study by the Boston Consulting Group of *all* hepatitis C drug development projects using private databases (Calcoen et al. 2015). Fourth, I reviewed a Harvard Business School case study on Gilead Sciences, which provided helpful historical context for the company's evolution as well as global access programs (Rangan and Lee 2009).

NOTES

PREFACE: PANDEMICS, WALL STREET, AND THE VALUE PLAYBOOK

1. Day (2020).
2. Luo, Gonsalves, and Kapczynski (2020).
3. Herper (2020).
4. Maybarduk (2020).
5. Quoted in Herper (2020).
6. O'Day (2020).
7. Armental and Walker (2020).
8. Quoted in O'Brien (2020).
9. Garthwaite (2020).
10. Roy and King (2016b).
11. Quoted in Liu (2020).

INTRODUCTION: THE POLITICS OF DRUG PRICING AND THE VALUE OF A CURE

1. Quoted in Barrett and Langreth (2015).
2. Quoted in Beckert (2011: 2).
3. Edlin et al. (2015); Hagan and Schinazi (2013).
4. Rosen (2011).
5. Rosen (2011).
6. Edlin et al. (2015); World Health Organization (2018).
7. Loftus (2015).
8. Hill et al. (2014).
9. Sanger-Katz (2014).

10. Canary, Klevens, and Holmberg (2015).

11. Neuman, Cubanski, and Hoadley (2014); Roehrig (2016).

12. Loftus (2014).

13. National Viral Hepatitis Roundtable (2015).

14. Reid (2015, 2016).

15. Barrett and Langreth (2015).

16. Barrett and Langreth (2015).

17. Gilead Sciences (2017).

18. Feugras and Ross (2014).

19. Gabble and Kohler (2014).

20. Kaiser Family Foundation (2020).

21. Post and BP-Weeks (2020).

22. Vey and Blamont (2016).

23. Nik-Khah (2014).

24. DiMasi, Grabowski, and Hansen (2016); DiMasi, Hansen, and Grabowski (2003); DiMasi et al. (1991).

25. Biagioli (2006).

26. Light and Warburton (2011).

27. Gregson et al. (2005).

28. Claxton et al. (2008); McCabe, Claxton, and Culyer (2008).

29. Bach and Pearson (2015); Pearson and Rawlins (2005).

30. Neumann, Cohen, and Ollendorf (2021); Saltzman (2019).

31. Zirkelbach (2015).

32. Kliff (2014).

33. Baker (2019).

34. World Medical Association (2020).

35. Leston and Finkbonner (2016).

36. Glabau (2016).

37. US Senate Committee on Finance (2015). To be sure, this investigation produced important insights into the pricing process that I use in this book. But the headline was less revealing.

38. "Frontiers in Drug Development for Hepatology" (2015).

39. Angell (2004).

40. Goozner (2005).

41. Sachs (2015).

42. Roy and King (2016b).

43. Alton (2016).

44. Roy and King (2016a).

45. Davis (2009); Krippner (2011); Lazonick (2015); van der Zwan (2014).

46. Schumpeter (1939, 1942).

47. Lazonick and O'Sullivan (2010).

48. Krippner (2011).

49. van der Zwan (2014).

50. Leyshon and Thrift (2007).

51. Davis (2009); Lazonick et al. (2016).

52. Davis (2009).
53. Faroohar (2016: 155).
54. Pisano (2006).
55. Lazonick and Tulum (2011); Lazonick et al. (2016); Montalban and Sakinc (2013).
56. Andersson et al. (2010); Birch (2016); Gleadle et al. (2014); Hopkins et al. (2007); Lazonick and Tulum (2011).
57. McCorvey (2015).
58. Gagnon (2016); Veblen (1908a, 1908b).
59. Birch (2016); Cochrane (2011); Nitzan and Bichler (2009); Veblen (1908b).
60. Cochrane (2011); Veblen (1908b).
61. Lazonick and Mazzucato (2013: 1097).
62. Knight (1921); see also Mazzucato (2013a, 2013b).
63. Vallas, Kleinman, and Biscotti (2011).
64. Freeman (1995).
65. Mazzucato (2013b).
66. Mazzucato (2013b).
67. Veblen (1908b).
68. Birch (2017); Birch and Muniesa (2020).
69. Nayak (2021).
70. Birch and Tyfield (2013).
71. My book chapter "The Crisis of Cures: Tracing Assetization and Value in Biomedical Innovation" (Roy 2020) describes why studying assets is particularly important when considering curative medicines that may diminish the potential for future revenue growth. While I prefer the term *financialization* for my broader political economy analysis of drug pricing in this book, I draw on theories of assets and assetization throughout this book.
72. Birch (2016); Muniesa (2011); Veblen (1908b).
73. Muniesa (2011); Nitzan and Bichler (2009).
74. Cochrane (2011); Nitzan and Bichler (2009).
75. Sunder Rajan (2017).
76. Beckert (2014).
77. Cochrane (2011); Gagnon (2016); Nitzan and Bichler (2009).
78. Nitzan and Bichler (2009).
79. Sunder Rajan (2017).
80. Galbraith (1993).
81. Goldstein (2015).
82. Mauss (1985).
83. Mazzucato (2018: 6).
84. Stark (2000).
85. Dumit (2012b: 51).

1. CAPITALIZING SCIENCE: PUBLIC KNOWLEDGE INTO PHARMACEUTICAL ASSETS

1. Quoted in Henderson and Schrage (1984).
2. Leyshon and Thrift (2007).

3. Alter et al. (1975).

4. Hoofnagle and Alter (1985).

5. Alter (2013).

6. Alter et al. (1989).

7. Blood banks were screened for the hepatitis C virus soon after its discovery and identification in 1989, significantly reducing transfusion-related transmission (Alter 2013).

8. Lindenbach and Rice (2005).

9. Ago et al. (1999); Kim et al. (1996); Lesburg et al. (1999); and Love et al. (1996) are the key papers on these subunits, citing work done at Japan Tobacco, Vertex Pharmaceuticals, Schering Plough, and Agouron Pharmaceuticals.

10. Pollack (2003).

11. Lindenbach and Rice (2005).

12. Bartenschlager's (2002) replicon research was funded by the German Ministry for Research and Technology (renamed the Federal Ministry for Education and Research in 1998) and the German Research Society.

13. Lohmann (1999).

14. Cohen (1999).

15. Quoted in Cohen (1999: 29).

16. Lohmann (1999).

17. Quoted in Nair (2011: 8452).

18. Blight, Kolykhalov, and Rice (2000).

19. Fenz (2020); Kolykhalov, Feinstone, and Rice (1996).

20. Bush (1945: 8–9).

21. Harden (2008); NIH (2017a).

22. Slaughter and Rhoades (1996).

23. Hoofnagle et al. (1986).

24. National Institutes of Health (2017a).

25. National Institutes of Health (2016).

26. Barenie et al. (2020).

27. Blight, Kolykhalov, and Rice (2000).

28. Blight, Kolykhalov, and Rice (2000); Nair (2011).

29. Marshall (2000).

30. Quoted in Marshall (2000).

31. Robbins (2016).

32. Apath (2016).

33. Marshall (2000).

34. Ceulemans and Kolls (2013); Keller and Block (2013).

35. Keller and Block (2013); Slaughter and Rhoades (1996).

36. SBIR-STTR (2016).

37. Keller and Block (2013).

38. SBIR-STTR (2016).

39. SBIR-STTR (2016).

40. Over a longer period, from 1999 to 2008, Apath received over $9 million in federal funding from the National Institutes of Health SBIR program, with funding for research across antiviral science (Apath 2016), National Institutes of Health (2015).

41. Blight, Kolykhalov, and Rice (2000).
42. Quoted in Blight, Kolykhalov, and Rice (2000).
43. Quoted in Pollack (2003).
44. Pharmasset (2009).
45. Barenie et al. (2020).
46. Mazzucato (2013b).
47. Mazzucato (2016).
48. The replicon technology was expanded to include multiple subtypes (called "geno-types") of the hepatitis C virus, such that drug developers could test compounds on all the variations of the virus which infect patients (Bartenschlager 2002; Blight et al. 2003; Horscroft et al. 2005).
49. Bartenschlager, Rice, and Sofia (2016).
50. Fenz (2020).
51. Quoted in Berkrot (2011).
52. De Clercq (2005).
53. Cohen (2015).
54. Cohen (2015).
55. Hays (2010).
56. Emory University (2016).
57. Veterans Affairs (2015).
58. National Institutes of Health (2017b).
59. Love (2014).
60. Cohen (2015).
61. Cohen (2015).
62. For more on the legal challenges around HIV nucleoside science out of which Pharmasset grew, see Bourgeron and Geiger (2022).
63. Robbins (1999).
64. Barenie et al. (2020).
65. Keller and Block (2013) argue that this is a striking figure, given that SBIR represents only 2.5% of all federal extramural research and development funding and is rarely cited as an important source of funding for biotechnology development. "The relationship between SBIR and VC is permeated by multiple logics in which venture capitalists use SBIR as a signaling and certification mechanism—investing in ideas developed through the program—and that they also use the program to develop ideas they already find promising" (645).
66. Pharmasset (2002).
67. Robbins (1999).
68. Robbins (1999).
69. Among these changes were the 1980 Supreme Court ruling in *Diamond v. Chakrabarty* that allowed genes to be patented; the Stephenson-Wydler Technology Innovation Act of 1980, which required federal agencies to engage in technology-transfer activities with private entities; and the Orphan Drug Act of 1983, which provided government support to companies for development of drugs for rare and genetic diseases (Slaughter and Rhoades 1996).
70. Rai and Eisenberg (2003).
71. Robertson (2015).

72. Mowery and Sampat (2004).

73. Mowery et al. (2001).

74. Cohen (2015).

75. Cohen (2015).

76. Emory University (2005).

77. Berkrot (2011).

78. Jasanoff (2011).

79. Pisano (2006).

80. Block and Keller (2008: 6).

81. Kesselheim (2011); Rai and Eisenberg (2003).

82. Maloney et al. (2010).

83. Krishtel (2019).

84. Emory University (2012).

85. Pisano (2006).

86. Furman, Otto, and Sofia (2011); Gounder (2013); Sofia, Furman, and Symonds (2010).

87. Sofia, Furman, and Symonds (2010).

88. Sofia, Furman, and Symonds (2010).

89. Sofia, Furman, and Symonds(2010).

90. Bartenschlager, Rice, and Sofia (2016).

91. McGuigan, Gilles, and Madela (2010); Perrone, Luoni, and Kelleher (2007).

92. Gounder (2013).

93. Balzarini et al. (1996); McGuigan, Cahard, and Sheeka (1996); Mehellou, Balzarini, and McGuigan (2009).

94. McGuigan, Gilles, and Madela (2010).

95. McGuigan et al. (1992).

96. McGuigan, Cahard, and Sheeka (1996); Siddiqui et al. (1999). The public funding sources named were the AIDS Directed Programme of the MRC, the Biomedical Research Programme and the Human Capital and Mobility Programme of the European Commission, the Belgian Geconcerteerde Onderzoeksacties, and the Belgian Natinoaal Fonds voor Wetenschlappelijk Onderzoek.

97. Cardiff University (2014).

98. Sofia, Furman, and Symonds (2010).

99. Bartenschlager, Rice, and Sofia (2016); Sofia, Furman, and Symonds (2010).

100. Roche, Merck, and AbbVie would all later sue Gilead over sofosbuvir's patents for different infringement claims.

101. Bourgeron and Geiger (2022).

102. Gilead Sciences, Inc. v. Merck & Co., Inc. (2016).

103. Cardiff University (2014).

104. Chung (2021).

105. Zeller (2007: 92).

106. World Health Organization (2016b).

107. Pharmasset (2009).

108. I use the term *speculative* to refer to the short-term and exit-oriented nature of these forms of capital. This contrasts with more *patient capital*, which is oriented toward long-term investment, performance measured by creditworthiness rather than share price,

and likelihood of maintaining investment (rather than exit) in adverse firm conditions. See Deeg and Hardie (2016) for more on patient capital.

109. Cohen (1999).

110. Broder (2010) tells the story of NIH's collaboration with Burroughs-Wellcome, now Glaxo-Smithkline (GSK), to develop the first antiretrovirals for HIV/AIDS. See also chapter 6 in Goozner (2005).

111. Groopman (1998).

112. Hopkins, Crane, and Nightingale (2013); Robbins-Roth (2001).

113. Robbins-Roth (2001).

114. Pharmasset (2006).

115. Rai and Eisenberg (2003).

116. On July 23, 1979, the Department of Labor amended a rule—the Employment Retirement Income Security Act of 1974's (ERISA) "prudent man rule"—that had prevented pension funds from investing substantial sums in venture capital funds or other "high-risk" asset classes (Gompers 1994).

117. Gompers (1994).

118. Gompers (1994).

119. Rudden (2019).

120. Robbins-Roth (2001).

121. Robbins-Roth (2001).

122. Clark vs. Schinazi, Emory University, Atlanta VA Medical Center (2010).

123. Furman, Otto, and Sofia (2011).

124. Pisano (2006).

125. PR Newswire (2004).

126. Heim (2013).

127. US Senate Committee on Finance (2015).

128. Pharmasset (2006).

129. Pharmasset (2009).

130. Pharmasset (2011).

131. Robbins-Roth (2001).

132. Reuters (2007).

133. Pharmasset (2006, 2010); Reuters (2007).

134. S&P Capital IQ (2016b).

135. Pharmasset (2011).

136. Carroll (2011); Feuerstein and Herper (2020).

137. Lazonick and Mazzucato (2013).

138. Lazonick and Mazzucato (2013).

139. Pharmasset (2006).

140. Beckert (2013).

141. Powell et al. (2001).

142. Lerner and Willinge (2011).

143. Robbins-Roth (2001).

144. Evnin (2014).

145. Lerner and Willinge (2011).

146. Evnin (2014).

147. Lazonick (2017).
148. Andersson et al. (2010); Hopkins, Crane, and Nightingale (2013).
149. Booth and Salehizadeh (2012).
150. Pisano (2006).
151. Beckert (2013).
152. Garber (2011); Heim (2013: 20).
153. Vernaz et al. (2016).
154. Pharmasset (2006, 2010, 2011).
155. Baum et al. (2010); Blackburn (2006); Ozmel, Robinson, and Stuart (2013).
156. Sofia, Furman, and Symonds (2010).
157. Garber (2011).
158. Flinn (2011).
159. Flinn (2011).
160. US Senate Committee on Finance (2015).
161. US Senate Committee on Finance (2015).

2. CAPITALIZING DRUGS: SHAREHOLDER POWER AND THE CANNIBALIZING COMPANY

1. Mirowski (2012).
2. Quoted in Berkrot (2011).
3. Pollack (2011).
4. Quoted in Pollack (2010).
5. Quoted in Knight (2013).
6. Jannarone (2011).
7. US Senate Committee on Finance (2015).
8. Brown (1997).
9. Riordan (1992).
10. Chandran et al. (2014).
11. Brown (1997).
12. Brown (1997).
13. Gilead Sciences (2014).
14. Gellene (2002).
15. Cohen (2015).
16. Rangan and Lee (2009).
17. Rangan and Lee (2009).
18. Gilead Sciences (2012).
19. Y Charts (2010).
20. Lazonick and O'Sullivan (2010).
21. Lazonick (2017).
22. Dodd (1932).
23. Davis (2009); Lazonick and O'Sullivan (2010).
24. Davis (2009); Lazonick and O'Sullivan (2010).
25. Fama and Jensen (1983).
26. This approach was also seen as resolving a principal–agent problem, in which managers (agents) were thought to have no incentive to return value to shareholders (principals)

and could thus pursue inefficient or management-enriching strategies at the expense of economic efficiency (Jensen and Meckling 1976).

27. Jensen (1986); Manne (1965).

28. Faroohar (2016); Lazonick and O'Sullivan (2010).

29. Davis (2009).

30. Davis (2009).

31. Damodaran (2017) estimates the cost of capital across US sectors using multiple data sets, arriving at 7.58% for established pharmaceutical companies and 9.25% annually for smaller biotechnology companies. Using a different method, Sunder Rajan (2012) notes a slightly higher expected growth rate of about 13% annually, with a realized growth rate typically in the 8–10% range.

32. Barton (2011).

33. Sunder Rajan (2012).

34. Rate of profitability is equal to net income divided by total revenue. See Gilead Sciences (2012) for financial data.

35. Gilead Sciences (2012).

36. Sunder Rajan (2017).

37. Rangan and Lee (2009).

38. Chandran et al. (2014).

39. S&P Capital IQ (2016a).

40. US Senate Committee on Finance (2015).

41. Jannarone (2011).

42. Seeking Alpha (2015).

43. Baum et al. (2010).

44. Terry and Lesser (2015).

45. Ha et al. (2011); Jannarone (2011).

46. Jannarone (2011).

47. Gilead Sciences (2010); Werth (2014).

48. US Senate Committee on Finance (2015).

49. US Senate Committee on Finance (2015).

50. This net present value thus represents the future stream of earnings less what a business would need to spend to gain control over this stream (Muniesa 2011).

51. Muniesa (2014).

52. US Senate Committee on Finance (2015).

53. Nitzan and Bichler (2009).

54. US Senate Committee on Finance (2015: 1000).

55. Chon (2016).

56. US Senate Committee on Finance (2015: 21).

57. Morgan (2018); OpenSecrets (2021).

58. US Senate Committee on Finance (2015: 1037).

59. Gilead Sciences (2012); S&P Capital IQ (2011, 2013).

60. Rode (2011).

61. Petersen (2016a); Pund, Lefert, and Bowes (2017).

62. Birch (2017).

63. Carroll (2011); Pharmasset (2011).

64. Pharmasset (2011).

65. Pollack and de la Merced (2011).

66. Ha et al. (2011); Krauskopf and Basu (2011); Winslow and Loftus (2011).

67. Swan (2014).

68. Quoted in Tirrell and Lachapelle (2011).

69. de la Merced (2012).

70. This escalation in speculative betting exposes one of the perils of financialized drug development: for the large companies pursuing acquisitions, the bets can sometimes be all or nothing. Just eight months after their acquisition, for example, BMS would end its hepatitis C development after a patient taking INX-89 died in phase III trials.

71. Pollack (2014a).

72. Pharmasset (2011).

73. Berkrot (2011).

74. de la Merced (2011); He et al. (2016); Krauskopf and Basu (2011); Winslow and Loftus (2011).

75. Jannarone (2011).

76. Pharmasset's founder, Ray Schinazi, summed up this view of technical and financial risk when he said to a journalist: "They [Gilead] could have had the company for $300 million or less in 2004. Somebody made a huge mistake. . . . Now they paid the premium. Of course, now the risk has been reduced significantly" (Berkrot 2011).

77. S&P Capital IQ (2011).

78. Lazonick (2017: 10).

79. Lazonick (2017: 10).

80. US Senate Committee on Finance (2015).

81. Afdhal, Reddy, et al. (2014); Afdhal, Zeuzem, et al. (2014); Jacobson et al. (2013); Lawitz et al. (2013).

82. Pollack (2014b).

83. Gilead Sciences (2017).

84. Gilead Sciences (2017).

85. Gross profit is total revenues minus the cost of goods sold (primarily the manufacturing and production costs of Gilead's medicines). I cite this figure here as it represents the total sum with which Gilead's senior leadership then made capital allocation decisions.

86. This figure includes a category of finance known as "marketable securities," which are liquid assets, such as stocks and bonds, that can be turned into cash in the market and used as capital by corporations.

87. Gilead Sciences (2017).

88. Of this total, $6.3 billion was dividends and the $26.3 billion was buybacks. Gilead began to offer dividends in the second quarter of 2015 (Gilead Sciences 2017).

89. Gilead Sciences (2017).

90. General operating expenses as well as taxes account for the remaining use of the gross profits.

91. This 86% figure represents $32.4 billion in additional cash and $32.6 billion in buybacks and dividends (for a total of $65 billion), divided by $75.9 billion in gross profits. For context, the annual budget for all of NIH hovered around $30 billion in this period (National Institutes of Health 2017a).

92. S&P Capital IQ (2015).

93. Mazzucato, Ryan-Collins, and Gouzoulis (2020).

94. Mazzucato et al. (2021).

95. Zeller (2007).

96. Birch (2019: 12).

97. Brettell, Gaffen, and Rohde (2015).

98. Gilead Sciences (2017).

99. Ezekoye, Koller, and Mittal (2016).

100. Ezekoye, Koller, and Mittal (2016).

101. Lazonick (2015).

102. Lazonick (2015).

103. Gerth (1981).

104. Lazonick (2015).

105. Lazonick and O'Sullivan (2010).

106. Lazonick (2017: 3).

107. Lazonick (2015).

108. Lazonick and Hopkins (2016).

109. Gilead Sciences (2017).

110. Gilead Sciences (2017).

111. S&P Capital IQ (2013).

112. S&P Capital IQ (2013).

113. Rice and Clemente (2016).

114. Rice and Clemente (2016).

115. Rice and Clemente (2016).

116. Kocieniewski (2016).

117. Heath (2018).

3. CAPITALIZING HEALTH: THE STRUGGLE OVER VALUE AND TREATMENT ACCESS

1. Quoted in "Nature, Politics, and Possibilities" (1995: 510).

2. Quoted in Walker (2015).

3. Gilead's initial wave of sofosbuvir would require interferon and ribavirin for 12 weeks, but its "wave 2" of sofosbuvir and ledipasvir (trade name Harvoni) would eliminate the need for interferon and ribavarin. It would ultimately be the first single-daily oral pill approved to cure hepatitis C (Loftus 2015; US Senate Committee on Finance 2015).

4. US Senate Committee on Finance (2015).

5. Both of these compounds attacked the NS3/4 protease in the hepatitis C virus, making them less potent inhibitors than sofosbuvir, which attacked the NS5b polymerase. These earlier medicines, which also required the toxic interferon regimens, were phased out within two years of the advent of sofosbuvir-based therapies.

6. Chaplin and Dusheiko (2012).

7. US Senate Committee on Finance (2015).

8. US Senate Committee on Finance (2015: 1349–51).

9. US Senate Committee on Finance (2015).

10. US Senate Committee on Finance (2015: 30).

11. US Senate Committee on Finance (2015: 101).

12. US Senate Committee on Finance (2015: 1836).

13. US Senate Committee on Finance (2015: 57).

14. Knox (2013); Pollack (2013).

15. Barrett and Langreth (2015).

16. OpenSecrets (2017).

17. US Senate Committee on Veterans' Affairs (2014).

18. Sunder Rajan (2017).

19. Quoted in Pollack (2014c).

20. Brookings Institution (2014).

21. Silverman (2015b).

22. Quoted in James (2015).

23. Quoted in Ollove (2018).

24. Ollove (2018).

25. Bach and Pearson (2015); Kaltenboeck and Bach (2018).

26. Saltzman (2019).

27. S&P Capital IQ (2014a).

28. Dumit (2012a).

29. Alter et al. (1992); Seeff et al. (1992).

30. Afdhal et al. (2014); Hoofnagle et al. (1986); McHutchison et al. (1998).

31. Castañeda (2016).

32. Pearson and Rawlins (2005).

33. McCabe, Claxton, and Culyer (2008).

34. For these studies, see Chahal et al. (2016); Chhatwal et al. (2015); Leidner et al. (2015); Najafzadeh et al. (2015); Rein et al. (2015); Tice, Chahal, and Ollendorf (2015); Van Nuys et al. (2015); Younossi et al. (2016).

35. Chahal et al. (2016).

36. Van Nuys et al. (2015).

37. Goldman, Chandra, and Lakdawalla (2014).

38. Quoted in Ollove (2018).

39. Kliff (2014).

40. Goldman, Chandra, and Lakdawalla (2014).

41. US Senate Committee on Finance (2015).

42. Vernaz et al. (2016).

43. Bach (2015).

44. Institute for Clinical and Economic Review (2020).

45. Institute for Clinical and Economic Review (2014). The public comments, particularly from Project INFORM and the National Viral Hepatitis Roundtable, highlight some of the criticisms of ICER's negative evaluation.

46. The Institute for Clinical and Economic Review (2015) would later assess the treatment to be of high value, when Gilead had dropped its price below $50,000.

47. Mazzucato and Roy (2018).

48. World Health Organization (2016a).

49. Galbraith (1993).

50. Buckley and Strom (2017: 152).

51. Edlin et al. (2015); Khullar and Chokshi (2016).
52. Chahal et al. (2016).
53. US Government Accountability Office (2021).
54. Gee (2019); Kapczynski and Kesselheim (2016).
55. Buckley and Strom (2017).
56. Buckley and Strom (2017: 152).
57. Bach (2009).
58. Centers for Medicare & Medicaid Services (2016).
59. Flynn (2015); Graham (2016); Rosenthal and Graham (2016).
60. Flynn (2015); Graham (2016).
61. Memorial Sloan Kettering Cancer Center (2017).
62. US Senate Committee on Finance (2015).
63. Barua et al. (2015); Canary, Klevens, and Holmberg (2015); Walker (2015).
64. Barua et al. (2015); Canary, Klevens, and Holmberg (2015).
65. Barua et al. (2015); Canary, Klevens, and Holmberg (2015); Ward and Mermin (2015).
66. Re et al. (2016).
67. Beckman et al. (2016); He et al. (2016).
68. Ayer et al. (2019); Loftus and Fields (2016); US Senate Committee on Finance (2015).
69. Barry-Jester (2015); He et al. (2016).
70. This is based on data from Medicare, Medicaid, the VA, prison systems, and the Indian Health Service (Beckman et al. 2016; Centers for Medicare & Medicaid Services 2016; Leston and Finkbonner 2016; US Senate Committee on Finance 2015).
71. Buckley and Strom (2016: 89, 118).
72. Nuys et al. (2015: 1673).
73. Nuys et al. (2015: 1673).
74. Yee (2014), emphasis added.
75. Quoted in Uyttebrouck (2015).
76. Quoted in Khazan (2015).
77. Centers for Disease Control and Prevention (2021).
78. World Health Organization (2017, 2021a).
79. Hoen et al. (2011).
80. Rangan and Lee (2009).
81. Harris (2014).
82. Momenghalibaf (2014).
83. Cullet (2007); Kapczynski (2009).
84. Rahmatian (2010).
85. Pollack (2015).
86. Gornall, Hoey, and Ozieranski (2016).
87. Hawkes (2019).
88. Cousins (2017).
89. World Health Organization (2018).
90. Treatment Action Group (2014).
91. Bourgeron and Geiger (2022).
92. Nocera (2018); Pollack (2015).
93. Nightingale (2016).

94. McNeil (2016).
95. Chen (2016b).
96. World Health Organization (2018).
97. See "The Triple Crisis of Financialization" in chapter 4 for more.
98. Moon and Erickson (2019).
99. Moon and Erickson (2019).
100. Gee (2019).
101. *Pharmaletter* (2017).
102. World Health Organization (2021b).
103. S&P Capital IQ (2014b: 12).
104. Gilead Sciences (2017).
105. S&P Capital IQ (2014a).
106. Chen (2017); Crow (2016); Nisen (2017).
107. Dumit (2012a).
108. Nisen (2016).
109. US Senate Committee on Finance (2015).
110. Crow (2015); Nisen (2017); Silverman (2016c).
111. Stynes (2016).
112. Silverman (2016c).
113. Jansen (2016).
114. Gilead Sciences (2017).
115. Quoted in Crow (2016).
116. Seeking Alpha (2016a).
117. S&P Capital IQ (2012).
118. S&P Capital IQ (2012).
119. Petersen (2016a).
120. Wang et al. (2016).
121. Hill et al. (2018); US Food & Drug Administration (2015).
122. While one lawsuit has been rejected, another was allowed to proceed in 2019. Gilead has argued that it had no duty to launch TAF drugs earlier than it did (Saganowsky 2019; Silverman 2016a).
123. Petersen (2016b).
124. Petersen (2016b).
125. Quoted in Terry (2018).
126. Fair Pricing Coalition (2015).
127. Silverman (2016b).
128. *Fly* (2019).
129. Grant et al. (2010).
130. Glazek (2013).
131. For more on US government patents and Truvada, see Rowland (2019).
132. Under public pressure for its price, in May 2019 the company announced the donation of 200,000 treatments of Truvada per year in the US. While some applauded the move, many observers saw it as a ploy by Gilead to prepare the HIV population for its next generation of PrEP treatments, which contain TAF (McNeil 2019).
133. Shefali and Gorman (2018).

134. Albeck-Ripka (2019).
135. Roy and King (2016).
136. Quoted in Silverman (2016c).
137. Quoted in Silverman (2016c).
138. Crow (2015).
139. Quoted in Crow (2015).
140. Quoted in Crow (2015).
141. Crow (2015); Nisen (2017).
142. Seeking Alpha (2016b).
143. Seeking Alpha (2016c), emphasis added.
144. Gilead Sciences (2017).
145. Budwell (2016).
146. Nisen (2017).
147. Quoted in Court (2018). Robin Washington, Gilead's CFO, gave a possible rationale for why companies continue to pursue buybacks: "We have purposely focused on share repurchases because in the absence of M&A it allows us to be flexible and more opportunistic. But when the right M&A opportunities present themselves, it allows us to reduce our share repurchases in order to make those necessary acquisitions and leverage our cash and debt and borrowing if we need to" (Seeking Alpha 2016c). Washington here focuses on buybacks as a form of *flexibility* in Gilead's strategy toward shareholders; where dividends create locked-in expectations among shareholders for a return at regular intervals, buybacks aim at directing capital to shareholders while also keeping cash and debt available for a future acquisition.
148. de la Merced (2017).
149. Quoted in Richtel and Pollack (2016).
150. Gilead Sciences (2021).
151. Jannarone (2011).
152. Joseph (2020).

4. FROM FINANCIALIZATION TO PUBLIC PURPOSE FOR HEALTH

1. See e.g. MacDavey (2018); McInnis (2006).
2. Polanyi (2014).
3. Chen (2016c).
4. Institute for Clinical and Economic Review (2019).
5. Yoxen (1981: 112).
6. Quoted in Pear (2019).
7. Sunder Rajan (2017).
8. Sunder Rajan (2017: 226).
9. Scherer (2004).
10. Lazonick (2015).
11. Sunder Rajan (2017).
12. Hopkins (2019).
13. Quoted in Kweon (2017).
14. Jannarone (2011).

15. Brown (2011).

16. Glabau (2017).

17. Arnold (2019).

18. Hartung et al. (2020).

19. Quoted in Silverman (2015a).

20. Mazzucato (2018: 271).

21. Mazzucato (2018: 271).

22. Mazzucato and Ryan-Collins (2019).

23. Lupkin (2016).

24. Mazzucato and Li (2020).

25. Lazonick et al. (2019). Corporations also use debt and previously stockpiled capital for shareholder payouts, which is why the figure can be greater than 100% of profits.

26. Lazonick and Mazzucato (2013: 1095).

27. Gebeloff (2021).

28. Stout (2013).

29. Lazonick (2015: 14).

30. Lazonick (2015: 14).

31. Kliff (2014).

32. Kim (2018).

33. Roy and King (2016).

34. Nisen (2017).

35. Dumit (2012a: 176).

36. Nocera (2018).

37. Light and Lexchin (2012) present data indicating that only one in ten approved medicines substantially benefit patients.

38. Birch and Muniesa (2020).

39. Buckley and Strom (2017).

40. Liu et al. (2021).

41. Rees (2020).

42. DeMartino, Miljković, and Prasad (2021).

43. Friedman, Gu, and Klausner (2019).

44. Bestvina et al. (2014).

45. Zafar et al. (2013).

46. Zafar (2015).

47. Abraham (2002); Galbraith (1973), Lazonick and Mazzucato (2013).

48. Sampat (2020).

49. Mole (2019).

50. Quoted in Gardner (2019).

51. Ledley et al. (2020).

52. Sachs (2019).

53. Swagel (2019).

54. Sitaraman and Alstott (2019).

55. Brown (2019); Quigley (2018).

56. Belluz (2019).

57 Muoio (2022).

58. See Bonvillian (2018) and Mazzucato (2013b) for more on these unique innovation agencies within the US government.

59. Reader (2021).

60. Singer, Kirchhelle, and Roberts (2020).

61. Olson and Sheiner (2017).

62. Mazzucato (2021).

63. Gates (2015); Lowy and Collins (2016).

64. Apuzzo and Gebrekidan (2021); Lupkin (2020).

65. Schlesinger (2020).

66. Warren (2018).

67. Gelles and Yaffe-Bellany (2019).

68. Stiglitz, Jayadev, and Prabhala (2020).

69. Scannell et al. (2012).

70. Brown (2019).

71. I-MAK (2018).

72. Pear (2019).

73. Ulrich (2015).

74 Maxmen (2022).

75. The Institute for Clinical and Economic Review's (2020) value assessment framework includes weighing a medicine's budgetary impact.

76. Patented Medicine Prices Review Board Canada (2020).

77. Doggett and Brown (2019).

78. Block (2001: xxviii).

79 Block (2001: xxviii).

80 Block (2001: xxviii).

CONCLUSION: RECKONING WITH PHARMACEUTICAL VALUE IN CRISIS TIMES

1. Quoted in Herman (2020).

2. Gelles and Drucker (2020).

3. Slaoui and Hepburn (2020); Weintraub and Weise (2020).

4. Quoted in McNamara (2021).

5. Fang (2021).

6. Fang (2021).

7. Mancini, Kuchler, and Khan (2021).

8. Smyth (2021).

9. Garde and Feuerstein (2020).

10. Ghosh (2020).

11. World Health Organization (2021c).

12. Van Trotsenburg (2021).

13. Krishtel and Hassan (2021).

14. Ren (2020).

15. LaFraniere and Zimmer (2021).

16. Wagner et al. (2021).

17. Kime (2017).
18. McAuliff (2020).
19. Silverman (2020).
20. Vandenberge (2020).
21. Steinberger (2020).
22. *Financial Times* Editorial Board (2020).
23. Mazzucato (2020).
24. Roy (2020).
25. Perez (2015).
26. Kaiser Family Foundation (2020).
27. Montazerhodjat, Weinstock, and Lo (2016).
28. Montazerhodjat, Weinstock, and Lo (2016: 2).

REFERENCES

Abraham, John. 2002. "The Pharmaceutical Industry as a Political Player." *The Lancet* 360 (9344): 1498–1502. https://doi.org/10.1016/s0140-6736(02)11477-2.

Afdhal, Nezam, K. Rajender Reddy, David R. Nelson, Eric Lawitz, Stuart C. Gordon, Eugene Schiff, Ronald Nahass, et al. 2014. "Ledipasvir and Sofosbuvir for Previously Treated HCV Genotype 1 Infection." *New England Journal of Medicine* 370 (16): 1483–93. https://doi.org/10.1056/nejmoa1316366.

Afdhal, Nezam, Stefan Zeuzem, Paul Kwo, Mario Chojkier, Norman Gitlin, Massimo Puoti, Manuel Romero-Gomez, et al. 2014. "Ledipasvir and Sofosbuvir for Untreated HCV Genotype 1 Infection." *New England Journal of Medicine* 370 (20): 1889–98. https://doi.org/10.1056/nejmoa1402454.

Ago, H., T. Adachi, A. Yoshida, M. Yamamoto, N. Habuka, K. Yatsunami, and M. Miyano. 1999. "Crystal Structure of the RNA-Dependent RNA Polymerase of Hepatitis C Virus." *Structure* 7 (11): 1417–26.

Albeck-Ripka, Livia. 2019. "How Australia Could Almost Eradicate H.I.V. Transmissions." *New York Times*, July 10. https://www.nytimes.com/2019/07/10/world/australia/hiv-aids-prep-prevention-drug.html.

Alter, Harvey. 2013. "The Road Not Taken or How I Learned to Love the Liver: A Personal Perspective on Hepatitis History." *Hepatology* 59 (1): 4–12. https://doi.org/10.1002/hep.26787.

Alter, Harvey, P. Holland, A. Morrow, R. Purcell, S. Feinstone, and Y. Moritsugu. 1975. "Clinical and Serological Analysis of Transfusion-Associated Hepatitis." *The Lancet* 306 (7940): 838–41. https://doi.org/10.1016/s0140-6736(75)90234-2.

Alter, Harvey, Robert H. Purcell, James W. Shih, Jacqueline C. Melpolder, Michael Houghton, Qui-Lim Choo, and George Kuo. 1989. "Detection of Antibody to Hepatitis C Virus in Prospectively Followed Transfusion Recipients with Acute and Chronic Non-A, Non-B Hepatitis." *New England Journal of Medicine* 321 (22): 1494–1500. https://doi.org/10.1056/nejm198911303212202.

Alter, M., Harold S. Margolis, Krzysztof Krawczynski, Franklyn N. Judson, Allene Mares, W. James Alexander, Pin Ya Hu, et al. 1992. "The Natural History of Community-Acquired Hepatitis C in the United States." *New England Journal of Medicine* 327 (27): 1899–1905. https://doi.org/10.1056/nejm199212313272702.

Alton, Gregg. 2016. "Re: Betting on Hepatitis C: How Financial Speculation in Drug Development Influences Access to Medicines." *British Medical Journal*, July 29. https://www.bmj.com/content/354/bmj.i3718/rr-0.

Andersson, Tord, Pauline Gleadle, Colin Haslam, and Nick Tsitsianis. 2010. "Bio-Pharma: A Financialized Business Model." *Critical Perspectives on Accounting* 21 (7): 631–41. https://doi.org/10.1016/j.cpa.2010.06.006.

Angell, Marcia. 2004. *The Truth about the Drug Companies: How They Deceive Us and What to Do about It*. New York: Random House.

Apath. 2016. "Apath Company Profile." http://www.apath.com/Company.htm.

Apuzzo, Matt, and Selam Gebrekidan. 2021. "Governments Sign Secret Vaccine Deals. Here's What They Hide." *New York Times*, January 28. https://www.nytimes.com/2021/01/28/world/europe/vaccine-secret-contracts-prices.html.

Armental, Maria, and Joseph Walker. 2020. "Gilead Raises 2020 Profit Outlook on Remdesivir Demand." *Wall Street Journal*, July 30. https://www.wsj.com/articles/gilead-swings-to-quarterly-loss-on-higher-costs-11596143000.

Arnold, John. 2019. Tweet, @JohnArnoldFndtn, May 27. https://twitter.com/JohnArnoldFndtn/status/1133091841484759040.

Ayer, Turgay, Can Zhang, Anthony Bonifonte, and Jagpreet Chhatwal. 2019. "Prioritizing Hepatitis C Treatment in U.S. Prisons." *Operations Research* 67 (3): 853–73. https://doi.org/10.1287/opre.2018.1812.

Bach, Peter B. 2009. "Limits on Medicare's Ability to Control Rising Spending on Cancer Drugs." *New England Journal of Medicine* 360 (6): 626–33. https://doi.org/10.1056/nejmhpr0807774.

———. 2015. "New Math on Drug Cost-Effectiveness." *New England Journal of Medicine* 373 (19): 1797–99. https://doi.org/10.1056/nejmp1512750.

Bach, Peter B., and Steven D. Pearson. 2015. "Payer and Policy Maker Steps to Support Value-Based Pricing for Drugs." *JAMA* 314 (23): 2503–4. https://doi.org/10.1001/jama.2015.16843.

Baker, Dean. 2019. "Government-Granted Patent Monopolies Are Driving Up Drug Prices." *Center for Economic and Policy Research* (blog), September 9. https://www.cepr.net/government-granted-patent-monopolies-are-driving-up-drug-prices/.

Balzarini, J., A. Karlsson, S. Aquaro, C. F. Perno, D. Cahard, L. Naesens, E. De Clercq, and C. McGuigan. 1996. "Mechanism of Anti-HIV Action of Masked Alaninyl D4T-MP Derivatives." *Proceedings of the National Academy of Sciences* 93 (14): 7295–99. https://doi.org/10.1073/pnas.93.14.7295.

Barenie, Rachel E., Jerry Avorn, Frazer A. Tessema, and Aaron S. Kesselheim. 2020. "Public Funding for Transformative Drugs: The Case of Sofosbuvir." *Drug Discovery Today*, October, S1359–6446(20)30381–0. https://doi.org/10.1016/j.drudis.2020.09.024.

Barrett, Paul, and Robert Langreth. 2015. "Pharma Execs Don't Know Why Anyone Is Upset by a $94,500 Miracle Cure." *Bloomberg*, June 3. https://www.bloomberg.com/news/articles/2015-06-03/specialty-drug-costs-gilead-s-hepatitis-c-cures-spur-backlash.

Barry-Jester, Anna Maria. 2015. "Eliminating Hepatitis C Means Treating Prisoners." *FiveThirtyEight*, August 31. https://fivethirtyeight.com/features/eliminating-hepatitis-c-means-treating-prisoners/.

Bartenschlager, Ralf. 2002. "Innovation: Hepatitis C Virus Replicons: Potential Role for Drug Development." *Nature Reviews Drug Discovery* 1 (11): 911–16. https://doi.org/10.1038/nrd942.

Bartenschlager, Ralf F. W., Charles M. Rice, and Michael J. Sofia. 2016. "Hepatitis C Virus— From Discovery to Cure: The 2016 Lasker-DeBakey Clinical Medical Research Award." *JAMA* 316 (12): 1254–55. https://doi.org/10.1001/jama.2016.13713.

Barton, Dominic. 2011. "Capitalism for the Long Term." *Harvard Business Review*, March. https://hbr.org/2011/03/capitalism-for-the-long-term.

Barua, Soumitri, Robert Greenwald, Jason Grebely, Gregory J. Dore, Tracy Swan, and Lynn E. Taylor. 2015. "Restrictions for Medicaid Reimbursement of Sofosbuvir for the Treatment of Hepatitis C Virus Infection in the United States." *Annals of Internal Medicine* 163 (3): 215–23. https://doi.org/10.7326/m15-0406.

Baum, A., P. Verdult, C. C. Chugbo, L. Abraham, and S. Mather. 2010. "Pharmaceuticals: Exit Research and Create Value." Morgan Stanley Research Europe.

Beckert, Jens. 2011. "Where Do Prices Come From? Sociological Approaches to Price Formation." *Socio-Economic Review* 9 (4): 757–86. https://doi.org/10.1093/ser/mwr012.

———. 2013. "Imagined Futures: Fictional Expectations in the Economy." *Theory and Society* 42 (3): 219–40. https://doi.org/10.1007/s11186-013-9191-2.

———. 2014. "Capitalist Dynamics: Fictional Expectations and the Openness of the Future." Discussion Paper 14/7, Max Planck Institute for the Study of Societies. https://doi.org/10.2139/ssrn.2463995.

Beckman, Adam L., Alyssa Bilinski, Ryan Boyko, George M. Camp, A. T. Wall, Joseph K. Lim, Emily A. Wang, R. Douglas Bruce, and Gregg S. Gonsalves. 2016. "New Hepatitis C Drugs Are Very Costly and Unavailable to Many State Prisoners." *Health Affairs* 35 (10): 1893–1901. https://doi.org/10.1377/hlthaff.2016.0296.

Belluz, Julia. 2019. "The Absurdly High Cost of Insulin, Explained." *Vox*, April 3. https://www.vox.com/2019/4/3/18293950/why-is-insulin-so-expensive.

Berkrot, Bill. 2011. "Gilead Could Have Had Pharmasset Cheap: Founder." *Reuters*, November 22. https://www.reuters.com/article/us-pharmasset-founder/gilead-could-have-had-pharmasset-cheap-founder-idUKTRE7AL2ES20111122.

Bestvina, Christine M., Leah L. Zullig, Christel Rushing, Fumiko Chino, Gregory P. Samsa, Ivy Altomare, James Tulsky, et al. 2014. "Patient-Oncologist Cost Communication, Financial Distress, and Medication Adherence." *Journal of Oncology Practice* 10 (3): 162–67. https://doi.org/10.1200/JOP.2014.001406.

Biagioli, M. 2006. "Patent Republic: Representing Inventions, Constructing Rights and Authors." *Social Research* 73 (4): 1129–72. https://doi.org/10.2307/40971878.

Birch, Kean. 2016. *Innovation, Regional Development and the Life Sciences: Beyond Clusters.* London: Routledge.

———. 2017. "Rethinking Value in the Bio-Economy: Finance, Assetization, and the Management of Value." *Science, Technology, & Human Values* 42 (3): 460–90. https://doi.org/10.1177/0162243916661633.

———. 2019. "Technoscience Rent: Toward a Theory of Rentiership for Technoscientific Capitalism." *Science, Technology, & Human Values* 45 (1): 3–33. https://doi.org/10.1177/0162243919829567.

Birch, Kean, and Fabian Muniesa, eds. 2020. *Assetization: Turning Things into Assets in Technoscientific Capitalism*. MIT Press.

Birch, Kean, and David Tyfield. 2013. "Theorizing the Bioeconomy: Biovalue, Biocapital, Bioeconomics or . . . What?" *Science, Technology, & Human Values* 38 (3): 299–327. https://doi.org/10.1177/0162243912442398.

Blackburn, R. 2006. "Finance and the Fourth Dimension." *New Left Review*, May/June, 39–70.

Blight, K. J., A. A. Kolykhalov, and C. M. Rice. 2000. "Efficient Initiation of HCV RNA Replication in Cell Culture." *Science* 290 (5498): 1972–74. https://doi.org/10.1126/science.290.5498.1972.

Blight, K. J., J. A. McKeating, J. Marcotrigiano, and C. M. Rice. 2003. "Efficient Replication of Hepatitis C Virus Genotype 1a RNAs in Cell Culture." *Journal of Virology* 77 (5): 3181–90. https://doi.org/10.1128/jvi.77.5.3181-3190.2003.

Block, F. 2001. "Introduction." In *The Great Transformation: The Political and Economic Origins of Our Time*. Boston, MA: Beacon Press.

Block, F., and M. Keller. 2008. "Where Do Innovations Come From? Transformations in the US National Innovation System 1970–2006." Information Technology and Innovation Foundation, July. http://www.itif.org/files/Where_do_innovations_come_from.pdf.

Bonvillian, William B. 2018. "DARPA and Its ARPA-E and IARPA Clones: A Unique Innovation Organization Model." *Industrial and Corporate Change* 27 (5): 897–914. https://doi.org/10.1093/icc/dty026.

Booth, Bruce L., and Bijan Salehizadeh. 2012. "Erratum: In Defense of Life Sciences Venture Investing." *Nature Biotechnology* 30 (1): 112. https://doi.org/10.1038/nbt0112-112a.

Bourgeron, Théo, and Susi Geiger. 2022. "(De-)Assetizing Pharmaceutical Patents: Patent Contestations behind a Blockbuster Drug." *Economy and Society* 51 (1): 23–45. https://doi.org/10.1080/03085147.2022.1987752.

Brettell, Karen, David Gaffen, and David Rohde. 2015. "As Stock Buybacks Reach Historic Levels, Signs that Corporate America Is Undermining Itself." *Reuters*, November 16. http://www.reuters.com/investigates/special-report/usa-buybacks-cannibalized/.

Broder, S. 2010. "The Development of Antiretroviral Therapy and Its Impact on the HIV-1/AIDS Pandemic." *Antiviral Research* 85 (1): 1–18. https://doi.org/10.1016/j.antiviral.2009.10.002.

Brookings Institution. 2014. "The Cost and Value of Biomedical Innovation: Implications for Health Policy," October 1. https://www.brookings.edu/events/the-cost-and-value-of-biomedical-innovation-implications-for-health-policy/.

Brown, Amy. 2011. "Pharmasset's Soaring Valuation Prompts Pressure to Deliver." Evaluate, July 6. https://www.evaluate.com/vantage/articles/news/pharmassets-soaring-valuation-prompts-pressure-deliver.

Brown, Dana. 2019. "Medicine for All: The Case for a Public Option in the Pharmaceutical Industry." Democracy Collaborative, August 31. https://democracycollaborative.org/learn/publication/medicine-all-case-public-option-pharmaceutical-industry.

Brown, Kathryn S. 1997. "Balms From Gilead: The Origins of Gilead Sciences and a New Era of Antiviral Medicines. Profile of Founder and Chairman Dr. Michael L. Riordan." *Washington University Magazine*, Spring 1997. https://www.slideshare.net/DigiAvenues/michael-riordan-ceo-and-founder-of-gilead-sciences-magazine-article.

Buckley, Gillian J., and Brian L. Strom, eds. 2016. *Eliminating the Public Health Problem of Hepatitis B and C in the United States: Phase One Report*. National Academies Press. https://doi.org/10.17226/23407.

———. 2017. *A National Strategy for the Elimination of Hepatitis B and C*. National Academies Press. https://doi.org/10.17226/24731.

Budwell, George. 2016. "41 Billion Reasons Why Gilead Sciences Might Need New Management." *Motley Fool*, October 19. https://www.fool.com/investing/2016/10/19/41-billion -reasons-why-gilead-sciences-might-need.aspx.

Bush, Vannevar. 1945. *Science, the Endless Frontier: A Report to the President on a Program for Postwar Scientific Research*. Washington, DC: National Science Foundation.

Calcoen, Dirk, Laura Elias, and Xiaomeng Yu. 2015. "What Does It Take to Produce a Breakthrough Drug?" *Nature Reviews Drug Discovery* 14 (3): 161–62. https://doi.org/10.1038 /nrd4570.

Canary, Lauren A., R. Monina Klevens, and Scott D. Holmberg. 2015. "Limited Access to New Hepatitis C Virus Treatment under State Medicaid Programs." *Annals of Internal Medicine* 163 (3): 226–28. https://doi.org/10.7326/M15-0320.

Cardiff University. 2014. "ProTide Technology: Transforming Drug Discovery of Nucleoside-Based Antiviral and Anti-Cancer Agents." Research Excellence Framework. https://ref2014impact.azurewebsites.net/casestudies2/refservice.svc/GetCaseStudy PDF/1929.

Carroll, John. 2011. "Report: How Savvy Pharmasset Persuaded Gilead to Boost Its Offer by 37%." *FierceBiotech*, December 7. http://www.fiercebiotech.com/biotech/report-how -savvy-pharmasset-persuaded-gilead-to-boost-its-offer-by-37.

Castañeda, Oscar Javier Maldonado. 2016. "Price-Effectiveness: Pharmacoeconomics, Value and the Right Price for HPV Vaccines." *Journal of Cultural Economy* 10 (2): 163–77. https://doi.org/10.1080/17530350.2016.1260041.

Centers for Disease Control and Prevention. 2021. "National Progress Report 2025 Goal: Reduce HCV Infections," February 10. https://www.cdc.gov/hepatitis/policy/NPR/2020 /NationalProgressReport-HepC-ReduceInfections.htm.

Centers for Medicare & Medicaid Services. 2016. "CMS Drug Spending Medicaid Dashboard." https://www.cms.gov/Research-Statistics-Data-and-Systems/Statistics-Trends-and -Reports/Information-on-Prescription-Drugs/.

Ceulemans, Steven, and Jay K. Kolls. 2013. "Can the SBIR and STTR Programs Advance Research Goals?" *Nature Immunology* 14 (3): 192–95. https://doi.org/10.1038/ni.2495.

Chahal, Harinder S., Elliot A. Marseille, Jeffrey A. Tice, Steve D. Pearson, Daniel A. Ollendorf, Rena K. Fox, and James G. Kahn. 2016. "Cost-Effectiveness of Early Treatment of Hepatitis C Virus Genotype 1 by Stage of Liver Fibrosis in a US Treatment-Naive Population." *JAMA Internal Medicine* 176 (1): 65–73. https://doi.org/10.1001/jamain ternmed.2015.6011.

Chandran, Karthik, Marcus Demaster, Pratyusha Ghoshal, and Candice Lo. 2014. "Gilead and the Pharmasset Deal." Keck Graduate Institute of Applied Life Sciences. https:// pdfslide.net/documents/gilead-and-the-pharmasset-deal-a-case-study.html.

Chaplin, Steve, and Geoffrey Dusheiko. 2012. "Review of Boceprevir and Telaprevir for the Treatment of Chronic Hepatitis C." *Prescriber* 23 (23-24): 42–46. https://doi.org/10.1002 /psb.998.

Chen, Caroline. 2016a. "Gilead Chief Has $21 Billion in Cash and an Itch to Do a Deal." *Bloomberg.* https://www.bloomberg.com/news/articles/2016-05-06/gilead-new-ceo-says -it-s-time-to-go-out-and-do-important-deals.

———. 2016b. "His Job Is to Sell a $1,000 Pill for $10 Without Losing Money." *Bloomberg,* February 29. https://www.bloomberg.com/news/articles/2016-02-29/his-job-is-to-sell -a-1-000-pill-for-10-without-losing-money.

———. 2016c. "Mutual Fund Industry to Drugmakers: Stand Up and Defend Yourself." *Bloomberg,* May 9. https://www.bloomberg.com/news/articles/2016-05-09/top-funds -said-to-tell-pharma-leaders-to-defend-drug-pricing.

———. 2017. "Gilead Plunges as Its Biggest Drug Blockbusters Are Fading Fast." *Bloomberg,* February 7. https://www.bloomberg.com/news/articles/2017-02-07/gilead-s-biggest-block busters-are-fading-fast-drugmaker-warns.

Chhatwal, Jagpreet, Fasiha Kanwal, Mark S. Roberts, and Michael A. Dunn. 2015. "Cost- Effectiveness and Budget Impact of Hepatitis C Virus Treatment with Sofosbuvir and Ledipasvir in the United States." *Annals of Internal Medicine* 162 (6): 397–406. https:// doi.org/10.7326/m14-1336.

Chon, Gina. 2016. "Rising Drug Prices Put Big Pharma's Lobbying to the Test." *New York Times,* September 2. https://www.nytimes.com/2016/09/02/business/dealbook/rising-drug -prices-put-big-pharmas-lobbying-to-the-test.html.

Chung, Andrew. 2021. "U.S. Supreme Court Rebuffs Merck Appeal in Hepatitis C Patent Fight with Gilead." *Reuters,* January 19. https://www.reuters.com/article/us-usa-court -merck-gilead-idUSKBN29O1PX.

Clark vs. Schinazi, Emory University, Atlanta VA Medical Center. 2010. US District Court for the Northern District of Alabama Northeastern Division.

Claxton, Karl, Andrew Briggs, Martin J. Buxton, Anthony J. Culyer, Christopher McCabe, Simon Walker, and Mark J. Sculpher. 2008. "Value Based Pricing for NHS Drugs: An Opportunity Not to Be Missed?" *BMJ* 336 (7638): 251–54. https://doi.org/10.1136 /bmj.39434.500185.25.

Cochrane, T. D. 2011. "Castoriadis, Veblen and the 'Power Theory of Capital.'" In *Depo- liticization: The Political Imaginary of Global Capitalism,* edited by I. S. Straume and J. F. Humphreys, 89–123. Aarhus University Press.

Cohen, Jon. 1999. "The Scientific Challenge of Hepatitis C." *Science* 285 (5424): 26–30. https://doi.org/10.1126/science.285.5424.26.

———. 2015. "King of the Pills." *Science* 348 (6235): 622–25. https://doi.org/10.1126/science .348.6235.622.

Court, Emma. 2018. "Big Biotech Companies Have Flushed $100 Billion in Stock Buy- backs down the Toilet." *Marketwatch,* November 4. https://www.marketwatch.com /story/big-biotech-companies-have-flushed-100-billion-in-stock-buybacks-down-the -toilet-2018-10-30.

Cousins, Sophie. 2017. "The Tasmanian Hep C Buyers' Club." *New York Times,* July 25. https://www.nytimes.com/2017/07/25/opinion/the-tasmanian-hep-c-buyers-club.html.

Crow, David. 2015. "Cash-Rich Gilead Hits Acquisition Trail." *Financial Times,* December 7. http://www.ft.com/cms/s/0/8a8e383e-9abc-11e5-a5c1-ca5db4add713.html.

———. 2016. "Gilead Risks Becoming Victim of Its Own Success." *Financial Times,* January 31. https://www.ft.com/content/ab14f1d6-c6d3-11e5-808f-8231cd71622e.

Cullet, Philippe. 2007. "Human Rights and Intellectual Property Protection in the TRIPS Era." *Human Rights Quarterly* 29 (2): 403–30.

Damodaran, Aswath. 2017. "Cost of Capital by Sector (US)." http://pages.stern.nyu.edu /~adamodar/New_Home_Page/datafile/wacc.htm.

Davis, Gerald. 2009. *Managed by Markets: How Finance Reshaped America*. Oxford University Press.

Day, Michael. 2020. "Covid-19: Experts Criticise Claim That Remdesivir Cuts Death Rates." *BMJ* 370: m2839. https://doi.org/10.1136/bmj.m2839.

de la Merced, Michael J. 2011. "Shareholders Whack Gilead and Alleghany for Expensive Deals." *New York Times*, November 21. https://dealbook.nytimes.com/2011/11/21/share holders-whack-gilead-and-alleghany-for-expensive-deals/.

———. 2012. "Bristol-Myers to Acquire Inhibitex for $2.5 Billion." *New York Times*, January 7. https://dealbook.nytimes.com/2012/01/07/bristol-myers-to-buy-inhibitex-for-2-5-billion/.

———. 2017. "Gilead to Buy Kite, Maker of Cancer Treatments, for $11.9 Billion." *New York Times*, August 29. https://www.nytimes.com/2017/08/28/business/dealbook/gilead-kite -gene-therapy.html.

De Clercq, Erik. 2005. "Recent Highlights in the Development of New Antiviral Drugs." *Current Opinion in Microbiology* 8 (5): 552–60. https://doi.org/10.1016/j.mib.2005.08.010.

Deeg, R., and I. Hardie. 2016. "What Is Patient Capital and Who Supplies It?" *Socio-Economic Review* 14 (4): 627–45. https://doi.org/10.1093/ser/mww025.

DeMartino, Patrick C., Miloš D. Miljković, and Vinay Prasad. 2021. "Potential Cost Implications for All US Food and Drug Administration Oncology Drug Approvals in 2018." *JAMA Internal Medicine* 181 (2): 162–67. https://doi.org/10.1001/jamainternmed .2020.5921.

DiMasi, Joseph A., Henry G. Grabowski, and Ronald W. Hansen. 2016. "Innovation in the Pharmaceutical Industry: New Estimates of R&D Costs." *Journal of Health Economics* 47: 20–33. https://doi.org/10.1016/j.jhealeco.2016.01.012.

DiMasi, Joseph A., Ronald W. Hansen, and Henry G. Grabowski. 2003. "The Price of Innovation: New Estimates of Drug Development Costs." *Journal of Health Economics* 22 (2): 151–85. https://doi.org/10.1016/s0167-6296(02)00126-1.

DiMasi, Joseph A., Ronald W. Hansen, Henry G. Grabowski, and Louis Lasagna. 1991. "Cost of Innovation in the Pharmaceutical Industry." *Journal of Health Economics* 10 (2): 107–42. https://doi.org/10.1016/0167-6296(91)90001-4.

Dodd, E. Merrick. 1932. "For Whom Are Corporate Managers Trustees?" *Harvard Law Review* 45 (7): 1145. https://doi.org/10.2307/1331697.

Doggett, Lloyd, and Sherrod Brown. 2019. "Doggett, Brown Announce Bicameral Medicare Drug Price Negotiation Bill." Press release, February 7. https://www.brown.senate.gov /newsroom/press/release/brown-doggett-announce-medicare-drug-price-negotiation -bill.

Dumit, Joseph. 2012a. *Drugs for Life*. Duke University Press.

———. 2012b. "Prescription Maximisation and the Accumulation of Surplus Health." In *Lively Capital*, edited by Kaushik Sundar Rajan. Duke University Press.

Edlin, Brian R., Benjamin J. Eckhardt, Marla A. Shu, Scott D. Holmberg, and Tracy Swan. 2015. "Toward a More Accurate Estimate of the Prevalence of Hepatitis C in the United States." *Hepatology* 62 (5): 1353–63. https://doi.org/10.1002/hep.27978.

Emory University. 2005. "Gilead Sciences and Royalty Pharma Announce $525 Million Agreement with Emory University to Purchase Royalty Interest for Emtricitabine." News release, July 18. http://www.emory.edu/news/Releases/emtri/.

———. 2012. "Emory Celebrates Top Biotech Innovations," March 20. http://news.emory.edu /stories/2012/03/tech_transfer_highlights/campus.html.

———. 2016. "Laboratory of Biochemical Pharmacology." http://www.pediatrics.emory.edu /divisions/biochem/.

Evnin, Luke. 2014. "For Venture Capital, Biotech Is Where It's Really At." *CB Insights* (blog), December 15. https://www.cbinsights.com/blog/biotech-venture-capital/.

Ezekoye, Obi, Tim Koller, and Ankit Mittal. 2016. "How Share Repurchases Boost Earnings without Improving Returns." McKinsey & Company. http://www.mckinsey.com/business -functions/strategy-and-corporate-finance/our-insights/how-share-repurchases-boost -earnings-without-improving-returns.

Fair Pricing Coalition. 2015. "Fair Pricing Coalition Blasts HIV Pharmaceutical Manufacturers for Unjustified 2015 Drug Price Increases." https://web.archive.org/web/201 50509093101/https://fairpricingcoalition.org/2015/01/.

Fama, Eugene F., and Michael C. Jensen. 1983. "Separation of Ownership and Control." *Journal of Law and Economics* 26 (2): 301–25. https://doi.org/10.1086/467037.

Fang, Lee. 2021. "Drugmakers Promise Investors They'll Soon Hike Covid-19 Vaccine Prices." *The Intercept*, March 18. https://theintercept.com/2021/03/18/covid-vaccine -price-pfizer-moderna/.

Faroohar, Rana. 2016. *Makers and Takers: The Rise of Finance and the Fall of American Business*. New York: Crown Business.

Fenz, Katherine. 2020. "Rockefeller's Charles M. Rice Honored with Nobel Prize for Research that Contributed to a Cure for Hepatitis C." Rockefeller University, October 5. https://www.rockefeller.edu/news/29292-rockefeller-virologist-charles-m-rice-hono red-with-nobel-prize-for-research-that-contributed-to-a-cure-for-hepatitis-c.

Feuerstein, Adam, and Matthew Herper. 2020. "Inside Gilead's $21 Billion Purchase of Immunomedics." *STAT*, September 14. https://www.statnews.com/2020/09/14/inside -gileads-21-billion-purchase-of-immunomedics-lamb-chops-steak-and-a-chance-for -transformation/.

Feugras, Laura, and Murray Ross. 2014. "Sovaldi, Harvoni, and Why It's Different This Time." *Health Affairs* (blog), November 21. https://www.healthaffairs.org/do/10.1377 /hblog20141121.042908/full/.

Financial Times Editorial Board. 2020. "Virus Lays Bare the Frailty of the Social Contract," April 3. https://www.ft.com/content/7eff769a-74dd-11ea-95fe-fcd274e920ca.

Flinn, R. 2011. "Gilead Increased Bid 37% as Rivals Demurred on Acquisition of Pharmasset." *Bloomberg*, December 6. http://www.bloomberg.com/news/2011-12-06/gilead-increased -bid-37-as-rivals-demurred-on-acquisition-of-pharmasset.html.

Fly, The. 2019. "Gilead HIV Drugs' Price Increase 30% Lower than Prior Years, Says Piper Jaffray," March 17. https://thefly.com/landingPageNews.php?id=2880214.

Flynn, Gerald. 2015. "The VA's Hepatitis C Problem." *Newsweek*, May 19. https://www.news week.com/vas-hepatitis-c-problem-330277.

Freeman, Chris. 1995. "The National System of Innovation in Historical Perspective." *Cambridge Journal of Economics* 19:5–24.

Friedman, Joseph, Fangning Gu, and Jeffrey D. Klausner. 2019. "Pursuing Global Equity in Access to Cancer Drugs: Lessons Learned from the HIV Epidemic." *JAMA Oncology* 5 (11): 1535–36. https://doi.org/10.1001/jamaoncol.2019.3811.

"Frontiers in Drug Development for Hepatology." 2015. HEP DART, Wailea, Hawaii.

Furman, Phillip A., Michael J. Otto, and Michael J. Sofia. 2011. "Discovery and Development of PSI-6130/RG7128." In *Antiviral Drugs: From Basic Discovery through Clinical Trials*, edited by Wieslaw M. Kazmierski, 305–15. Hoboken, NJ: Wiley. https://doi.org/10.1002/9780470929353.ch21.

Gabble, Ravinder, and Jillian Clare Kohler. 2014. "To Patent or Not to Patent? The Case of Novartis' Cancer Drug Glivec in India." *Globalization and Health* 10:3–3. https://doi.org/10.1186/1744-8603-10-3.

Gagnon, Marc-André. 2016. "Capital, Power and Knowledge according to Thorstein Veblen: Reinterpreting the Knowledge-Based Economy." *Journal of Economic Issues* 41 (2): 593–600. https://doi.org/10.1080/00213624.2007.11507049.

Galbraith, John Kenneth. 1973. *Economics and the Public Purpose*. Boston: Houghton Mifflin.

———. 1993. *American Capitalism: The Concept of Countervailing Power*. New Brunswick, NJ: Transaction.

Garber, Ken. 2011. "Hepatitis C: Move Over Interferon." *Nature Biotechnology* 29 (11): 963–66. https://doi.org/10.1038/nbt.2031.

Garde, Damian, and Adam Feuerstein. 2020. "Selling Stock Like Clockwork, Top Moderna Doctor Gets $1 Million Richer Each Week." *STAT*, October 13. https://www.statnews.com/2020/10/13/selling-stock-like-clockwork-modernas-top-doctor-gets-1-million-richer-every-week/.

Gardner, Jonathan. 2019. "House Passes Drug Pricing Bill that Pharma Warned Would Bring 'Nuclear Winter.'" *BioPharma Dive*, December 12. https://www.biopharmadive.com/news/house-approves-hr3-drug-pricing-bill-pharma/568966/.

Garthwaite, Craig. 2020. "Beware of Underpriced Drugs for Covid-19 Treatments." *Washington Post*, May 18. https://www.washingtonpost.com/opinions/2020/05/18/beware-underpriced-drugs-covid-19-treatments/.

Gates, Bill. 2015. "The Next Epidemic: Lessons from Ebola." *New England Journal of Medicine* 372 (15): 1381–84. https://doi.org/10.1056/nejmp1502918.

Gebeloff, Robert. 2021. "Who Owns Stocks? Explaining the Rise in Inequality during the Pandemic." *New York Times*, January 26. https://www.nytimes.com/2021/01/26/upshot/stocks-pandemic-inequality.html.

Gee, Rebekah E. 2019. "Louisiana's Journey toward Eliminating Hepatitis C." *Health Affairs* (blog), April 1. https://www.healthaffairs.org/do/10.1377/hblog20190327.603623/full/.

Gellene, Denise. 2002. "Gilead Sciences to Buy Triangle Pharmaceuticals." *Los Angeles Times*, December 5. http://articles.latimes.com/2002/dec/05/business/fi-gilead5.

Gelles, David, and Jesse Drucker. 2020. "Corporate Insiders Pocket $1 Billion in Rush for Coronavirus Vaccine." *New York Times*, July 25.

Gelles, David, and David Yaffe-Bellany. 2019. "Shareholder Value Is No Longer Everything, Top C.E.O.s Say." *New York Times*, August 19. https://www.nytimes.com/2019/08/19/business/business-roundtable-ceos-corporations.html.

Gerth, Jeff. 1981. "Shad of SEC Favors Bright Corporate Image." *New York Times*, August 3. http://www.nytimes.com/1981/08/03/business/shad-of-sec-favors-bright-corporate-image.html.

Ghosh, Jayati. 2020. "Vaccine Apartheid." *Project Syndicate*, November 16. https://www
.project-syndicate.org/commentary/pfizer-vaccine-doses-claimed-by-rich-countries
-weakens-covax-by-jayati-ghosh-2020-11.

Gilead Sciences. 2010. "John G. McHutchison, MD, to Join Gilead Sciences as Senior Vice
President, Liver Disease Therapeutics," June 8. https://www.gilead.com/news-and-press
/press-room/press-releases/2010/6/john-g-mchutchison-md-to-join-gilead-sciences-as
-senior-vice--president-liver-disease-therapeutics.

———. 2012. "Gilead 2011 10-K." Securities and Exchange Commission.

———. 2014. "Gilead Sciences Company Factsheet." http://www.gilead.com/~/media/Files/pdfs
/other/Gilead_Sciences_Company_Overview_FactSheet_080514.pdf.

———. 2017. "Gilead 2016 10-K." Securities and Exchange Commission.

———. 2021. "Gilead Sciences Announces Fourth Quarter and Full Year 2020 Financial
Results," February 4. https://www.gilead.com/news-and-press/press-room/press-releases
/2021/2/gilead-sciences-announces-fourth-quarter-and-full-year-2020-financial
-results.

Gilead Sciences, Inc. v. Merck & Co., Inc., Case No. 13-Cv-04057-BLF. 2016. Casetext.
https://casetext.com/case/gilead-scis-inc-v-merck-co-7.

Glabau, Danya. 2016. "Why Does Everyone Hate Martin Shkreli?" *Somatosphere*, January 14.
http://somatosphere.net/2016/01/why-does-everyone-hate-martin-shkreli.html.

———. 2017. "Conflicting Assumptions: The Meaning of Price in the Pharmaceutical Economy." *Science as Culture* 26 (4): 455–67. https://doi.org/10.1080/09505431.2017.1356280.

Glazek, Christopher. 2013. "Why Is No One on the First Treatment to Prevent H.I.V.?" *New
Yorker*, September 30. https://www.newyorker.com/tech/annals-of-technology/why-is
-no-one-on-the-first-treatment-to-prevent-h-i-v.

Gleadle, Pauline, Stuart Parris, Alan Shipman, and Roberto Simonetti. 2014. "Restructuring
and Innovation in Pharmaceuticals and Biotechs: The Impact of Financialisation." *Critical Perspectives on Accounting* 25 (1): 67–77. https://doi.org/10.1016/j.cpa.2012.10.003.

Goldman, Dana, Amitabh Chandra, and Darius Lakdawalla. 2014. "It's Easier to Measure
the Cost of Health Care than Its Value." *Harvard Business Review*, November 18. https://
hbr.org/2014/11/its-easier-to-measure-the-cost-of-health-care-than-its-value.

Goldstein, Amy. 2015. "Sharp Increases in Drug Costs Draw Hundreds to Government
Forum." *Washington Post*, November 20. https://www.washingtonpost.com/news/to
-your-health/wp/2015/11/20/sharp-increases-in-drug-costs-draw-hundreds-to-government
-forum/.

Gompers, Paul Alan. 1994. "The Rise and Fall of Venture Capital." *Business and Economic
History* 23 (2). https://thebhc.org/sites/default/files/beh/BEHprint/v023n2/p0001-p0026
.pdf.

Goozner, Merrill. 2005. *The $800 Million Pill*. University of California Press.

Gornall, Jonathan, Amanda Hoey, and Piotr Ozieranski. 2016. "A Pill Too Hard to Swallow:
How the NHS Is Limiting Access to High Priced Drugs." *BMJ* 354:i4117. https://doi.org
/10.1136/bmj.i4117.

Gounder, Celine. 2013. "A Better Treatment for Hepatitis C." *New Yorker*, December 9.
https://www.newyorker.com/tech/annals-of-technology/a-better-treatment-for-hepatitis-c.

Graham, Judith. 2016. "VA Extends New Hepatitis C Drugs to All Veterans in Its Health
System." *JAMA* 316 (9): 913–15. https://doi.org/10.1001/jama.2016.8669.

Grant, R. M., Javier R. Lama, Peter L. Anderson, and Vanessa McMahan. 2010. "Preexposure Chemoprophylaxis for HIV Prevention in Men Who Have Sex with Men." *New England Journal of Medicine* 363:2587–99. https://doi.org/DOI:10.1056/NEJMoa1011205.

Gregson, Nigel, Keiron Sparrowhawk, Josephine Mauskopf, and John Paul. 2005. "A Guide to Drug Discovery: Pricing Medicines: Theory and Practice, Challenges and Opportunities." *Nature Reviews Drug Discovery* 4 (2): 121–30. https://doi.org/10.1038/nrd1633.

Groopman, Jerome. 1998. "The Shadow Epidemic." *New Yorker*, May 11. http://www.newyorker.com/magazine/1998/05/11/the-shadow-epidemic.

Ha, Kimberly, Claudia Montato, Yana Morris, and Ashley Armstrong. 2011. "Gilead's 'Big Bet' on Pharmasset Hinges on Future Results." *Financial Times*, November 22.

Hagan, Liesl M., and Raymond F. Schinazi. 2013. "Best Strategies for Global HCV Eradication." *Liver International* 33:68–79. https://doi.org/10.1111/liv.12063.

Harden, Victoria A. 2008. "A Short History of the National Institutes of Health." National Institutes of Health. https://history.nih.gov/display/history/A+Short+History+of+the+National+Institutes+of+Health.

Harris, Gardiner. 2014. "Maker of Costly Hepatitis C Drug Sovaldi Strikes Deal on Generics for Poor Countries." *New York Times*, September 15. https://www.nytimes.com/2014/09/16/business/international/maker-of-hepatitis-c-drug-strikes-deal-on-generics-for-poor-countries.html.

Hartung, Daniel M., Lindsey Alley, Kirbee A. Johnston, and Dennis N. Bourdette. 2020. "Qualitative Study on the Price of Drugs for Multiple Sclerosis." *Neurology* 94 (4): e368. https://doi.org/10.1212/WNL.0000000000008653.

Hawkes, Nigel. 2019. "NHS England Finalises Procurement to Eliminate Hepatitis C." *BMJ* 365. https://doi.org/10.1136/bmj.l1994.

Hays, Marguerite T. 2010. "VA Research: Improving Veterans' Lives." Department of Veterans Affairs. http://www.research.va.gov/pubs/docs/ORD-85yrHistory.pdf.

He, Tianhua, Kan Li, Mark S. Roberts, Anne C. Spaulding, Turgay Ayer, John J. Grefenstette, and Jagpreet Chhatwal. 2016. "Prevention of Hepatitis C by Screening and Treatment in U.S. Prisons." *Annals of Internal Medicine* 164 (2): 84–92. https://doi.org/10.7326/m15-0617.

Heath, T. 2018. "A Year after Their Tax Cuts, How Have Corporations Spent the Windfall?" *Washington Post*, December 14. https://www.washingtonpost.com/business/economy/a-year-after-their-tax-cuts-how-have-corporations-spent-the-windfall/2018/12/14/e966d98e-fd73-11e8-ad40-cdfdoeodd65a_story.html.

Heim, M. H. 2013. "25 Years of Interferon-Based Treatment of Chronic Hepatitis C: An Epoch Coming to an End." *Nature Reviews Immunology* 13 (7): 535–42. https://doi.org/10.1038/nri3463.

Henderson, Nell, and Michael Schrage. 1984. "Government R&D." *Washington Post*, December 16. https://www.washingtonpost.com/archive/politics/1984/12/16/government-r38/cb580e3d-4ce2-4950-bf12-a717b4d3ca36/.

Herman, Bob. 2020. "The NIH Claims Joint Ownership of Moderna's Coronavirus Vaccine." *Axios*, June 25. https://www.axios.com/moderna-nih-coronavirus-vaccine-ownership-agreements-22051c42-2dee-4b19-938d-099afd71f6a0.html.

Herper, Matthew. 2020. "Gilead Announces Long-Awaited Price for Covid-19 Drug Remdesivir." *STAT*, June 29. https://www.statnews.com/2020/06/29/gilead-announces-remdesivir-price-covid-19/.

Hill, Andrew, Sophie L. Hughes, Dzintars Gotham, and Anton L. Pozniak. 2018. "Tenofovir Alafenamide Versus Tenofovir Disoproxil Fumarate: Is There a True Difference in Efficacy and Safety?" *Journal of Virus Eradication* 4 (2): 72–79.

Hill, Andrew, Saye Khoo, Joe Fortunak, Bryony Simmons, and Nathan Ford. 2014. "Minimum Costs for Producing Hepatitis C Direct-Acting Antivirals for Use in Large-Scale Treatment Access Programs in Developing Countries." *Clinical Infectious Diseases* 58 (7): 928–36. https://doi.org/10.1093/cid/ciu012.

Hoen, Ellen 't, Jonathan Berger, Alexandra Calmy, and Suerie Moon. 2011. "Driving a Decade of Change: HIV/AIDS, Patents and Access to Medicines for All." *Journal of the International AIDS Society* 14 (March): 15. https://doi.org/10.1186/1758-2652-14-15.

Hoofnagle, J., and H. Alter. 1985. "Chronic Non-A, Non-B Hepatitis." *Progress in Clinical and Biological Research* 182:63–69.

Hoofnagle, Jay H., Kevin D. Mullen, D. Brian Jones, Vinod Rustgi, Adrian Di Bisceglie, Marion Peters, Jeanne G. Waggoner, Yoon Park, and E. Anthony Jones. 1986. "Treatment of Chronic Non-A, Non-B Hepatitis with Recombinant Human Alpha Interferon." *New England Journal of Medicine* 315 (25): 1575–78. https://doi.org/10.1056/NEJM1986 12183152503.

Hopkins, Jared S. 2019. "Drugmakers Raise Prices on Hundreds of Medicines." *Wall Street Journal*, January 2. https://www.wsj.com/articles/drugmakers-raise-prices-on-hundreds -of-medicines-11546389293.

Hopkins, M. M., P. A. Crane, and P. Nightingale. 2013. "Buying Big into Biotech: Scale, Financing, and the Industrial Dynamics of UK Biotech, 1980–2009." *Industrial and Corporate Change* 22 (4): 903–52. https://doi.org/10.1093/icc/dtt022.

Hopkins, Michael M., Paul A. Martin, Paul Nightingale, Alison Kraft, and Surya Mahdi. 2007. "The Myth of the Biotech Revolution: An Assessment of Technological, Clinical and Organisational Change." *Research Policy* 36 (4): 566–89. https://doi.org/10.1016/j .respol.2007.02.013.

Horscroft, N., V. C. Lai, W. Cheney, N. Yao, J. Z. Wu, Z. Hong, and W. Zhong. 2005. "Replicon Cell Culture System as a Valuable Tool in Antiviral Drug Discovery against Hepatitis C Virus." *Antiviral Chemistry and Chemotherapy* 16 (1): 1–12. https://doi.org /10.1177/095632020501600101.

I-MAK. 2018. *Overpatented, Overpriced: How Excessive Pharmaceutical Patenting Is Extending Monopolies and Driving Up Drug Prices.* https://www.i-mak.org/overpatented-over priced-excessive-pharmaceutical-patenting-extending-monopolies-driving-drug -prices/.

Institute for Clinical and Economic Review. 2014. "Hepatitis C: An Assessments of Treatments, Including Harvoni and Sovaldi." https://icer.org/assessment/hepatitis-c-december -2014/.

Institute for Clinical and Economic Review. 2015. "New Lower Prices for Gilead Hepatitis C Drugs Reach CTAF Threshold for High Health System Value," February 17. https://icer .org/news-insights/press-releases/new-lower-prices-for-gilead-hepatitis-c-drugs -reach-ctaf-threshold-for-high-health-system-value/.

Institute for Clinical and Economic Review. 2019. "ICER Comments on the FDA Approval of Zolgensma for the Treatment of Spinal Muscular Atrophy," May 24. https://icer.org /news-insights/press-releases/icer_comment_on_zolgensma_approval/.

———. 2020. "Value Assessment Framework." https://icer.org/our-approach/methods -process/value-assessment-framework/.

Jacobson, Ira M., Stuart C. Gordon, Kris V. Kowdley, Eric M. Yoshida, Maribel Rodriguez-Torres, Mark S. Sulkowski, Mitchell L. Shiffman, et al. 2013. "Sofosbuvir for Hepatitis C Genotype 2 or 3 in Patients without Treatment Options." *New England Journal of Medicine* 368 (20): 1867–77. https://doi.org/10.1056/nejmoa1214854.

James, Davy. 2015. "Gilead Limits Enrollment in Hepatitis C Drug Patient Assistance Program." *Pharmacy Times*, July 24. https://www.pharmacytimes.com/view/gilead-limits -enrollment-in-hepatitis-c-drug-patient-assistance-program.

Jannarone, John. 2011. "Gilead's Risky Revival Procedure." *Wall Street Journal*, November 22. https://www.wsj.com/articles/SB10001424052970203710704577052553063879174.

Jansen, Bret. 2016. "Gilead: Like Waiting For Godot." *Seeking Alpha*, June 21. https://seeking alpha.com/article/3983359-gilead-like-waiting-godot.

Jasanoff, Sheila. 2011. *Designs on Nature: Science and Democracy in Europe and the United States*. Princeton University Press.

Jensen, Michael C. 1986. "Agency Cost of Free Cash Flow, Corporate Finance, and Takeovers." *American Economic Review* 76 (2): 323–29.

Jensen, Michael C., and William H Meckling. 1976. "Theory of the Firm: Managerial Behavior, Agency Costs and Ownership Structure." *Journal of Financial Economics* 3 (4): 305–60. http://www.sciencedirect.com/science/article/pii/0304405X7690026X.

Joseph, Andrew. 2016. "Where Hepatitis C Rates Are Seven Times the US Average—and a Cure Is Kept out of Reach." *STAT*, November 14. https://www.statnews.com/2016/11/14 /hepatitis-c-cure-kentucky/.

Kaiser Family Foundation. 2020. "Public Opinion on Prescription Drugs and Their Prices," October 16. https://www.kff.org/slideshow/public-opinion-on-prescription-drugs-and -their-prices/.

Kaltenboeck, Anna, and Peter B Bach. 2018. "Value-Based Pricing for Drugs: Theme and Variations." *JAMA* 319 (21): 2165–66.

Kapczynski, Amy. 2009. "Harmonization and Its Discontents: A Case Study of TRIPS Implementation in India's Pharmaceutical Sector." *California Law Review* 97 (6): 1571–1649. https://www.jstor.org/stable/20677920.

Kapczynski, Amy, and Aaron S. Kesselheim. 2016. "'Government Patent Use: A Legal Approach To Reducing Drug Spending." *Health Affairs* 35 (5): 791–97. https://doi.org /10.1377/hlthaff.2015.1120.

Keller, Matthew R., and Fred Block. 2013. "Explaining the Transformation in the US Innovation System: The Impact of a Small Government Program." *Socio-Economic Review* 11 (4): 629–56. https://doi.org/10.1093/ser/mws021.

Kesselheim, Aaron S. 2011. "An Empirical Review of Major Legislation Affecting Drug Development: Past Experiences, Effects, and Unintended Consequences." *Milbank Quarterly* 89 (3): 450–502. https://doi.org/10.1111/j.1468-0009.2011.00636.x.

Khazan, Olga. 2015. "The True Cost of an Expensive Medication." *The Atlantic*, September 25. https://www.theatlantic.com/health/archive/2015/09/an-expensive-medications -human-cost/407299/.

Khullar, Dhruv, and Dave A. Chokshi. 2016. "Toward an Integrated Federal Health System." *JAMA* 315 (23): 2521–22. https://doi.org/10.1001/jama.2016.4641.

Kim, J. L., K. A. Morgenstern, C. Lin, T. Fox, and M. D. Dwyer. 1996. "Crystal Structure of the Hepatitis C Virus NS3 Protease Domain Complexed with a Synthetic NS4A Cofactor Peptide." *Cell* 87 (2): 343–55. https://doi.org/10.1016/s0092-8674(00)81351-3.

Kim, Tae. 2018. "Goldman Sachs Asks in Biotech Research Report: 'Is Curing Patients a Sustainable Business Model?'" *CNBC*, April 11. https://www.cnbc.com/2018/04/11/gold man-asks-is-curing-patients-a-sustainable-business-model.html.

Kime, Patricia. 2017. "Hepatitis C Drug Maker Is Price-Gouging, GOP Lawmaker Says." *Military Times*, August 8. https://www.militarytimes.com/pay-benefits/military-benefits /health-care/2016/01/27/hepatitis-c-drug-maker-is-price-gouging-gop-lawmaker-says/.

Kliff, Sarah. 2014. "Each of These Hepatitis C Pills Cost $1,000. That's Actually a Great Deal." *Vox*, July 16. https://www.vox.com/2014/7/16/5902271/hepatitis-c-drug-sovaldi-price.

Knight, Frank. 1921. *Risk, Uncertainty and Profit*. New York: Houghton and Mifflin.

Knight, Sam. 2013. "Hepatitis C: The Cure?" *Financial Times*, March 15. https://www.ft.com /content/542ad524-8b77-11e2-b1a4-00144feabdc0.

Knox, R. 2013. "'1,000 Pill for Hepatitis C Spurs Debate on Drug Prices." *NPR* (blog), December 30. http://www.npr.org/blogs/health/2013/12/30/256885858/-1-000-pill-for -hepatitis-c-spurs-debate-over-drug-prices.

Kocieniewski, D. 2016. "Gilead Seen Cutting Taxes by $10 Billion as Pricey Drug Took Off." *Bloomberg*, July 13. https://www.bloomberg.com/news/articles/2016-07-13/gilead-seen -cutting-taxes-by-10-billion-as-pricey-drug-took-off.

Kolykhalov, A. A., S. M. Feinstone, and C. M. Rice. 1996. "Identification of a Highly Con- served Sequence Element at the 3′ Terminus of Hepatitis C Virus Genome RNA." *Journal of Virology* 70 (6): 3363–71. https://doi.org/10.1128/JVI.70.6.3363-3371.1996.

Krauskopf, Lewis, and Anand Basu. 2011. "Gilead Bets $11 Billion on Hepatitis in Pharmas- set Deal." *Reuters*, November 21. http://www.reuters.com/article/us-gilead-pharmasset -idUSTRE7AK0XU20111121.

Krippner, Greta R. 2011. *Capitalizing on Crisis: The Political Origins of the Rise of Finance*. Harvard University Press.

Krishtel, Priti. 2019. "Why Are Drug Prices So High? Investigating the Outdated US Patent System." TED Talk. https://www.ted.com/talks/priti_krishtel_why_are_drug_prices_so _high_investigating_the_outdated_us_patent_system.

Krishtel, Priti, and Fatima Hassan. 2021. "Share Vaccine Know-How." *Science* 364 (6566): 379.

Kweon, Alex. 2017. "As Promised, Allergan Unveils Single-Digit Price Hikes for 9 Brand Name Drugs." *BioSpace*, January 4. https://www.biospace.com/article/as-promised -allergan-unveils-single-digit-price-hikes-for-9-brand-name-drugs-/.

LaFraniere, Sharon, and Carl Zimmer. 2021. "Pfizer and BioNTech Say a Third Shot Boosts Antibodies against the Virus." *New York Times*, August 25. https://www.nytimes .com/2021/08/25/us/politics/pfizer-vaccine-booster-trial-results.html.

Lawitz, Eric, Alessandra Mangia, David Wyles, Maribel Rodriguez-Torres, Tarek Hassanein, Stuart C. Gordon, Michael Schultz, et al. 2013. "Sofosbuvir for Previously Untreated Chronic Hepatitis C Infection." *New England Journal of Medicine* 368 (20): 1878–87. https://doi.org/10.1056/nejmoa1214853.

Lazonick, W. 2015. "Share Buybacks: From Retain-and-Reinvest to Downsize-and-Distribute." Brookings Institution, April 17. http://www.brookings.edu/research/papers/2015/04/17 -stock-buybacks-lazonick.

———. 2017. "The Functions of the Stock Market and the Fallacies of Shareholder Value." Working paper no. 58, Institute for New Economic Thinking. https://papers.ssrn.com /sol3/papers.cfm?abstract_id=2993978.

Lazonick, W., and Matt Hopkins. 2016. "Corporate Executives Are Making Way More Money than Anybody Reports." *The Atlantic*, September 15. https://www.theatlantic .com/business/archive/2016/09/executives-making-way-more-than-reported/499850/.

Lazonick, William, Matt Hopkins, Ken Jacobson, Mustafa Erdem Sakinç, and Öner Tulum. 2016. "Life Sciences? How 'Maximizing Shareholder Value' Increases Drug Prices, Restricts Access, and Stifles Innovation." UN Secretary-General's High-Level Panel on Access to Medicines. https://static1.squarespace.com/static/562094dee4b0d00c1a3ef761 /t/56d53437c6fc08c537794d78/1456813112051/theAIRnet+Life+Sciences_+SUBMIT TED+20160228+%28002%29.pdf.

Lazonick, W., and M. Mazzucato. 2013. "The Risk-Reward Nexus in the Innovation-Inequality Relationship: Who Takes the Risks? Who Gets the Rewards?" *Industrial and Corporate Change* 22 (4): 1093–1128. https://doi.org/10.1093/icc/dtt019.

Lazonick, W., and Mary O'Sullivan. 2010. "Maximizing Shareholder Value: A New Ideology for Corporate Governance." *Economy and Society* 29 (1): 13–35. https://doi.org/10.1080 /030851400360541.

Lazonick, W., and Ö. Tulum. 2011. "US Biopharmaceutical Finance and the Sustainability of the Biotech Business Model." *Research Policy* 40 (9). https://doi.org/10.1016/j.respol .2011.05.021.

Lazonick, William, Öner Tulum, Matt Hopkins, Mustafa Erdem Sakinç, and Ken Jacobson. 2019. "Financialization of the U.S. Pharmaceutical Industry." Institute for New Economic Thinking. https://www.ineteconomics.org/uploads/papers/Lazonick-financialization-of -the-US-pharmaceutical-industry-20191202_1-final.pdf.

Ledley, Fred D., Sarah Shonka McCoy, Gregory Vaughan, and Ekaterina Galkina Cleary. 2020. "Profitability of Large Pharmaceutical Companies Compared with Other Large Public Companies." *JAMA* 323 (9): 834–43. https://doi.org/10.1001/jama.2020.0442.

Leidner, Andrew J., Harrell W. Chesson, Fujie Xu, John W. Ward, Philip R. Spradling, and Scott D. Holmberg. 2015. "Cost-Effectiveness of Hepatitis C Treatment for Patients in Early Stages of Liver Disease." *Hepatology* 61 (6): 1860–69. https://doi.org/10.1002/hep .27736.

Lerner, Josh, and John Willinge. 2011. "A Note on Valuation in Private Equity Settings." Background Note 297–050, Harvard Business School.

Lesburg, C. A., M. B. Cable, E. Ferrari, Z. Hong, A. F. Mannarino, and P. C. Weber. 1999. "Crystal Structure of the RNA-Dependent RNA Polymerase from Hepatitis C Virus Reveals a Fully Encircled Active Site." *Nature Structural Biology* 6 (10): 937–43. https:// doi.org/10.1038/13305.

Leston, Jessica, and Joe Finkbonner. 2016. "The Need to Expand Access to Hepatitis C Virus Drugs in the Indian Health Service." *JAMA* 316 (8): 817–18. https://doi.org/10.1001 /jama.2016.7186.

Leyshon, A., and N. Thrift. 2007. "The Capitalization of Almost Everything: The Future of Finance and Capitalism." *Theory, Culture & Society* 24 (7–8): 97–115. https://doi.org /10.1177/0263276407084699.

Light, Donald W., and Joel R. Lexchin. 2012. "Pharmaceutical Research and Development: What Do We Get for All That Money?" *BMJ* 345. https://doi.org/10.1136/bmj.e4348.

Light, Donald W., and Rebecca Warburton. 2011. "Demythologizing the High Costs of Pharmaceutical Research." *BioSocieties* 6 (1): 34–50. https://doi.org/10.1057/biosoc.2010.40.

Lindenbach, Brett D., and Charles M. Rice. 2005. "Unravelling Hepatitis C Virus Replication from Genome to Function." *Nature* 436 (7053): 933–38. https://doi.org/10.1038/nature04077.

Liu, Angus. 2020. "Gilead Should Be Allowed 'Real Pricing' for Remdesivir—and a Sizable Profit, Analyst Says." *FiercePharma*, June 11. https://www.fiercepharma.com/pharma/gilead-should-be-allowed-remdesivir-real-pricing-and-sizeable-profit-covid-19-says-analyst.

Liu, Patrick, Sanket S. Dhruva, Nilay D. Shah, and Joseph S. Ross. 2021. "Trends in Within-Class Changes in US Average Wholesale Prices for Brand-Name Medications for Common Conditions From 2015 to 2020." *JAMA Network Open* 4 (1): e2035064–e2035064. https://doi.org/10.1001/jamanetworkopen.2020.35064.

Loftus, Peter. 2014. "Senate Committee Is Investigating Pricing of Hepatitis C Drug." *Wall Street Journal*, July 11. http://online.wsj.com/articles/senate-finance-committee-is-investigating-pricing-of-hepatitis-c-drug-1405109206.

———. 2015. "Gilead Knew Hepatitis C Drug Price Was High, Senate Says." *Wall Street Journal*, December 1. https://www.wsj.com/articles/gilead-knew-hepatitis-drug-price-was-high-senate-says-1449004771.

Loftus, Peter, and Gary Fields. 2016. "High Cost of New Hepatitis C Drugs Strains Prison Budgets, Locks Many Out of Cure." *Wall Street Journal*, September 12. https://www.wsj.com/articles/high-cost-of-new-hepatitis-c-drugs-strains-prison-budgets-locks-many-out-of-cure-1473701644.

Lohmann, V. 1999. "Replication of Subgenomic Hepatitis C Virus RNAs in a Hepatoma Cell Line." *Science* 285 (5424): 110–13. https://doi.org/10.1126/science.285.5424.110.

Love, J. 2014. "HCV Timeline." Knowledge Ecology International. https://docs.google.com/document/d/18usDcyubX_HgnYvK5i7Re7E8L3nAC52AqRFjssHBsPQ/pub.

Love, Robert A., Hans E. Parge, John A. Wickersham, Zdenek Hostomsky, Noriyuki Habuka, Ellen W. Moomaw, Tsuyoshi Adachi, and Zuzana Hostomska. 1996. "The Crystal Structure of Hepatitis C Virus NS3 Proteinase Reveals a Trypsin-like Fold and a Structural Zinc Binding Site." *Cell* 87 (2): 331–42. https://doi.org/10.1016/s0092-8674(00)81350-1.

Lowy, D. R., and F. S. Collins. 2016. "Aiming High: Changing the Trajectory for Cancer." *New England Journal of Medicine* 374 (20): 1901–04. https://doi.org/10.1056/nejmp1600894.

Luo, Jing, Gregg Gonsalves, and Amy Kapczynski. 2020. "Treatments Don't Work If We Can't Afford Them: The Global Need for Open and Equitable Access to Remdesivir." *BMJ Opinion*, June 3. https://blogs.bmj.com/bmj/2020/06/03/treatments-dont-work-if-we-cant-afford-them-the-global-need-for-open-and-equitable-access-to-remdesivir/.

Lupkin, Sydney. 2016. "A Frenzy of Lobbying on 21st Century Cures." *Kaiser Health News*, November 28. https://khn.org/news/a-frenzy-of-lobbying-on-21st-century-cures/.

———. 2020. "Pfizer's Coronavirus Vaccine Supply Contract Excludes Many Taxpayer Protections." National Public Radio, November 24. https://www.npr.org/sections/health-shots/2020/11/24/938591815/pfizers-coronavirus-vaccine-supply-contract-excludes-many-taxpayer-protections.

MacDavey, Megan. 2018. "System Redesign Part I: Why It Matters." *Tower Foundation* (blog), April 26. https://thetowerfoundation.org/2018/04/26/system-redesign-part-i-why-it-matters-html/.

Maloney, Timothy P., Richard A. Kaba, James P. Krueger, Rudy Kratz, and Calista J. Mitchell. 2010. "Intellectual Property in Drug Discovery and Biotechnology." In *Burger's Medicinal Chemistry and Drug Discovery*, edited by Donald J. Abraham and David P. Rotella, 101–86. https://doi.org/10.1002/0471266949.bmc040.pub2.

Mancini, Donato Paolo, Hannah Kuchler, and Mehreen Khan. 2021. "Pfizer and Moderna Raise EU Covid Vaccine Prices." *Financial Times*, August 1. https://www.ft.com/content/d415a01e-d065-44a9-bad4-f9235aa04c1a.

Manne, H. G. 1965. "Mergers and the Market for Corporate Control." *Journal of Political Economy* 73 (2): 110–20.

Marshall, E. 2000. "Hepatitis C: New 'Replicon' Yields Viral Proteins." *Science* 290 (5498): 1870–71. https://doi.org/10.1126/science.290.5498.1870b.

Mauss, Marcel. 1985. "A Category of the Human Mind: The Notion of Person; the Notion of Self." In *A Category of the Human Mind: Anthropology, History, Philosophy*, edited by Michael Carrithers, Steven Collins, and Steven Lukes, 1–25. Cambridge University Press.

Maxmen, Amy. 2022. "Unseating Big Pharma: The Radical Plan for Vaccine Equity." *Nature*, July 13. https://www.nature.com/immersive/d41586-022-01898-3/.

Maybarduk, Peter. 2020. "Gilead's Remdesivir Price Is Offensive." *Public Citizen*, June 29. https://www.citizen.org/news/gileads-remdesivir-price-is-offensive/.

Mazzucato, Mariana. 2013a. "Financing Innovation: Creative Destruction vs. Destructive Creation." *Industrial and Corporate Change* 22 (4): 851–67. https://doi.org/10.1093/icc/dtt025.

———. 2013b. *The Entrepreneurial State: Debunking Public vs. Private Sector Myths*. London: Anthem Press.

———. 2016. "From Market Fixing to Market-Creating: A New Framework for Innovation Policy." *Industry and Innovation* 23 (2): 140–56. https://doi.org/10.1080/13662716.2016.1146124.

———. 2018. *The Value of Everything*. New York: Penguin.

———. 2020. "Capitalism Is Broken. The Fix Begins with a Free Covid-19 Vaccine." *New York Times*, October 8. https://www.nytimes.com/2020/10/08/opinion/international-world/capitalism-covid-19-vaccine.html.

———. 2021. *Mission Economy: A Moonshot Guide to Changing Capitalism*. New York: Harper Collins.

Mazzucato, Mariana, Rainer Kattel, Tim O'Reilly, and Josh Entsminger. 2021. "Reimagining the Platform Economy." *Project Syndicate*, February 5. https://www.project-syndicate.org/onpoint/platform-economy-data-generation-and-value-extraction-by-mariana-mazzucato-et-al-2021-02.

Mazzucato, Mariana, and Henry Li. 2020. "The Entrepreneurial State and Public Options: Socialising Risks and Rewards." UCL Institute for Innovation and Public Purpose. https://www.ucl.ac.uk/bartlett/public-purpose/wp2020-20.

Mazzucato, Mariana, and Victor Roy. 2018. "Rethinking Value in Health Innovation: From Mystifications towards Prescriptions." *Journal of Economic Policy Reform* 73 (2): 1–19. https://doi.org/10.1080/17487870.2018.1509712.

Mazzucato, Mariana, and Josh Ryan-Collins. 2019. "Putting Value Creation Back into 'Public Value': From Market Fixing to Market Shaping." Working paper WP 2019–05, UCL Institute for Innovation and Public Purpose. https://www.ucl.ac.uk/bartlett/public-purpose/publications/2019/jun/putting-value-creation-back-public-value-market-fixing-market-shaping.

Mazzucato, Mariana, Josh Ryan-Collins, and Giorgos Gouzoulis. 2020. "Theorising and Mapping Modern Economic Rents." Working paper WP 2020–13, UCL Institute for Innovation and Public Purpose. https://www.ucl.ac.uk/bartlett/public-purpose/publi cations/2020/jun/theorising-and-mapping-modern-economic-rents.

McAuliff, Michael. 2020. "High Drug Prices Driven by Profits, House Committee Reports Find." NBC News, September 30. https://www.nbcnews.com/health/health-news/high -drug-prices-driven-profits-house-panel-report-finds-n1241589.

McCabe, Christopher, Karl Claxton, and Anthony J. Culyer. 2008. "The NICE Cost-Effective-ness Threshold." *PharmacoEconomics* 26 (9): 733–44. https://doi.org/10.2165/00019053 -200826090-00004.

McCorvey, J. J. 2015. "How Drug Company Gilead Sciences Outpaces Its Competitors—and Common Diseases." *Fast Company*, February 18. https://www.fastcompany.com/3041565 /how-drug-company-gilead-outpaces-its-competitors-and-common-d.

McGuigan, C., D. Cahard, and H. M. Sheeka. 1996. "Aryl Phosphoramidate Derivatives of D4T Have Improved Anti-HIV Efficacy in Tissue Culture and May Act by the Genera-tion of a Novel Intracellular Metabolite." *Journal of Medicinal Chemistry* 39 (8): 1748–53. https://doi.org/10.1021/jm950605j.

McGuigan, C., A. Gilles, and K. Madela. 2010. "Phosphoramidate ProTides of 2′-C-Methyl-guanosine as Highly Potent Inhibitors of Hepatitis C Virus. Study of Their In Vitro and In Vivo Properties." *Journal of Medicinal Chemistry* 53 (13): 4949–57. https://doi .org/10.1021/jm1003792.

McGuigan, Christopher, Ranjith N. Pathirana, Naheed Mahmood, Kevin G. Devine, and Alan J. Hay. 1992. "Aryl Phosphate Derivatives of AZT Retain Activity against HIV1 in Cell Lines Which Are Resistant to the Action of AZT." *Antiviral Research* 17 (4): 311–21. https://doi.org/10.1016/0166-3542(92)90026-2.

McHutchison, John G., Stuart C. Gordon, Eugene R. Schiff, Mitchell L. Shiffman, William M. Lee, Vinod K. Rustgi, Zachary D. Goodman, Mei-Hsiu Ling, Susannah Cort, and Janice K. Albrecht. 1998. "Interferon Alfa-2b Alone or in Combination with Ribavirin as Initial Treatment for Chronic Hepatitis C." *New England Journal of Medicine* 339 (21): 1485–92. https://doi.org/10.1056/nejm199811193392101.

McInnis, Doug. 2006. "What System?" *Dartmouth Medicine*, Summer. https://dartmed .dartmouth.edu/summer06/html/what_system.php.

McNamara, Audrey. 2021. "Pfizer Execs Discuss Hiking Vaccine Price after Pandemic Wanes." *CBS News*, March 17. https://www.cbsnews.com/news/pfizer-covid-vaccine -price-hike-post-pandemic/.

McNeil, Donald G., Jr. 2016. "Curing Hepatitis C, in an Experiment the Size of Egypt." *New York Times*, December 15. http://www.nytimes.com/2015/12/16/health/hepatitis-c-treat ment-egypt.html.

McNeil, Donald G., Jr. 2019. "Gilead Will Donate Truvada to U.S. for H.I.V. Prevention." *New York Times*, May 10. https://www.nytimes.com/2019/05/09/health/gilead-truvada -hiv-aids.html.

Mehellou, Youcef, Jan Balzarini, and Christopher McGuigan. 2009. "Aryloxy Phosphorami-date Triesters: A Technology for Delivering Monophosphorylated Nucleosides and Sug-ars into Cells." *ChemMedChem* 4 (11): 1779–91. https://doi.org/10.1002/cmdc.200900289.

Memorial Sloan Kettering Cancer Center. 2017. "Louisiana Budget Allocator." Drug Pricing Lab. https://drugpricinglab.org/louisiana-budget-allocator/.

Mirowski, P. 2012. "The Modern Commercialization of Science Is a Passel of Ponzi Schemes." *Social Epistemology* 26 (3–4): 285–310.

Mole, Beth. 2019. "Big Pharma's Image Sinks to New Low amid Opioid Crisis, High Drug Prices." *Ars Technica*, September 4. https://arstechnica.com/science/2019/09/big-pharmas-image-sinks-to-new-low-amid-opioid-crisis-high-drug-prices/.

Momenghalibaf, Azzi. 2014. "License to Deceive? A Big Drug Company's Smokescreen on Hepatitis C." Open Society Foundations, September 24. https://www.opensocietyfoundations.org/voices/license-deceive-big-drug-company-s-smokescreen-hepatitis-c.

Montalban, Matthieu, and Mustafa Erdem Sakinc. 2013. "Financialization and Productive Models in the Pharmaceutical Industry." *Industrial and Corporate Change* 22 (4): 981–1030. https://doi.org/10.1093/icc/dtt023.

Montazerhodjat, Vahid, David M. Weinstock, and Andrew W. Lo. 2016. "Buying Cures versus Renting Health: Financing Health Care with Consumer Loans." *Science Translational Medicine* 8 (327): 327ps6–327ps6. https://doi.org/10.1126/scitranslmed.aad6913.

Moon, Suerie, and Elise Erickson. 2019. "Universal Medicine Access through Lump-Sum Remuneration: Australia's Approach to Hepatitis C." *New England Journal of Medicine* 380 (7): 607–10. https://doi.org/10.1056/NEJMp1813728.

Morgan, John. 2018. "A Bitter Pill: How Big Pharma Lobbies to Keep Prescription Drug Prices High." Citizens for Responsibility and Ethics in Washington. https://www.citizensforethics.org/reports-investigations/crew-reports/a-bitter-pill-how-big-pharma-lobbies-to-keep-prescription-drug-prices-high/.

Mowery, David C., Richard R. Nelson, Bhaven N. Sampat, and Arvids A. Ziedonis. 2001. "The Growth of Patenting and Licensing by U.S. Universities: An Assessment of the Effects of the Bayh–Dole Act of 1980." *Research Policy* 30 (1): 99–119. https://doi.org/10.1016/s0048-7333(99)00100-6.

Mowery, David C., and Bhaven N. Sampat. 2004. "The Bayh-Dole Act of 1980 and University–Industry Technology Transfer: A Model for Other OECD Governments?" *Journal of Technology Transfer* 30 (1–2): 115–27. https://doi.org/10.1007/s10961-004-4361-z.

Muniesa, Fabian. 2011. "A Flank Movement in the Understanding of Valuation." *Sociological Review* 59 (2_suppl): 24–38. https://doi.org/10.1111/j.1467-954x.2012.02056.x.

———. 2014. *The Provoked Economy: Economic Reality and the Performative Turn*. London: Routledge.

Muoio, Dave. 2022. "California Will Tackle High Drug Prices by Making Its Own Low-Cost Insulin, Newsom Says." *Fierce Healthcare*, July 8. https://www.fiercehealthcare.com/payers/california-aims-tackle-high-drug-prices-making-its-own-low-cost-insulin-newsome-says.

Nair, Prashant. 2011. "Profile of Charles M. Rice." *Proceedings of the National Academy of Sciences* 108 (21): 8541–43. https://doi.org/10.1073/pnas.1105050108.

Najafzadeh, Mehdi, Karin Andersson, William H. Shrank, Alexis A. Krumme, Olga S. Matlin, Troyen Brennan, Jerry Avorn, and Niteesh K. Choudhry. 2015. "Cost-Effectiveness of Novel Regimens for the Treatment of Hepatitis C Virus." *Annals of Internal Medicine* 162 (6): 407–19. https://doi.org/10.7326/m14-1152.

National Institutes of Health. 2015. "Research Portfolio Online Reporting Tools (RePORT)." https://reporter.nih.gov/search/ofCzSNqRUo-SPkNYPX48kw/projects.

National Institutes of Health. 2016. "NIH Research Project Grant Program (R01)." https://grants.nih.gov/grants/funding/r01.htm.

————. 2017a. "History." Office of Budget. https://officeofbudget.od.nih.gov/history.html.

————. 2017b. "NIGMS MERIT Awards." https://www.nigms.nih.gov/Research/Pages/meri tawards.aspx.

National Viral Hepatitis Roundtable. 2015. World Hepatitis Day Meeting, Washington, DC.

"Nature, Politics, and Possibilities: A Debate and Discussion with David Harvey and Donna Haraway." 1995. *Environment and Planning D: Society and Space* 13 (5): 507–27. https://doi.org/doi:10.1068/d130507.

Nayak, Malathi. 2021. "Costs Soar for Trade Secrets, Pharma Patent Suits, Survey Finds." *Bloomberg Law*, December 19. https://news.bloomberglaw.com/ip-law/costs-soar-for -trade-secrets-pharma-patent-suits-survey-finds.

Neuman, T., J. Cubanski, and J. Hoadley. 2014. "The Cost of a Cure: Medicare's Role in Treating Hepatitis C." *Health Affairs*, June 4. https://www.healthaffairs.org/do/10.1377 /hblog20140605.039396/full/.

Neumann, Peter J., Joshua T. Cohen, and Daniel A. Ollendorf. 2021. "Drug-Pricing Debate Redux: Should Cost-Effectiveness Analysis Be Used Now to Price Pharmaceuticals?" *New England Journal of Medicine* 385 (21): 1923–24. https://doi.org/10.1056/NEJMp2113323.

Nightingale, A. "Partial Revocation of EPO Patent on Sofosbuvir." *Intellectual Property Watch*, October 5. https://www.ip-watch.org/2016/10/05/partial-revocation-of-epo-pat ent-on-sofosbuvir-key-for-hepatitis-c/.

Nik-Khah, E. 2014. "Neoliberal Pharmaceutical Science and the Chicago School of Economics." *Social Studies of Science* 44 (4): 489–517. https://doi.org/10.1177/0306312714520864.

Nisen, Max. 2016. "Pharma's Game of (Hep C) Thrones." *Bloomberg*, May 12. https://www .bloomberg.com/gadfly/articles/2016-05-12/hepatitis-c-cure-game-of-thrones-far -from-over.

————. 2017. "Gilead Mismanaged Its Gold Mine." *Bloomberg*, February 8. https://www .bloomberg.com/gadfly/articles/2017-02-08/gilead-earnings-mismanaging-a-goldmine.

Nitzan, Jonathan, and Shimshom Bichler. 2009. *Capital as Power: A Study of Order and Creorder*. London: Routledge.

Nocera, Joe. 2018. "Wall Street Wants the Best Patents, Not the Best Drugs." *Bloomberg*, November 27. https://www.bloomberg.com/opinion/articles/2018-11-27/gilead-s-cures -for-hepatitis-c-were-not-a-great-business-model.

O'Brien, Timothy L. 2020. "$600 or $3,120? Gilead Puts a Price Tag on Covid-19 Relief." *Bloomberg*, July 2. https://www.bloomberg.com/opinion/articles/2020-07-02/gilead-s-covid -drug-remdesivir-shows-fuzzy-math-of-pricing.

O'Day, Daniel. 2020. "An Open Letter from Daniel O'Day, Chairman & CEO, Gilead Sciences." Gilead Sciences, June 29. https://www.gilead.com/news-and-press/press -room/press-releases/2020/6/an-open-letter-from-daniel-oday-chairman--ceo-gilead -sciences.

Ollove, Michael. 2018. "Courts Force States to Provide Costly Hep C Treatment." Pew Trusts, September 25. https://www.pewtrusts.org/en/research-and-analysis/blogs/state line/2018/09/25/courts-force-states-to-provide-costly-hep-c-treatment.

Olson, Peter, and Louise Sheiner. 2017. "The Hutchins Center Explains: Prescription Drug Spending." *Brookings* (blog), April 26. https://www.brookings.edu/blog/up -front/2017/04/26/the-hutchins-center-explains-prescription-drug-spending/.

OpenSecrets. 2017. "Lobbying Spending Database: Gilead Sciences." https://www.opense crets.org/lobby/clientsum.php?id=D000026221&year=2017.

————. 2021. "Pharmaceutical Manufacturing Lobbying Profile." https://www.opensecrets
.org/federal-lobbying/industries/summary?cycle=2011&id=h4300.

Ozmel, U., D. T. Robinson, and T. E. Stuart. 2013. "Strategic Alliances, Venture Capital, and Exit Decisions in Early Stage High-Tech Firms." *Journal of Financial Economics* 107 (3): 655–70. https://doi.org/10.1016/j.jfineco.2012.09.009.

Patented Medicine Prices Review Board Canada. 2020. "PMPRB Guidelines," October 23. https://www.canada.ca/en/patented-medicine-prices-review/services/legislation/about -guidelines/guidelines.html.

Pear, Robert. 2019. "Drug Makers Try to Justify Prescription Prices to Senators at Hearing." *New York Times*, February 26. https://www.nytimes.com/2019/02/26/us/politics /prescription-drug-prices.html.

Pearson, Steven D., and Michael D. Rawlins. 2005. "Quality, Innovation, and Value for Money." *JAMA* 294 (20): 2618–22. https://doi.org/10.1001/jama.294.20.2618.

Perez, Carlota. 2015. "Capitalism, Technology and a Green Global Golden Age: The Role of History in Helping to Shape the Future." *Political Quarterly* 86 (December): 191–217. https://doi.org/10.1111/1467-923X.12240.

Perrone, P., G. M. Luoni, and M. R. Kelleher. 2007. "Application of the Phosphoramidate ProTide Approach to 4'-Azidouridine Confers Sub-Micromolar Potency versus Hepatitis C Virus on an Inactive Nucleoside." *Journal of Medicinal Chemistry* 50 (8): 1840–49. https://doi.org/10.1021/jm0613370.

Petersen, Melody. 2016a. "A History of Gilead's Biggest HIV Drug." *Los Angeles Times*, May 29. http://www.latimes.com/business/la-fi-gilead-timeline-20160527-snap-story.html.

————. 2016b. "A Question of Timing: A Lawsuit Claims Gilead Sciences Could Have Developed a Less-Harmful Version of Its HIV Treatment Sooner." *Los Angeles Times*, May 29. http://www.latimes.com/business/la-fi-gilead-20160529-snap-story.html.

Pharmaletter. 2017. "Gilead Has Directly Cured 1.5 Million HCV Patients—Just Another 70 Million to Go, Says Michael Mertens," August 16. https://www.thepharmaletter.com /article/gilead-has-directly-cured-1-5-million-hcv-patients-just-another-70-million-to -go-says-michael-mertens.

Pharmasset. 2002. "Phase 1 Clinical Study for HIV is Underway: A Promising New Antiviral Agent." Press release, May 21 (Wayback Machine). https://web.archive.org/web /20020607191100/http://www.pharmasset.com/press_&_news.htm.

————. 2006. "Pharmasset S-1 2006."

————. 2009. "Pharmasset 2008 10-K." Securities and Exchange Commission.

————. 2010. "Pharmasset 2009 10-K." Securities and Exchange Commission.

————. 2011. "Pharmasset 2010 10-K." Securities and Exchange Commission.

Pisano, Gary P. 2006. *Science Business*. Cambridge, MA: Harvard Business School Press.

Polanyi, Karl. 2014. *The Great Transformation: The Political and Economic Origins of Our Time*. Boston, MA: Beacon Press.

Pollack, Andrew. 2003. "H.I.V. Lessons Used in Hepatitis C Treatment." *New York Times*, March 11. http://www.nytimes.com/2003/03/11/health/hiv-lessons-used-in-hepatitis-c -treatment.html.

————. 2010. "Hope against Hepatitis C." *New York Times*, June 22. https://www.nytimes .com/2010/07/22/business/22hepatitis.html.

————. 2011. "Second Drug Wins Approval For Treatment of Hepatitis C." *New York Times*, May 24. https://www.nytimes.com/2011/05/24/business/24drug.html.

———. 2013. "F.D.A. Approves Pill to Treat Hepatitis C." *New York Times*, December 7. http://www.nytimes.com/2013/12/07/business/fda-approves-pill-to-treat-hepatitis-c.html.

———. 2014a. "Merck Bids $3.8 Billion for an Edge in Hepatitis." *New York Times*, June 9. https://dealbook.nytimes.com/2014/06/09/merck-to-acquire-idenix-pharmaceuticals/.

———. 2014b. "Gilead's Hepatitis C Drug, Sovaldi, Is on Pace to Become a Blockbuster." *New York Times*, July 23. https://www.nytimes.com/2014/07/24/business/sales-of-hepatitis-c-drug-sovaldi-soar.html.

———. 2014c. "Harvoni, a Hepatitis C Drug from Gilead, Wins F.D.A. Approval." *New York Times*, October 10. https://www.nytimes.com/2014/10/11/business/harvoni-a-hepatitis-c-drug-from-gilead-wins-fda-approval.html.

———. 2015. "High Cost of Sovaldi Hepatitis C Drug Prompts a Call to Void Its Patents." *New York Times*, May 20. https://www.nytimes.com/2015/05/20/business/high-cost-of-hepatitis-c-drug-prompts-a-call-to-void-its-patents.html.

Pollack, Andrew, and Michael J. de la Merced. 2011. "Gilead to Buy Pharmasset for $11 Billion." *New York Times*, November 21. https://dealbook.nytimes.com/2011/11/21/gilead-to-buy-pharmasset-for-11-billion/.

Post, Sharon, and Maurice BP-Weeks. 2020. *Poi$on: How Big Pharma's Racist Price Gouging Kills Black and Brown Folks*. Action Center on Race & the Economy. https://acrecampaigns.org/wp-content/uploads/2020/08/new-poison-final.pdf.

Powell, W., K. Koput, J. Bowie, and L. Smith-Doerr. 2001. "The Spatial Clustering of Science and Capital: Accounting for Biotech Firm-Venture Capital Relationships." *Regional Studies* 36 (3): 291–305.

PR Newswire. 2004. "Roche and Pharmasset Join Forces to Develop New Generation of Hepatitis C Therapies," October 27. http://www.prnewswire.com/news-releases/roche-and-pharmasset-join-forces-to-develop-new-generation-of-hepatitis-c-therapies-75009282.html.

Pund, Britten, Ann Lefert, and Amanda Bowes. 2017. "National ADAP Monitoring Project." NASTAD. https://nastad.org/sites/default/files/2021-12/PDF-2017-ADAP-Report.pdf.

Quigley, Fran. 2018. "Building a NASA for Prescription Drugs." *New Republic*, May 10. https://newrepublic.com/article/148361/building-nasa-prescription-drugs.

Rahmatian, Andreas. 2010. "Neo-Colonial Aspects of Global Intellectual Property Protection." *Journal of World Intellectual Property* 12 (1): 40–74.

Rai, Arti, and Rebecca Eisenberg. 2003. "Bayh-Dole Reform and the Progress of Biomedicine." *Law and Contemporary Problems* 66. https://doi.org/10.1511/2003.11.842.

Rangan, V. Kasturi, and K. Lee. 2009. "Gilead Sciences, Inc.: Access Program." Case 510–029, Harvard Business School. http://www.hbs.edu/faculty/Pages/item.aspx?num=37998.

Re, Vincent Lo, Charitha Gowda, Paul N. Urick, Joshua T. Halladay, Amanda Binkley, Dena M. Carbonari, Kathryn Battista, et al. 2016. "Disparities in Absolute Denial of Modern Hepatitis C Therapy by Type of Insurance." *Clinical Gastroenterology and Hepatology* 14 (7): 1035–43. https://doi.org/10.1016/j.cgh.2016.03.040.

Reader, Ruth. 2021. "Meet HARPA, the Bold Way Biden Can Jump-Start Health Innovation." *Fast Company*, February 12. https://www.fastcompany.com/90598254/meet-harpa-the-bold-way-biden-can-jump-start-health-innovation.

Rees, Victoria. 2020. "Almost 400 Cell and Gene Therapies in US Pipeline, Finds Report." *European Pharmaceutical Review*, March 11. https://www.europeanpharmaceuticalreview.com/news/114971/almost-400-cell-and-gene-therapies-in-us-pipeline-finds-report/.

Reid, Chip. 2015. "VA Can't Afford Drug for Veterans Suffering from Hepatitis C." CBS News, December 1. https://www.cbsnews.com/news/va-cant-afford-drug-for-veterans -suffering-from-hepatitis-c/.

———. 2016. "Lawmaker: Costly Hepatitis C Drug 'A Slap in the Face to the Veterans.'" CBS News, February 3. https://www.cbsnews.com/news/hepatitis-c-cure-veterans-affairs -congressional-hearing-cbs-news-investigation/.

Rein, David B., John S. Wittenborn, Bryce D. Smith, Danielle K. Liffmann, and John W. Ward. 2015. "The Cost-Effectiveness, Health Benefits, and Financial Costs of New Antiviral Treatments for Hepatitis C Virus." *Clinical Infectious Diseases* 61 (2): 157–68. https://doi.org/10.1093/cid/civ220.

Ren, Grace. 2020. "Progress on COVID-19 Technology Pool Inches Along as Sister Initiative to Pool Vaccine Procurement Accelerates." *Health Policy Watch*, September 25. https://healthpolicy-watch.news/progress-on-covid-19-technology-pool-inches-along -as-sister-initiative-to-pool-vaccine-procurement-accelerates/.

Reuters. 2007. "Pharmasset IPO Raises $45 Mln at Bottom of Range." Reuters, April 26. https://www.reuters.com/article/pharmasset-ipo/update-1-pharmasset-ipo-raises -45-mln-at-bottom-of-range-idUSN2618890820070426.

Rice, William, and Frank Clemente. 2016. *Gilead Sciences: Price Gouger, Tax Dodger.* Americans for Tax Fairness. https://americansfortaxfairness.org/new-report-taxpayer -supported-gilead-sciences-is-price-gouging-the-public-then-dodging-taxes-on-the -huge-profits/.

Richtel, Matt, and Andrew Pollack. 2016. "Harnessing the U.S. Taxpayer to Fight Cancer and Make Profits." *New York Times*, December 19. https://www.nytimes.com/2016/12/19 /health/harnessing-the-us-taxpayer-to-fight-cancer-and-make-profits.html.

Riordan, Michael. 1992. "State of the Gilead." https://www.slideshare.net/presentation select/a-few-slides-from-state-of-the-gilead-presentation-by-founder-michael-l-riordan -in-july-1992/2.

Robbins, Rebecca. 2016. "The Lab Breakthrough that Paved the Way for Today's Pricey Hepatitis C Cures." *STAT*, September 13. https://www.statnews.com/2016/09/13/lab -breakthrough-hepatitis-c/.

Robbins, Roni B. 1999. "HIV Drug Company Moves on Fast Track." *Atlanta Business Chronicle*, October 18. https://www.bizjournals.com/atlanta/stories/1999/10/18/story7 .html.

Robbins-Roth, Cynthia. 2001. *From Alchemy to IPO: The Business of Biotechnology.* New York: Basic Books.

Robertson, Melva. 2015. "OTT30: Emory Tech Transfer Office Celebrates 30 Years of Innovation." Emory University, March 1. http://news.emory.edu/stories/2015/02/ott_30 _and_celebration_of_innovation_and_technology/campus.html.

Rode, Margaret. 2011. "Stop Price Increases for H.I.V. and AIDS Prescriptions." *Pharmacy-Checker Blog*, May 12. https://www.pharmacycheckerblog.com/stop-price-increases-for -h-i-v-and-aids-prescriptions.

Roehrig, Charles. 2016. "CSHS Health Sector Trend Report." Altarum Institute. https:// altarum.org/sites/default/files/uploaded-publication-files/Altarum%20RWJF %20Trend%20Report%20February%202016_2.pdf.

Rosen, Hugo R. 2011. "Chronic Hepatitis C Infection." *New England Journal of Medicine* 364 (25): 2429–38. https://doi.org/10.1056/nejmcp1006613.

Rosenthal, Elana S., and Camilla S. Graham. 2016. "Price and Affordability of Direct-Acting Antiviral Regimens for Hepatitis C Virus in the United States." *Infectious Agents and Cancer* 11 (1): 24. https://doi.org/10.1186/s13027-016-0071-z.

Rowland, Christopher. 2019. "Gilead Defied a Government HIV Patent. The Justice Department Has Opened a Review." *Washington Post*, April 24. https://www.washingtonpost.com/business/economy/gilead-defied-a-government-hiv-patent-the-justice-department-has-opened-a-review/2019/04/24/16e4e20e-62bc-11e9-bfad-36a7eb36cb60_story.html.

Roy, Arundhati. 2020. "The Pandemic Is a Portal." *Financial Times*, April 3. https://www.ft.com/content/10d8f5e8-74eb-11ea-95fe-fcd274e920ca.

Roy, Victor. 2020. "A Crisis for Cures? Tracing Assetization and Value in Biomedical Innovation." In *Assetization: Turning Things into Assets in Technoscientific Capitalism*, edited by Kean Birch and Fabian Muniesa. MIT Press. https://direct.mit.edu/books/book/4848/AssetizationTurning-Things-into-Assets-in.

Roy, Victor, and Lawrence King. 2016a. "A Focus on Acquisitions and Buybacks." *BMJ* 345 (August 9). http://www.bmj.com/content/354/bmj.i3718/rr-3.

———. 2016b. "Betting on Hepatitis C: How Financial Speculation in Drug Development Influences Access to Medicines." *BMJ* 354:i3718. https://doi.org/10.1136/bmj.i3718.

Rudden, Jennifer. 2019. "Value of Venture Capital Investment in the United States from 1995 to 2018 (in Billion U.S. Dollars)." *Statista*. https://www.statista.com/statistics/277501/venture-capital-amount-invested-in-the-united-states-since-1995/.

S&P Capital IQ. 2011. "Gilead Pharmasset LLC M&A Call."

———. 2012. "Gilead Sciences Inc. FQ1 2012 Earnings Call Transcript."

———. 2013. "Gilead Sciences Inc. FQ4 2012 Earnings Call Transcript."

———. 2014a. "Gilead Sciences Inc. FQ1 2014 Earnings Call Transcripts."

———. 2014b. "Gilead Sciences Inc. FQ3 2014 Earnings Call Transcripts."

———. 2015. "Gilead Sciences Inc. FQ1 2015 Earnings Call Transcripts."

———. 2016a. "Gilead Sciences, Inc Financial Statements."

———. 2016b. "Pharmasset Financial Statements."

Sachs, Jeffrey. 2015. "Gilead's Greed that Kills." *Huffington Post*, July 27. https://www.huffpost.com/entry/gileads-greed-that-kills_b_7878102.

Sachs, Rachel. 2019. "Understanding the House Democrats' Drug Pricing Package." *Health Affairs*, September 19. https://www.healthaffairs.org/do/10.1377/hblog20190919.459441/full/.

Saganowsky, Eric. 2019. "Gilead Tries—and Fails—to Dodge Lawsuit Claiming It Delayed Safer HIV Meds." *FiercePharma*, May 14. https://www.fiercepharma.com/pharma/gilead-fails-to-convince-judge-to-toss-hiv-drug-case.

Saltzman, Jonathan. 2019. "Boston Drug-Pricing Watchdog Group Is 'Mouse that Roared.'" *Boston Globe*, June 19. https://www.bostonglobe.com/business/2019/06/19/boston-drug-pricing-watchdog-group-has-pharma-companies-attention/opfu6zAa3TKecdshGc2hsI/story.html.

Sampat, Bhaven. 2020. "Whose Drugs Are These?" *Issues in Science and Technology*, July 16. https://issues.org/drug-pricing-and-taxpayer-funded-research/.

Sanger-Katz, M. 2014. "$1,000 Hepatitis Pill Shows Why Fixing Health Costs Is So Hard." *New York Times*, August 2. http://www.nytimes.com/2014/08/03/upshot/is-a-1000-pill-really-too-much.html.

SBIR-STIR. 2016. "Birth & History of the SBIR Program." https://www.sbir.gov/birth-and -history-of-the-sbir-program.

Scannell, Jack W., Alex Blanckley, Helen Boldon, and Brian Warrington. 2012. "Diagnosing the Decline in Pharmaceutical R&D Efficiency." *Nature Reviews Drug Discovery* 11 (3): 191–200. https://doi.org/10.1038/nrd3681.

Scherer, F M. 2004. "The Pharmaceutical Industry: Prices and Progress." *New England Journal of Medicine* 351 (9): 927–32. https://doi.org/10.1056/nejmhpr040117.

Schlesinger, Jacob M. 2020. "Coronavirus Stimulus Package to Include Curbs on Share Buybacks." *Wall Street Journal*, March 25. https://www.wsj.com/articles/coronavirus -stimulus-package-to-include-curbs-on-share-buybacks-11585160044.

Schumpeter, Joseph. 1939. *Business Cycles: A Theoretical Historical, and Statistical Analysis of the Capitalist Process.* New York: McGraw-Hill.

———. 1942. *Capitalism, Socialism, and Democracy.* Harper Brothers.

Seeff, Leonard B., Zelma Buskell-Bales, Elizabeth C. Wright, Stephen J. Durako, H. Alter, Frank L. Iber, F. Blaine Hollinger, et al. 1992. "Long-Term Mortality after Transfusion-Associated Non-A, Non-B Hepatitis." *New England Journal of Medicine* 327 (27): 1906–11. https://doi.org/10.1056/nejm199212313272703.

Seeking Alpha. 2015. "Gilead Sciences Q1 FY2015 Earnings Call Transcript." https://seeking alpha.com/article/3126056-gilead-sciences-gild-ceo-john-martin-on-q1-2015-results -earnings-call-transcript.

———. 2016a. "Gilead Sciences' CEO John Milligan Presents at Morgan Stanley Global Healthcare Conference (Transcript)." https://seekingalpha.com/article/4005708-gilead -sciences-gild-ceo-john-milligan-presents-morgan-stanley-global-healthcare-conference.

———. 2016b. "Gilead Sciences (GILD) John C. Martin on Q4 2015 Results—Earnings Call Transcript." https://seekingalpha.com/article/3858206-gilead-sciences-gild-john-c -martin-q4-2015-results-earnings-call-transcript.

———. 2016c. "Gilead Sciences (GILD) John F. Milligan on Q1 2016 Results—Earnings Call Transcript," April 28. https://seekingalpha.com/article/3969438-gilead-sciences-gild -john-f-milligan-q1-2016-results-earnings-call-transcript.

Shefali, Luthra, and Anna Gorman. 2018. "Rising Cost of PrEP to Prevent HIV Infection Pushes It Out of Reach for Many." *NPR*, June 30. https://www.npr.org/sections/health -shots/2018/06/30/624045995/rising-cost-of-prep-a-pill-that-prevents-hiv-pushes-it -out-of-reach-for-many.

Siddiqui, Adam Q., Carlo Ballatore, Christopher McGuigan, Erik De Clercq, and Jan Balzarini. 1999. "The Presence of Substituents on the Aryl Moiety of the Aryl Phosphoramidate Derivative of D4T Enhances Anti-HIV Efficacy in Cell Culture: A Structure–Activity Relationship." *Journal of Medicinal Chemistry* 42 (3): 393–99. https://doi.org /10.1021/jm9803931.

Silverman, Ed. 2015a. "Multiple Sclerosis Drug Prices Rose at an 'Alarming' Rate: Study." *Wall Street Journal*, April 24. https://blogs.wsj.com/pharmalot/2015/04/24/multiple -sclerosis-drug-prices-rose-at-an-alarming-rate-study/.

———. 2015b. "Gilead Limits Enrollment in Its Hep C Patient Program to Pressure Insurers." *Wall Street Journal*, July 16. https://blogs.wsj.com/pharmalot/2015/07/16/gilead-limits -enrollment-in-its-hep-c-patient-program-to-pressure-insurers/.

———. 2016a. "Gilead Accused of Manipulating HIV Patents." *STAT*, February 1. https:// www.statnews.com/pharmalot/2016/02/01/gilead-patents-hiv/.

———. 2016b. "Gilead's New Price Hikes on HIV Drugs Anger AIDS Activists." *STAT*, July 5. https://www.statnews.com/pharmalot/2016/07/05/gilead-hiv-aids-drug-prices/.

———. 2016c. "As Hep C Sales Decline, Wall Street Wonders What Gilead Does for Its Next Act." *STAT*, July 26. https://www.statnews.com/pharmalot/2016/07/26/hepatitis-wall -street-gilead/.

———. 2020. "Despite the Pandemic, Prices for Many Drugs Keep Rising." *STAT*, July 9. https://www.statnews.com/pharmalot/2020/07/09/drug-pricing-pandemic-goodrx/.

Singer, Andrew C., Claas Kirchhelle, and Adam P. Roberts. 2020. "(Inter)Nationalising the Antibiotic Research and Development Pipeline." *Lancet Infectious Diseases* 20 (2): e54–62. https://doi.org/10.1016/S1473-3099(19)30552-3.

Sitaraman, Ganesh, and Anne Alstott. 2019. *The Public Option: How to Expand Freedom, Increase Opportunity, and Promote Equality*. Harvard University Press.

Slaoui, Moncef, and Matthew Hepburn. 2020. "Developing Safe and Effective Covid Vaccines: Operation Warp Speed's Strategy and Approach." *New England Journal of Medicine* 383 (18): 1701–3. https://doi.org/10.1056/NEJMp2027405.

Slaughter, Sheila, and Gary Rhoades. 1996. "The Emergence of a Competitiveness Research and Development Policy Coalition and the Commercialization of Academic Science and Technology." *Science, Technology, & Human Values* 21 (3): 303–39. https://doi .org/10.1177/016224399602100303.

Smyth, Jamie. 2021. "Pfizer and Moderna Forecast to Almost Double Vaccine Sales in 2022." *Financial Times*, October 17. https://www.ft.com/content/e7865240-88cc-41ba-86c2 -3a020d1431f9.

Sofia, Michael J., Donghui Bao, Wonsuk Chang, Jinfa Du, Dhanapalan Nagarathnam, Suguna Rachakonda, P. Ganapati Reddy, et al. 2010. "Discovery of a β-d-2′-Deoxy-2′- α-Fluoro-2′-β-C-Methyluridine Nucleotide Prodrug (PSI-7977) for the Treatment of Hepatitis C Virus." *Journal of Medicinal Chemistry* 53 (19): 7202–18. https://doi.org /10.1021/jm100863x.

Sofia, Michael J., P. A. Furman, and William T. Symonds. 2010. "2′-F-2′-C-Methyl Nucleosides and Nucleotides for the Treatment of Hepatitis C Virus: From Discovery to the Clinic." In *Accounts in Drug Discovery: Case Studies in Medicinal Chemistry*, edited by Joel Barrish, Percy Carter, Peter Cheng, and Robert Zahler, 238–66. Royal Society of Chemistry. https://pubs.rsc.org/en/content/chapter/bk9781849731263-00238/978-1 -84973-126-3.

Stark, David. 2000. "For a Sociology of Worth." Center on Organizational Innovation, Columbia University. https://www.researchgate.net/publication/251651120_For_a_Sociology _of_Worth.

Steinberger, Michael. 2020. "What Is the Stock Market Even For Anymore?" *New York Times*, May 27. https://www.nytimes.com/interactive/2020/05/26/magazine/stock-market -coronavirus-pandemic.html.

Stiglitz, Joseph E., Arjun Jayadev, and Achal Prabhala. 2020. "Patents vs. the Pandemic." *Project Syndicate*, April 23. https://www.project-syndicate.org/commentary/covid19 -drugs-and-vaccine-demand-patent-reform-by-joseph-e-stiglitz-et-al-2020-04.

Stout, Lynn. 2013. *The Shareholder Value Myth: How Putting Shareholders First Harms Investors, Corporations, and the Public*. New York: Penguin Random House.

Stynes, Tess. 2016. "Gilead Sales of Hepatitis C Drugs Fall 19%." *Wall Street Journal*, July 25. https://www.wsj.com/articles/gilead-sales-of-hepatitis-c-drugs-fall-19-1469479592.

Sunder Rajan, Kaushik. 2012. "Pharmaceutical Crises and Questions of Value: Terrains and Logics of Global Therapeutic Politics." *South Atlantic Quarterly* 111 (2): 321–46. https://doi.org/10.1215/00382876-1548239.

———. 2017. *Pharmocracy: Value, Politics, and Knowledge in Global Biomedicine.* Duke University Press.

Swagel, Phillip L. 2019. "CBO's Model of Drug Price Negotiations under the Elijah E. Cummings Lower Drug Costs Now Act." Working Paper 2021–01, Congressional Budget Office. https://www.cbo.gov/system/files/2019-10/hr3ltr.pdf.

Swan, Tracy. 2014. "Bonanza! The Gold Rush Is Under Way." *HIV Treatment Bulletin*, July 19. https://i-base.info/htb/26977.

Terry, Colin, and Neil Lesser. 2015. "Measuring the Return from Pharmaceutical Innovation 2015: Transforming R&D Returns in Uncertain Times." Deloitte Centre for Health Solutions. https://www2.deloitte.com/am/en/pages/life-sciences-and-healthcare/articles/measuring-return-from-pharmaceutical-innovation.html.

Terry, Mark. 2018. "Can Gilead Develop a Cure for HIV?" *BioSpace*, March 20. https://www.biospace.com/article/can-gilead-develop-a-cure-for-hiv-/.

Tice, Jeffrey A., Harinder S. Chahal, and Daniel A. Ollendorf. 2015. "Comparative Clinical Effectiveness and Value of Novel Interferon-Free Combination Therapy for Hepatitis C Genotype 1: Summary of California Technology Assessment Forum Report." *JAMA Internal Medicine* 175 (9): 1559–60. https://doi.org/10.1001/jamainternmed.2015.3348.

Tirrell, Meg, and Tara Lachapelle. 2011. "Pharmasset Sets Inhibitex-to-Achillion Drugmaker Deals: Real M&A." *Bloomberg*, November 23. https://www.bloomberg.com/news/articles/2011-11-22/pharmasset-shows-inhibitex-to-achillion-drugmakers-up-for-grabs-real-m-a.

Treatment Action Group. 2014. "Activists Hold Die-In to Protest High Price of Gilead's Hepatitis C Drug," July 24. https://www.treatmentactiongroup.org/statement/activists-hold-die-in-to-protest-high-price-of-gileads-hepatitis-c-drug/.

Ulrich, Lauren. 2015. "TRIPS and Compulsory Licensing: Increasing Participation in the Medicines Patent Pool in the Wake of an HIV/AIDS Treatment Timebomb." Emory University School of Law. http://law.emory.edu/eilr/content/volume-30/issue-1/comments/trips-compulsory-medicines-patent-wake-hiv-aids.html.

US Food & Drug Administration. 2015. Center for Drug Evaluation and Research Approval Package for Application Number 207561Orig1s000. November 5. https://www.accessdata.fda.gov/drugsatfda_docs/nda/2015/207561Orig1s000Approv.pdf.

US Government Accountability Office. 2021. "Prescription Drug Spending." https://www.gao.gov/prescription-drug-spending.

US Senate Committee on Finance. 2015. "The Price of Sovaldi and Its Impact on the U.S. Health Care System." https://www.finance.senate.gov/ranking-members-news/wyden-grassley-sovaldi-investigation-finds-revenue-driven-pricing-strategy-behind-84-000-hepatitis-drug.

US Senate Committee on Veterans' Affairs. 2014. "Hepatitis C and Veterans." Hearing. Washington, DC, December 3. https://www.govinfo.gov/content/pkg/CHRG-113shrg91803/html/CHRG-113shrg91803.htm.

Uyttebrouck, Olivier. 2015. "'Amazing' Drug to Cost NM Medicaid $140M." *Albuquerque Journal*, August 3. https://www.abqjournal.com/622285/amazing-drug-to-cost-nm-medicaid-140m.html.

Vallas, Paul, Daniel L. Kleinman, and Dina Biscotti. 2011. "Political Structures and the Making of U.S. Biotechnology." In *State of Innovation: The U.S. Government's Role in Technology Development*, edited by Fred Block and Matthew R. Keller. Boulder, CO: Paradigm.

van der Zwan, Natascha. 2014. "Making Sense of Financialization." *Socio-Economic Review* 12 (1): 99–129. https://doi.org/10.1093/ser/mwt020.

Van Nuys, Karen, Ronald Brookmeyer, Jacquelyn W. Chou, David Dreyfus, Douglas Dieterich, and Dana P. Goldman. 2015. "Broad Hepatitis C Treatment Scenarios Return Substantial Health Gains, but Capacity Is a Concern." *Health Affairs* 34 (10): 1666–74. https://doi.org/10.1377/hlthaff.2014.1193.

Van Trotsenburg, Axel. 2021. "Tackling Vaccine Inequity for Africa." *Voices* (blog), World Bank, October 8. https://blogs.worldbank.org/voices/tackling-vaccine-inequity-africa.

Vandenberge, Jordan. 2020. "The Dow Hit a Record High. So Did the Greater Cleveland Food Bank." *News 5 Cleveland*, November 25. https://www.news5cleveland.com/news/local-news/cleveland-metro/the-dow-hit-a-record-high-so-did-the-greater-cleveland-food-bank.

Veblen, Thorstein. 1908a. "On the Nature of Capital." *Quarterly Journal of Economics* 22 (4): 517. https://doi.org/10.2307/1884915.

———. 1908b. "On the Nature of Capital: Investment, Intangible Assets, and the Pecuniary Magnate." *Quarterly Journal of Economics* 23 (1): 104. https://doi.org/10.2307/1883967.

Vernaz, Nathalie, François Girardin, Nicolas Goossens, Urs Brügger, Marco Riguzzi, Arnaud Perrier, and Francesco Negro. 2016. "Drug Pricing Evolution in Hepatitis C." *PLOS ONE* 11 (6): e0157098. https://doi.org/10.1371/journal.pone.0157098.

Veterans Affairs. 2015. "Raymond Schinazi, Drug-Development Pioneer, Earns VA's Highest Honor for Biomedical Research," August 10. https://www.research.va.gov/currents/0815-10.cfm.

Vey, Jean-Baptiste, and Matthias Blamont. 2016. "France Gets G7 to Discuss Global Regulation of Medicine Prices." *Reuters*, May 3. https://www.reuters.com/article/us-g7-japan-pharmaceuticals/france-gets-g7-to-discuss-global-regulation-of-medicine-prices-idUSKCN0XT0TU.

Wagner, Caroline E., et al. 2021. "Vaccine Nationalism and the Dynamics and Control of SARS-CoV-2." *Science* 373 (6562): eabj7364. https://doi.org/10.1126/science.abj7364.

Walker, Joseph. 2015. "Gilead's $1,000 Pill Is Hard for States to Swallow." *Wall Street Journal*, April 8. https://www.wsj.com/articles/gileads-1-000-hep-c-pill-is-hard-for-states-to-swallow-1428525426.

Wang, H., X. Lu, X. Yang, and N. Xu. 2016. "The Efficacy and Safety of Tenofovir Alafenamide versus Tenofovir Disoproxil Fumarate in Antiretroviral Regimens for HIV-1 Therapy: Meta-Analysis." *Medicine* 95 (41): e5146. https://doi.org/10.1097/md.0000000000005146.

Ward, John W., and Jonathan H. Mermin. 2015. "Simple, Effective, but Out of Reach? Public Health Implications of HCV Drugs." *New England Journal of Medicine* 373 (27): 2678–80. https://doi.org/10.1056/nejme1513245.

Warren, Elizabeth. 2018. "Warren Introduces Accountable Capitalism Act." Press release, August 15. https://www.warren.senate.gov/newsroom/press-releases/warren-introduces-accountable-capitalism-act.

Weintraub, Karen, and Elizabeth Weise. 2020. "Federal Spending on COVID-19 Vaccine Candidates Tops \$9 Billion, Spread among 7 Companies." *USA Today*, August 8. https://www.usatoday.com/story/news/health/2020/08/08/feds-spending-more-than-9-billion-covid-19-vaccine-candidates/5575206002/.

Werth, Barry. 2014. *The Antidote: Inside the World of New Pharma*. New York: Simon and Schuster.

Winslow, Ron, and Peter Loftus. 2011. "Gilead's \$11 Billion Gambit." *Wall Street Journal*, November 22. https://www.wsj.com/articles/SB1000142405297020444340457705180064 0024264.

World Health Organization. 2016a. "Draft Global Health Sector Strategies, Viral Hepatitis 2016–21." EB138/30. Geneva. https://apps.who.int/gb/ebwha/pdf_files/WHA69/A69_32 -en.pdf.

———. 2016b. "SOFOSBUVIR: Patent Situation of Key Products for Treatment of Hepatitis C." Geneva. https://cdn.who.int/media/docs/default-source/essential-medicines/intellectual -property/sofosbuvir-report.pdf.

———. 2017. *Global Hepatitis Report, 2017*. https://www.who.int/publications-detail-redi rect/global-hepatitis-report-2017.

———. 2018. "Progress Report on Access to Hepatitis C Treatment." https://apps.who.int /iris/handle/10665/260445/.

———. 2021a. "Hepatitis C." https://www.who.int/news-room/fact-sheets/detail/hepatitis-c.

———. 2021b. *Accelerating Access to Hepatitis C Diagnostics and Treatment: Overcoming Barriers in Low and Middle-Income Countries*. Geneva. https://www.who.int/publications/i /item/9789240019003.

———. 2021c. "WHO Director-General's Opening Remarks at the Media Briefing on COVID-19," September 8. https://www.who.int/director-general/speeches/detail/who -director-general-s-opening-remarks-at-the-media-briefing-on-covid-19---8-september -2021.

World Medical Association. 2020. "WMA Declaration of Geneva." https://www.wma.net /policies-post/wma-declaration-of-geneva/.

Y Charts. 2010. "Cash Rich but What's Gilead's Next Big Drug?" *Forbes*, December 3. https://www.forbes.com/sites/investor/2010/12/03/cash-rich-but-whats-gileads-next -big-drug/.

Yee, Michael. 2014. "Gilead Sciences: MRK Hep C Derivative Thoughts, and Our Interesting Thought on Treating Only F3–4?" RBC Capital Markets, Toronto, Canada.

Younossi, Zobair M., Haesuk Park, Douglas Dieterich, Sammy Saab, Aijaz Ahmed, and Stuart C. Gordon. 2016. "The Value of Cure Associated with Treating Treatment-Naïve Chronic Hepatitis C Genotype 1: Are the New All-Oral Regimens Good Value to Society?" *Liver International* 37 (5): 662–68. https://doi.org/10.1111/liv.13298.

Yoxen, Ed. 1981. "Life as a Productive Force: Capitalizing upon Research in Molecular Biology." In *Science, Technology, and the Labour Process*, edited by Les Levidov and Bob Young, 66–122. London: Blackrose Press.

Zafar, S. Yousuf. 2015. "Financial Toxicity of Cancer Care: It's Time to Intervene." *Journal of the National Cancer Institute* 108 (5): djv370. https://doi.org/10.1093/jnci/djv370.

Zafar, S. Yousuf, Jeffrey M. Peppercorn, Deborah Schrag, Donald H. Taylor, Amy M. Goetzinger, Xiaoyin Zhong, and Amy P. Abernethy. 2013. "The Financial Toxicity of Cancer Treatment: A Pilot Study Assessing Out-of-Pocket Expenses and the Insured Cancer Patient's Experience." *The Oncologist* 18 (4): 381–90. https://doi.org/10.1634/the oncologist.2012-0279.

Zeller, Christian. 2007. "From the Gene to the Globe: Extracting Rents Based on Intellectual Property Monopolies." *Review of International Political Economy* 15 (1): 86–115. https://doi.org/10.1080/09692290701751316.

Zirkelbach, Robert. 2015. "The Five Essential Truths about Prescription Drug Spending." Pharmaceutical Research and Manufacturers of America, March 10. https://catalyst.phrma.org/the-five-essential-truths-about-prescription-drug-spending.

INDEX

Abbott Laboratories, 128
AbbVie company, 88, 95, 114, 118, 150n100
Accountable Capitalism Act, 126
activism, 79, 91, 93–94, 102
Allergan company, 110
Alstott, Anne, 123
Alter, Harvey, 23, 26–27, 31
Alton, Gregg H., 3, 9, 71*tab.*, 79, 107
American Association for the Study of Liver
  Diseases, 64
American Economics Association, 83
Americans for Tax Fairness, 71
American Society of Health Economists, 116
Angell, Marcia, 8
Apath company, 28–29, 33, 148n40
Arnold, John, 113
Arora, Sanjeev, 90
Atripla treatment, 53, 63
Australia, 86, 93, 95, 102, 118

Bach, Peter, x, 84
Balzarini, Jan, 37–38
Barclays Capital, 59–60*tab.*, 61–63
Bartenschlager, Ralf, 25, 31, 148n12
Bayh-Dole Act (1980), 34–36, 41
Beckert, Jens, 15, 44, 46
Belldegrun, Arie, 104
Berens, Andrew, 64
Berwick, Donald, 107
Bichler, Shimshon, 15

Biden, President Joe, 123
Bill and Melinda Gates Foundation, 101
biomedicine: capital and finance analytics, 17;
  financialization mechanisms, 16, 20, 107,
  108–12; financialization threats, 117–20.
  See also pharmaceutical industry
biotechnology companies: awards, 32;
  commercialization, 34–36, 149n69; innovation
  factors, 13; research and development (R&D)
  investments, 26–28, 49–50; speculative
  capital, 49–50; strategic partnerships, 41–43;
  value creation, 49–50; venture capital, 11,
  44–46. *See also* pharmaceutical industry;
  specific names of companies
Birch, Kean, 14, 63, 64, 69, 118
Bischofberger, Norbert, 71*tab.*, 102–3
Blight, Keril, 27, 29
Block, Fred, 33, 129–30, 149n65
Bloomberg, 3, 58, 64, 97, 103, 106, 117
boceprevir drug, 76, 78
Boston Consulting Group, 58
Bourgeron, Théo, 38
Brazil, 91, 92, 118, 128
Bristol Myers Squibb, 37, 48, 64, 154n70
Brookings Institution, 80, 143
Burr, Richard, 80
Burroughs-Wellcome company, 151n110
Bush, Laura, 90
Bush, Vannevar, 26, 121
Business Roundtable, 126

Founded in 1893,
UNIVERSITY OF CALIFORNIA PRESS
publishes bold, progressive books and journals
on topics in the arts, humanities, social sciences,
and natural sciences—with a focus on social
justice issues—that inspire thought and action
among readers worldwide.

The UC PRESS FOUNDATION
raises funds to uphold the press's vital role
as an independent, nonprofit publisher, and
receives philanthropic support from a wide
range of individuals and institutions—and from
committed readers like you. To learn more, visit
ucpress.edu/supportus.